Essays on the Modern Identity

Studies on Themes and Motifs in Literature

Horst S. Daemmrich
General Editor

Vol. 55

PETER LANG
New York • Washington, D.C./Baltimore • Boston • Bern
Frankfurt am Main • Berlin • Brussels • Vienna • Oxford

Essays on the
Modern Identity

Edited by
William D. Brewer
and Carole J. Lambert

PETER LANG
New York • Washington, D.C./Baltimore • Boston • Bern
Frankfurt am Main • Berlin • Brussels • Vienna • Oxford

Library of Congress Cataloging-in-Publication Data

Essays on the modern identity / edited by
William D. Brewer and Carole J. Lambert.
p. cm. — (Studies on themes and motifs in literature; vol. 55)
Includes bibliographical references.
1. Literature, Modern—History and criticism. 2. Self in literature.
3. Identity (Psychology) in literature. I. Brewer, William D.
(William Dean). II. Lambert, Carole J. III. Series.
PN56.S46 E74   809'.93384—dc21   99-055825
ISBN 0-8204-4900-8
ISSN 1056-3970

Die Deutsche Bibliothek-CIP-Einheitsaufnahme

Essays on the modern identity / ed. by:
William D. Brewer and Carole J. Lambert.
−New York; Washington, D.C./Baltimore; Boston; Bern;
Frankfurt am Main; Berlin; Brussels; Vienna; Oxford: Lang.
(Studies on themes and motifs in literature; Vol. 55)
ISBN 0-8204-4900-8

The paper in this book meets the guidelines for permanence and durability
of the Committee on Production Guidelines for Book Longevity
of the Council of Library Resources.

© 2000 Peter Lang Publishing, Inc., New York

Printed in the United States of America

Table of Contents

Illustrations

Acknowledgments

This collection of essays grew out of an NEH Summer Seminar directed by Professor Leo Damrosch at Harvard University entitled "Rousseau and Blake: Inventing the Modern Self." The editors would like to express their appreciation for Professor Damrosch's guidance and for the financial support provided by the National Endowment of the Humanities, which made this collaboration possible.

Many citations in Mira Morgenstern's essay, "Self and the Other in Rousseau: Love, Equality and Equity in a World of Flux," are based on work that has been published previously in her *Rousseau and the Politics of Ambiguity* (University Park: The Pennsylvania State University Press, 1996) and are reproduced here with permission of the publisher. We would also like to thank the editor of *The Comparatist* for permission to reprint Dan Latimer's essay, "Piracquo's Missing Finger, or, The Utility of the Liberal Arts," and Sage Publications, Inc., for permission to reprint a slightly revised portion of W. Jay Reedy's article, "Rousseau and Communitarian Individualism in 'Late Modern' America: The Interpretation of Benjamin Barber." Quotations from Samuel Taylor Coleridge's *Notebooks* (ed. Kathleen Coburn) and *Biographia Literaria* (ed. James Engell and W.J. Bate) are reprinted by permission of Princeton University Press; quotations from Virginia Woolf's *The Diary of Virginia Woolf* (ed. Anne Olivier Bell) are reprinted by permission of the Hogarth Press and of the executors of the Virginia Woolf estate, and quotations from Dorothy Wordsworth's *Journals* are reprinted by permission of Oxford University Press.

Finally, we would like to thank the Office of Graduate Studies and Research at Appalachian State University for its financial support of this project.

Contributors

William D. Brewer (co-editor) is professor of English at Appalachian State University in Boone, North Carolina. He is the author of *The Shelley-Byron Conversation* (Univ. Press of Florida, 1994), *The Mental Anatomies of William Godwin and Mary Shelley* (Fairleigh Dickinson Univ. Press, 2000), and articles in *Papers on Language & Literature, Philological Quarterly, Keats-Shelley Journal, European Romantic Review, Southern Humanities Review, Studies in Browning and His Circle*, and *John Clare Society Journal*.

Kent Brudney teaches political science at Cuesta College, in San Luis Obispo, California. He is the author of articles in a variety of political science journals, including *Political Theory*.

Ann Glenn Crowe is associate professor of art history at Virginia Commonwealth University. She is the author of critical essays on modern and contemporary artists including sculptor Naum Gabo for *American National Biography* (Oxford, 1999), architects Frank Gehry and Arata Isozaki and the Los Angeles Museum of Contemporary Art for the *International Dictionary of Architects and Architecture* (St. James Press, 1993), and sculptors Siah Armajani, Alice Aycock, and Michael Heizer for *Contemporary Masterworks* (St. James, 1991). She is a frequent contributor of critical reviews to the international monthly *Art Papers* (Atlanta). Her doctoral dissertation on Goya is in the process of revision for publication.

Howard Giskin is associate professor of English at Appalachian State University. He is the author of articles on Latin American literature, Yves Bonnefoy, Ortega y Gasset, and Taoism, and has published a volume of Chinese folktales (NTC/Contemporary, 1997). He is also co-editor of *An Introduction to Chinese Culture Through the Family* (SUNY Press, forthcoming).

Anthony John Harding is professor of English at the University of Saskatchewan, Canada. He is the author of *The Reception of Myth in*

English Romanticism (Univ. of Missouri Press, 1995), "Coleridge, Subjectivity, and the Mirror of Mysteries," *European Romantic Review* 5 (1995): 193–213; and *Milton, the Metaphysicals, and Romanticism* (Cambridge UP, 1994). He is editing volume 5 of the *Notebooks* of S. T. Coleridge for Princeton University Press. His other current projects include an article on how perceptions of racial otherness contributed to the concept of personal identity in British literature 1790–1830.

Carole J. Lambert (co-editor) is professor at Azusa Pacific University. She is the author of *The Empty Cross: Medieval Hopes, Modern Futility in the Theater of Maurice Maeterlinck, Paul Claudel, August Strindberg, and Georg Kaiser* (Garland, 1990), "Postmodern Biography: Lively Hypotheses and *Dead Certainties*" (*Biography*, Fall 1995), and several book reviews (*Southern Humanities Review*, 1995).

Dan Latimer is professor of English at Auburn University and co-editor of *Southern Humanities Review*. He is the author of *Contemporary Critical Theory* (Harcourt Brace Jovanovich, 1989) as well as recent essays on Melville (*Essays in Literature*, Fall 1994), on Paul de Man for the *Encyclopedia of Contemporary Literary Theory* (Toronto, 1993), on Nietzsche's *Birth of Tragedy* and Joseph Roth's *Radetzky March* for the *Reference Guide to World Literature* (St. James Press, 1995), and on Schiller and Eichendorff for the *Encyclopedia of German Literature* (Fitzroy Dearborn, 1999). An essay on American Neopragmatism will appear in the *Cambridge History of Literary Criticism*, volume 9 (in 2000).

Ronnie Littlejohn is professor of Philosophy and Chair of the Department at Belmont University in Nashville, Tennessee. He is the author of *Ethics: Studying the Art of Moral Appraisal* (1993) and *Exploring Christian Theology* (1984). His work is intentionally Wittgensteinian in method, and his most recent publication is "Comparative Moral Grammars: Studying Japanese Moral Culture," in *The Transformation of Japan in the 21ˢᵗ Century* for the University of California at Berkeley series on *East Asian Studies*.

Mira Morgenstern is assistant professor of political science at Kingsborough/CUNY. She is the author of *The Politics of Ambiguity* (Pennsylvania State Press, 1996) and of articles on Rousseau in *Pensée*

Libre, the *Actes du Colloque de Montmorency*, and *Historical Reflections*. She has also published on Biblical studies in *Judaism* and on cultural transmission in *Jewish Mothers*.

Marjean D. Purinton is associate professor of English at Texas Tech University. She is the author of *Romantic Ideology Unmasked: The Mentally Constructed Tyrannies in Dramas of William Wordsworth, Lord Byron, Percy Shelley, and Joanna Baillie* (Univ. of Delaware Press, 1994) as well as numerous articles on Romantic drama, early nineteenth-century women writers, and Women's Studies issues. She is currently working on a book project entitled *British Romantic Drama and Cultural Identity*.

W. Jay Reedy is associate professor of history at Bryant College, Smithfield, RI. He is the author of a dozen essays in such journals as *Historical Reflections*, *Studies on Voltaire and the Eighteenth Century*, *History of Political Thought*, the *Proceedings of the American Philosophical Society*, and the *Journal of the History of Ideas*. The latter journal, in conjunction with the University of Rochester Press, has recently republished on of his *JHI* articles in a collection entitled *Language and the History of Thought*, edited by Nancy Struever (1995).

Sally Silk is associate professor of French at Oakland University in Rochester, Michigan. She is the author of essays on Céline, Butor, Blanchot, and Jorge Semprun in *MLN*, *Style*, *Romanic Review*, *CLIO*, and *Neophilologus*. She is currently working on the relationship of the early nineteenth-century concept of taste in bourgeois France to Habermans's work on public and private spheres.

Introduction:
Essays on the Modern Identity

It may seem odd, in this postmodern age, for us to concern ourselves with questions about identity, or the self. After all, as Martin E. Gloege asserts, "The most recent chapter in the history of the self is the story of its debunking, its fragmentation, its dismemberment, its explosion, dissolution, destruction, its scattering or dispersal, and, finally, its annihilation."[1] While some theorists consider the self a complete illusion, others regard it as a social construct, an idea that tells us more about a person's position in society than about the person's "essential" identity. In fact, essentialist conceptions of the self are frequently seen as myths created by a given society to justify its laws, economic system, or patriarchal worldview. This essentialism, theorists argue, is illusory and, in some cases, even sinister in nature, embodying phallocentric, restrictive, or repressive values.[2]

Despite its elusiveness, deceptiveness, and controversiality, however, the notion of a human identity or identities is presented as an important and perhaps even indispensable concept in many modern texts. In some of these texts, the establishment of a personal identity is seen as particularly crucial from a psychological point of view. For example, in the "Profession of Faith of the Savoyard Vicar" section of *Emile* (1762), Jean-Jacques Rousseau introduces the reader to a clergyman who, victimized by a scandal, falls into "that frame of mind of uncertainty and doubt that Descartes demands for the quest for truth."[3] This uncertain mental state causes him much suffering: "I have never led a life so constantly disagreeable as during those times of perplexity and anxiety, when I ceaselessly wandered from doubt to doubt and brought back from my long meditations only uncertainty, obscurity, and contradictions about the cause of my being and the principle of my duties" (268). He overcomes this crisis of uncertainty through turning within himself, to an "inner light" or conscience, which appears more trustworthy than books of philosophy: "Let us consult the inner light; it will lead me astray less than [the philosophers] lead me astray; or at least my error will be my own, and I will deprave myself less in following my own illusions than in yielding to their lies" (269).

According to the Savoyard Vicar, one must be true to oneself in order to attain psychological equilibrium and even to discover what is right and wrong: "I do not draw…rules [for conduct] from the principles of high philosophy, but find them written by nature with ineffaceable characters in the depth of my heart" (286). In fact, the Vicar's sense of self becomes so strong that he longs to die so as to become completely himself: "I aspire to the moment when, after being delivered from the shackles of the body, I shall be *me* without contradiction or division and shall need only myself in order to be happy" (293). Although this view of the modern identity embodies some postmodern concerns about "contradiction or division" (at least during one's mortal existence), there is nevertheless a faith in a basic, core self which can rescue an individual from the psychological distress brought on by philosophical skepticism and can even provide moral guidance.

In *The Prelude* (1805 version), William Wordsworth describes his own identity crisis, a period of psychological and conceptual confusion which resembles, in some ways, the Vicar's experience in *Emile*. For Wordsworth, the catalyst is his loss of faith in the French Revolution after he learns that the Republican armies have "become oppressors in their turn."[4] Like the Vicar, his first response is a turn toward philosophy. In Wordsworth's case, William Godwin's *Enquiry Concerning Political Justice* seems most relevant, and, following Godwin, he dedicates himself to "the human reason's naked self" (10:817), "The freedom of the individual mind, / Which…/…adopts / One guide—the light of circumstances, flashed / Upon an independent intellect" (10:825–829). Wordsworth's decision to use his individual reason to resolve life's confusions leads, however, to despair: "demanding proof, / And seeking it in every thing, I lost / All feeling of conviction, and, in fine, / Sick, wearied out with contrarieties, / Yielded up moral questions in despair" (10:896–900). Having been misled by "external accidents" (10:886), such as the French Revolution, and by a Godwinian faith in reason, Wordsworth finds himself in a state of profound psychological and moral disorientation.

Like Rousseau's Vicar, Wordsworth must turn inward to a basic, core self in order to overcome his crisis, and, for Wordsworth, this requires the emotional support of his sister Dorothy:

The belovèd woman in whose sight

Those days were passed...
Maintained for me a saving intercourse
With my true self (for, though impaired, and changed
Much, as it seemed, I was no further changed
Than as a clouded, not a waning moon) (10:908–917).

Not only do the Savoyard Vicar and Wordsworth reflect a belief in a core self which is both authentic and essentially unchangeable, they also repudiate external ideas and occurrences (such as philosophical writings and historical events) which distract them from communion with their "true" selves. In the case of Wordsworth, there does, however, seem to be a need for the creation of a healing community (consisting of himself and Dorothy)—he is not as self-reliant as the Vicar.

From a postmodern point of view, this reliance on a true self may seem naive and even delusional. If the idea of the self is a social construct, how can there be a self apart from ideology and history? Recent studies by psychologists have, however, suggested that the belief of the Savoyard Vicar and Wordsworth in a true or core self is not necessarily misguided. In an article on the core self, William R. Caspary uses the example of narcissistic parents' children who have had to develop a false self: "In order to gain even the minimal love these parents can give, in order to escape being annihilated psychologically if not physically, the infant learns to read every subtle cue about the parents' wishes and to act out the desired demeanor and behavior....[T]hese children who developed a false self grow up to experience profound doubts about who they are, or whether they really exist as persons at all. This absence of a sense of identity, of personhood, of selfhood leads to persistent feelings of emptiness and depression."[5] The therapy for this "false self" syndrome involves recovering "certain intense spontaneous emotions that are recognized by the clients as genuinely their own. The awareness of these emotions is followed, momentarily at least, by a feeling of integration and relief from emptiness and terror."[6] While the children of narcissistic parents are presumably in more psychological conflict than either the Savoyard Vicar or Wordsworth, Caspary's analysis of their plight suggests that the modern sense of a core self is not irrelevant in our postmodern period. Moreover, as James M. Glass has observed in his critique of the postmodern "decentered self," schizophrenics and multiple personality disorder patients suffer tremendously as a result of their lack of a coherent self.[7]

Of course, conceptions of the modern identity also have moral ramifications. In fact, Charles Taylor argues that "[s]elfhood and the good, or in another way selfhood and morality, turn out to be inextricably intertwined themes."[8] Taylor contends that the lack of a self-concept can lead to an "identity crisis," the results of which may be psychological suffering, moral disorientation, and social irresponsibility: people who have no identities "lack a frame or horizon within which things can take on a stable significance, within which some life possibilities can be seen as good or meaningful, others as bad or trivial. The meaning of all these possibilities is unfixed, labile, or undetermined. This is a painful and frightening experience."[9] If we do not have a sense of self, we do not know where we stand, and we cannot know how to be good or how to do good. Our disorientation is moral as well as psychological.

The relationship of the self to the broader community has become an important issue in governmental as well as academic circles. There has been, in fact, a movement to construct a "communitarian" conception of self in American politics, a movement which has been supported to a degree by the Clinton administration.[10] In some ways, Communitarian theorists are continuing the discussion initiated in Rousseau's *On Social Contract* (1762) regarding the optimal relationship in society between individual and general will.[11] According to William A. Galston, "Communitarianism is a movement that seeks to balance rights and responsibilities and to nourish the moral ties of family, neighborhood, workplace, and citizenship as a basis for innovative public policy."[12] Rather than adamantly insisting on their "rights," citizens should be willing to take on social responsibilities, or even sacrifice their interests on occasion to promote the welfare of various social groups. What is at stake in this conception of the self, communitarians suggest, is nothing less than the cohesion and viability of human society. Selfishness, in other words, is not a morally or socially defensible basis for public policy decisions.

Another important issue addressed in this volume is the construction of gender and its relation to modern and postmodern conceptions of identity. The modern self exemplified by James Joyce's Stephen Dedalus—unique, strong, independent of nationality, religion, and others—has been attacked by some exponents of postmodernism. The Cartesian self/other dichotomy, including the self regarding itself as other, is felt by them to be the rationalist basis of a patriarchal culture that is no longer tolerable. Theoretically, a "decentered" self should eliminate this dichotomy and lead to increased freedom. Psychological evidence suggests, however, that decentered selves are often incapable of making important choices and meaningfully following through on their decisions. They risk becoming victimized by powerful "centered" selves who are able to do what they cannot do. Truly decentered selves, schizophrenic patients and others approaching mental illness, often express severe anxiety about becoming absorbed in the identity of another. Thus the loss of a sense of self, a continuing identity, does not result in freedom but rather in bondage to another who is self-centered.

Feminists are particularly concerned about the reduction of agency that the postmodern decentered self implies. Lacking in autonomy in the past because of familial, social, and cultural constraints, many women strongly desire coherent self-determination and liberated self-expression. They do not want to be reduced to a nexus of circulating discourses, a prisoner of incessant language games. In fact, some women have already felt for too long decentered and defined by others; these women know from experience that such a position is the antithesis of freedom. As with many other topics relating to identity, the issue of gender and the self is much debated at present, and this debate has important and widespread ramifications with respect to our evolving attitudes toward social roles and individual self-concepts.

Thus the modern identity is not a dead issue—the essays in this collection attest to its continuing relevance in the postmodern world. Of course, the essays in this book also suggest that it is difficult to draw a sharp line between the concepts of the modern and the postmodern identity, which can easily blur into one another in a given text. It is, however, difficult to understand postmodernism without having some grasp of the modernist assumptions which precede it, and the debate between modern and postmodern conceptions of the self can give us important perspectives on the questions of identity, autonomy, individual rights, and public interest. Moreover, as we have already indicated, the shattering, fragmenting, decentering, or annihilation of the self have important psychological, moral, and social ramifications: modern views on the self provide postmodernists with warnings as well as historical insights.

Essays on the Modern Identity selectively represents the developing understanding of the modern self from the time of Jean-Jacques Rousseau to the present. The articles grouped under the heading of Early Modern Self-Understanding highlight perceptions of the self found in literary and philosophical texts by Rousseau, G. W. F. Hegel, Samuel Taylor Coleridge, Dorothy Wordsworth, and William Blake, and in the pictorial art of Francisco de Goya. Those articles, collected under the heading of Modern Identity in a Postmodern World, emphasize the difficulty of both maintaining identity, a continuing sense of self, in a postmodern world and sharing this self in community with others. The theoretical positions concerning the self postulated by Gilles Deleuze, Félix Guattari, James M. Glass, Diane Meyers, and Heinz Kohut are followed by pieces which demonstrate the mutations that the embodied self undergoes when experiencing travel and oppression as exemplified in Céline's *Voyage au bout de la nuit* and Jorge Semprun's *The Long Voyage*. The self is then considered in community: its shaping through the liberal arts education and its political responsibilities in society.

Since World War II, the meaning of the term "postmodern" has been gradually evolving. Patricia Waugh describes postmodernism as "a late phase in a tradition of specifically *aestheticist* modern thought inaugurated by philosophers such as Kant and embodied in Romantic *and* modernist art;" thus she views postmodernism not as a strident reaction to modernism but as "a late-flowering Romanticism." She continues, "What distinguishes its mood from earlier Romanticisms, however, is that its aesthetic impulses have spilled out of the self-consciously defined sphere of art and into the spheres of what Kant referred to as the cognitive and scientific on the one hand and the practical or moral on the other."[13] Postmodernism is a term now applied to all domains of life. Specific stylistic qualities signal it.

Because the Grand Narratives of Platonic truths, Marxist materialism, theological dogmas, and patriarchal rationalism have been placed in doubt and are now thought to be ideologies derived from a will to power rather than objective verities, a pervasive cynicism penetrates postmodernist texts and critiques. Ironic tones, parodies parasitical of earlier texts, self-conscious narration, pastiche, focus on simulacrum rather than original, unstable meanings, and fragmentation of time and space are marks of the new era. Some commentators attribute this shift in mentality and style to the effects of full-blown capitalism. As Waugh notes, "capitalism, in its latest consumerist phase, invades everything including the aesthetic, the post-colonial world and the unconscious…leaving no remaining oppositional space."[14]

This cultural milieu, of course, will affect the self. Recognizing that what were formerly considered to be transcendental truths are now ideological discourses, one may choose one's ideology, but it is as dispensable as many of the items produced in the consumerist culture. One can master the language games of particular ideologies and can play to win, but the transaction is only a culturally constructed sport, not concrete verity.

It is not surprising that many theoreticians of postmodernism speak of the decentered self. This self is subject to surrounding discourses with no center to serve as a filter or moral guide. There is little difference between stylistically constructing one's self and being constructed by stylized ideologies. Indeed, the individual becomes a vehicle traversed by discourses. The modernist self, the controlling subjectivity originally derived from the medieval soul, has fragmented. Waugh describes this phenomenon well: "In this world, not only self but also consciousness is discovered to be adrift, increasingly unable to anchor itself to any universal ground of justice, truth or reason, and is thus itself 'decentered'...: no longer agent, origin, author, but a function through which impersonal forces pass and intersect."[15]

Waugh provides an interesting critique of the postmodernist view of the self. First, she notes that postmodernism paradoxically attacks all Grand Narratives and yet, in doing so, replaces them: it becomes the only remaining explanatory narrative for all cultural phenomena. She wonders, "Is Postmodernism a phenomenon in the world or a theoretical construction projected on the world...?"[16]

Second, she suggests that theories about the fragmented postmodern self may result from the theoretician's "collective psychological response to the recognition that the ideal autonomy of Enlightenment cannot be possessed."[17] In other words, Stephen Dedalus's dream of flying by the nets of family, church, and country was realized neither by him, as he reappears in *Ulysses*, nor by others who still find themselves bound by the responsibilities of real life. The fragmentation of the self now recognized to be less that omnipotent would then be an immature, dangerous response to the inevitability of limitations. The Faustian desire to surpass all boundaries would no longer result in a pact with the devil leading to a descent to hell, as in Marlowe's version, or miraculous ascension into heaven because of a loving woman's intervention, as in Goethe's interpretation, but rather in total self-annihilation; devils and saints become unnecessary.

There is always tension between self-creation, the self one wants to be, and the responsibilities of self to others in society. The "private self" dreams, hopes, interprets life, stores memories, and acts; the "public self" situated in community also acts, sometimes for self and often for others. As one acts, one gains an identity—a sense of personal continuity in terms of language, habits, and values—which is nurtured and maintained by memory. Yet this self-continuity is constantly being modified by new experiences so that, paradoxically, the self has identity—a recognizable consistency about it—and yet is always new. Arnold H. Modell explains this paradox: "The self endures through time as a sense of identity, yet consciousness of self is always changing...The self is paradoxical: it is an enduring structure and at the same time nearly coterminus with an ever-changing consciousness. Furthermore, the private self supports a relative self-sufficiency, whereas from another perspective the self is not at all autonomous but can be seen as vulnerable in its dependence upon others for a sense of coherence and continuity."[18]

When the private self enters public space, its identity is modified, for better or for worse. This inevitable shaping of the self cannot be prevented, but it can be better understood through theoretical discussions of the self, alone and in community, and through exploration of how others, fictional and real characters, have experienced this process. *Essays on the Modern Identity* reveals how the self can never be neutral and is always modified by certain environments. The authors' goals are to create greater self-understanding within the reader and to sharpen the reader's comprehension of how his or her own self can best function in community. Modell has remarked that "the coherence and continuity of the self are augmented when the self extends its agency through the creation of new meanings."[19] It is hoped that readers will find just this kind of self-growth through experiencing the "new meanings" offered in this text.

Early Modern Self-Understanding

Subjectivity evolved during the Renaissance from a medieval understanding that the signs of the universe revealed God communicating with humankind to a modern belief that these now multivalent signs require a responsible subject to interpret them. As Luiz Costa Lima remarks, "because the traditional cosmic order, formulated theologically and grounded in the faith, was being found insufficient, the individual subject was charged with the discovery of a guiding logic."[20] Since the subject became the interpreter and organizer of external phenomena, increased attention was given to the internal processes of this thinking subject and to his or her agency in acting upon the world as a result of interpretations of it.

In "Self and Other in Rousseau: Love, Equality, and Equity in a World of Flux," Mira Morgenstern analyzes the significance of love, *amour-propre* and *amour de soi*, in theoretical texts by Jean-Jacques Rousseau but especially in the fictional social constructs designed by Wolmar in *La Nouvelle Héloïse* and by the tutor in *Emile*. While the construction of seemingly utopian situations represents modernism *par excellence*, the contradictions in Rousseau's treatment of his novels' characters and their love for each other foreshadow postmodern understandings of the self. Morgenstern notes how Rousseau's supposedly perfect society and ideal system of education deconstruct themselves and how the usual dualities of self and other, public and private, *amour-propre* and *amour de soi* elide and separate, never remaining in any category of essentiality. Rousseau's texts resist systematization but do show love, liberty, and authenticity to be foundational for the self, family, and broader society. He predicated the modernist assumption that an integrated self, open to change yet basically stable, is necessary for meaningful existence.

Morgenstern highlights the difficulties that Rousseau's characters experience in sharing themselves with others in a loving relationship. *Amour-propre*, an inauthentic love based on comparisons of self to others and resulting in the valuing of self over others, causes ephemeral relationships filled with passion and jealousy. *Amour de soi*, an authentic love founded on a healthy sense of self-preservation, enables one to love others reciprocally in relationships of equality and justice. The lover is able to identify empathically and freely with the beloved.

Yet the lover expects and perhaps needs to be loved in return. One is limited because one is dependent upon the other, but there is no happiness without a loving relationship. Morgenstern shrewdly demonstrates Rousseau's deconstruction of his own philosophy of love: "fermented" *amour de soi* can become inauthentic *amour-propre*; the beloved's "beauty" can be manipulated to fool the lover; "beauty," life, and hence love change and do not endure; and language can be finessed to disguise inauthenticity.

Julie in *La Nouvelle Héloïse* dies unhappily, and Emile and Sophie in *Emile* separate tragically. Julie fears losing her self to Saint-Preux, but she remains ignorant of the manipulation of the seemingly loving, but actually absolutely controlling, Wolmar; her true self is destroyed.

Sophie has little self-understanding in her education that can lead her to affirm adequate values. Morgenstern shows that the failure of the loving relationships within Rousseau's novels does not negate his belief in love and freedom as foundational for the family and society but rather demonstrates how difficult these qualities are to achieve and maintain in reciprocal, just relationships. Love means that self will be expanded and changed, possibly for the worse but hopefully for the better. As Morgenstern states, "Loving another person means being willing to risk one's own identity in the hope of enriching two lives."

In "Rousseau's Beautiful Soul: A Hegelian Reading," Ronnie L. Littlejohn demonstrates how Hegel's view of the self, in contrast to Rousseau's, keeps the self in motion, always experiencing the flux resulting from an irreducible dialectical interaction with the other. Hegel reflects philosophically on what Rousseau examined in his autobiographies and fiction: the relationship between self and other and the building of a society of selves. A self withdrawn from others, indeed a "beautiful soul" created when "the law of the heart elevates the individual conscience to moral supremacy," dissolves into a mad "lost soul." Littlejohn explores Hegel's position that being a person results from the dialectic between subject and object, freedom and nature, independence and dependence, and equality and reciprocity. He analyzes particularly Hegel's "Master and Slave" parable, in which the roles of the oppressed and the oppressor keep reversing themselves.

Rousseau, along with Descartes, Leibniz, Kant, Locke, and Hume, presents a fixed self known intuitively and formed by oneself in virtual isolation from others. Rousseau believed that his true self could not be known by others and that only he could understand that self and experience it fully in solitude, freed from the presence of others. Emile as a sort of modern "natural man" necessarily must be raised in isolation; Rousseau always feared the loss of his own and Emile's natural, basically good selves in society. By briefly comparing Hegel's and Rousseau's biographies, Littlejohn suggests that while Rousseau's unstable, impoverished beginnings could have motivated him to compose autobiographical works, Hegel's stable and successful life may have freed him from the need to write deeply personal journals and memoirs. Rousseau feared losing himself to others while Hegel, in his early "Materials for a Philosophy of Subjective Psychology" and later *Phenomenology of Spirit* (mostly written in 1806), posited that self-consciousness can only be derived from the dialectical struggle with others and that this struggle is never brought to a synthesizing conclusion. Society, then, "is not what is created by a set of rules agreed to by isolated individuals. It is that webbing of shared practices born of innumerable master-slave struggles which make possible not only human flourishing but the very emergence of persons themselves."

In "Goya and the Duchess of Alba: A Pictorial Confession Revealed," Ann Glenn Crowe documents passion's conquest over a famous artist, Francisco de Goya (1746–1828). Goya confesses his ill-fated love affair with the Duchess of Alba in five inter-related images produced within less than a decade. These images reveal, whether consciously or unconsciously, the artist's increasing anguish over this lady's inconstancy. This pictorial confession graphically demonstrates Goya's need to leave visual signs of his private feelings in works of art intended for public viewing.

Crowe's detective work in linking the five images that convey Goya's ardor is convincing. The first image is Goya's famous portrait, *The Duchess of Alba in Black* (1797). Three more are etchings from Goya's series of eighty etchings of social satire published in 1799, *Los Caprichos*. These are *Capricho 19*, "Volaverunt," and the etching intended for *Los Caprichos* but withheld from publication until 1940: "Dream. Of Lies and Inconstancy" (1798). The fifth image examined is Goya's notorious unsigned and undated painting *The Maja Vestida*. Although sometimes dated as late as 1805, Crowe demonstrates that it, too, may well date from the turn of the century. Each of these images display repeating items of clothing and physical features that signal the Duchess of Alba. Only on this Duchess did Goya paint the red satin sash and gold tufted sleeves of the bull fighter's bolero jacket in combination with the *mantilla* (shawl), the *camaisa* (slip), the *basquina* (overskirt), and the distinguishing "beauty spot" on her right temple. To these visual signs, Goya added other repeating physical features of the Duchess: her narrow waist, full bosom, proud carriage, oval face, long, straight nose, small mouth, large eyes, and thick, slanting eyebrows. With each image examined the "accretion of meanings" accumulates, so that ultimately Goya's passionate preoccupation with the Duchess of Alba is visually documented. Goya's "highly personal, psychic narrative" demonstrates that "the depth of his illicit passion for the aristocratic Duchess was considerable, even obsessive, however disjunctive the narrative by which he reveals it."

Anthony John Harding, in "The Romantic Subject and the Betrayals of the Text," explores a genre that, unlike Goya's disjunctive images, is traditionally thought to embody the plenitude of subjectivity. Modernist readings, for example, of Samuel Taylor Coleridge's notebooks and letters and of Dorothy Wordsworth's journals would seem to invite privileged access to their authors' unified consciousness and perceptions. Conventionally, the journal has been thought to contain the "real self" of the writer.

While Crowe considers dispersed images of Goya and creates a unity from them, Harding finds enormous disunity in texts that would seem to reveal the authentic self fully. Harding discovers in Coleridge's and Wordsworth's writings "the figurative nature of the private self, and its highly oblique and fitful relationship to the material texts." He recommends that journals be read "slant"—against the grain of their authors' and other modernists' assumptions about the unified continuity of the writing subject.

Harding, along with many postmodern thinkers, sees subjectivity as a product of specific historical circumstances, not as a universal given. He reiterates Michel Foucault's belief that writing creates "a space into which the writing subject constantly disappears." He agrees with Jane Flax that subjectivities are "fluid rather than solid, contextual rather than universal, and process oriented rather than topographical." Hence a careful deconstructive reading of journals is necessary in order to avoid fixing the writer's self into a mold or an essentialism that will resist further understanding of that self. Journal entries provide a textual self grounded in a particular time and space and composed of a network of other writings. These entries also present partial accounts of historical circumstances as well as information about the conditions of production of other works. Journal literature, Harding affirms, "exists for us as a textual space where subjectivity exists only from moment to moment, in evident incompleteness and temporality."

The concept of a fluid self in process is vividly exemplified in the texts of William Blake. Marjean D. Purinton, in "The De-Gendered Self in William Blake's poetry," argues that Blake's myth seeks to dissolve gender distinctions. The Eternal Imagination "is not a state; it is a Human Existence itself, and it is not defined by sex or gender." The violent conflicts between male and female entities in *America: A Prophecy, Europe: A Prophecy, The Book of Urizen, Thel, Visions of the Daughters of Albion, The Four Zoas, Milton*, and *Jerusalem* are the tragic result of gendered relationships. Purinton's reading of these texts thus reveals the artist not to be misogynistic but rather deeply troubled by the cruel outcomes of interactions grounded upon gendered selfhood.

The postlapsarian self is a cultural and political construction that fluctuates violently between the polarities of male and female, oppressor and oppressed. As soon as the oppressed gains power, he or she becomes an oppressor. Blake's texts destabilize these dichotomies and deconstruct unitary models of gender identity. They expose the oppression incorporated into the Western philosophical understanding of selfhood, and they challenge the reader to imagine a self not defined and delimited by gender. Purinton asserts, "To redeem ourselves from this system, we must, like Ololon, Milton, Los, and the Daughters of Albion, put off Selfhood, or gender, and work with—not against—Humanity as a genderless Divine being."

Each of these five chapters reveals that early modern self-understanding was much less essentialist than has been believed in the past. Every essay shows that, within the early modern writers' texts themselves, a self in motion is ever present. These readings exemplify how fresh understandings of the self combined with careful textual analysis can place in doubt the traditional assumptions about stable, gendered identities.

Modern Identity in a Postmodern World

The topic of subjectivity or its demise is popular among postmodern theoreticians. Some, like Jane Flax, link the concept of a unified self to the "metanarratives" of modernism. These metanarratives have oppressed the Other who embodies differences unrecognized by the definers of subjectivity. Flax states, "the unitary self is an effect of many kinds of relations of domination. It can only sustain its unity by splitting off or repressing other parts of its own and others' subjectivity."[21] Polarized terminology such as public/private, male/female, mind/body, white/black, and heterosexual/homosexual favors the first term of these dichotomies. One way to destabilize these descriptors is to redefine the self.

The self can be considered abstractly as an intellectual concept or more viscerally as "a being who is simultaneously embodied, fantasizing, rational, language-using, related to others, endowed with a distinctive temperament and inner world, socially constituted, and desiring."[22] Such a subject will be considered in the following essays. No attempt will be made to provide a conclusive definition of this subject because each subject is, of course, unique and free to view itself and others from either a modern, essentialist perspective or a postmodern, fluid point of view. These essays show that both perspectives still prevail simultaneously.

In "The Postmodern Self: 'Decentered,' 'Shattered,' 'Autonomous,' or What? A Study of Theoretical Texts by Deleuze and Guattari, Glass, Kohut, and Meyers," Carole J. Lambert explores four theories about the self which have been proposed in the postmodern era since 1946. She analyzes Gilles Deleuze and Félix Guattari's *Anti-Oedipus, Capitalism and Schizophrenia*, James M. Glass's *Private Terror/Public Life, Psychosis and the Politics of Community* and *Shattered Selves, Multiple Personality in a Postmodern World*, Heinz Kohut's *The Restoration of the Self*, and Diane Meyers's *Self, Society, and Personal Choice*. She notes that the goal of all of these theoreticians of the self is personal, individual freedom, an end already sought by Jean-Jacques Rousseau and writers of both the Romantic and Modern western European eras.

As we have seen in the first part of this book, authors and their subjects strongly *desired* a unified self which could ward off the threats to autonomy of an increasingly fragmented world. This desire was, however, often frustrated; subjectivity, as we noted for Rousseau, Coleridge, Dorothy Wordsworth, and many of Blake's mythological characters, was more slippery and out of control than these people or literary creations fully realized. If the essentialist self never completely existed in reality or fiction, then perhaps new understandings of the self may be necessary.

What differentiates modernists from postmodernists is how one arrives at personal liberation. Kohut proposes his psychotherapeutic theory, an improvement, he believes, on the Freudian paradigm, as a means of restoring a fragmented self to wholesome centeredness. Meyers's "autonomy competency," "autobiographical retrospection, detection, and reconciliation of conflicts within the self, and identification with preferred components of the self," secures "an integrated personality." Thus Kohut's and Meyers's approaches favor a unified self as the chief source of freedom.

The concept of the postmodern "decentered" self, as described by Deleuze and Guattari, suggests an introverted modern self without a center. The self operates according to freed unconscious desires, liberated from the oppressive metanarratives of Freudianism and capitalism. Glass opposes this postmodern paradigm with case studies of authentic "decentered" selves, those diagnosed as schizophrenics or sufferers of multiple personality disorder. He shows how very "unfree" these persons are, particularly in their inability to share a consensual reality with others and hence to live and work in communities.

Lambert's essay raises two questions that will necessitate an ongoing dialogue across the disciplines: how centered, decentered, or communal is the postmodern self, and how can the postmodern self's desire for freedom—from metanarratives, social conventions, internal pathology, and other restraints—best be achieved and expressed?

In "Discourse, Home, and Travel: The Place of the Self in Modern Travel Writing," Sally M. Silk emphasizes the relationship of language to the constitution of the self. Through her analysis of Céline's *Voyage au bout de la nuit*, she demonstrates her concept of "discursive homelessness": "a condition of language in which the self is understood as a transitive activity because it keeps moving from one voice to another, provoking transitions as it eludes centering." There is a continual disjunction between Bardamu, the narrator's voice, and Bardamu, the protagonist's characterization, in this story. The narrator's voice remains "free-floating" and separate from the story of its younger self. The two never really cohere. This lack of coherence, the eluding of a centering integration, represents linguistically a decentered self. Thus the act of writing problematizes rather than resolves the self's encounter with itself.

Bardamu's desire for freedom expresses itself in his unwillingness to accept the rules of any discursive process—namely that language is shared with others and thus runs the risk of being appropriated by them. Bardamu, the protagonist, is repeatedly taken advantage of when he does confide in others, so he evolves into a skilled escape artist, abandoning one situation after another. Bardamu, the narrator, compensates for his lack of control over his own words by creating a sympathetic ideal addressee. Thus the confessional mode of Rousseau and the Romantics, previously thought to represent unified subjectivity (although, as we have seen above, this may be a false assumption), now explodes into a frustrated, abject attempt "to bring discourse home once and for all." Both Bardamus try to hold back the threat of the other who will misuse their words, but this can never be achieved since language, narrative, and ultimately the self narrating and being narrated always remain in motion, available for new interpretations.

If the self is primarily defined and represented in disjunctive, ever mobile language, then two more key questions arise: who controls the self's language, and how can this "other" be controlled?

Howard Giskin, in "Lest We Not Forget: Memory in Semprun's *The Long Voyage*," argues that "activation of memory and reconciliation of the psychic split created by Gérard's war trauma in effect provide an antidote to the threat of totalitarianism." Jorge Semprun's Gérard, a thinly disguised autobiographical character, like Bardamu in Céline's *Voyage au bout de la nuit*, tries to make sense of a life badly disrupted because of the powerful discourses of others. Gérard (and Semprun) believe that through recalling extremely painful memories of victimization by the Nazis and by writing or telling about these memories three goals may be accomplished: personal psychological healing, negation of Nazi inhumanity through revealing this inhumanity to the world, and prevention of atrocities as horrendous as those that occurred during the Holocaust. Unlike the decentered Bardamu, Gérard, according to Giskin, transforms into a coherent account the "jumbled mass of disjointed memories" about his train ride to the concentration camp, the shattering of mind and body that occurred there, and the frustration of post-liberation encounters with persons who refuse to become fully aware of the horrible acts which took place during the Holocaust. Given the one voiced "truth" which the Nazis imposed on their victims and many persons' silent denial of distressing history, the Holocaust's historicity must be guarded and then exposed by a centered, somewhat autonomous self. This historicity is lost if the self becomes "decentered," either through agreeing with the Nazi discourse or through suffering a psychic splitting off of the memories, the experience of those who refuse to acknowledge painful truths.

One means that Gérard uses to avoid self-decentering is to analyze the predominant Nazi discourse which tries to control the self's language. Knowledge of how this discourse works is already a means of gaining some control over it. Gérard ascertains that the Nazi credo advocates "the submission of individuality and the death of critical self-consciousness." Thus Nazis are *intentionally* trying to decenter the self so that the recreated self is shaped according to their desires and loses the centeredness which would allow a critique of their actions. The inhumane, violent acts of German soldiers, functionaries, and civilians, including small children, result from their adherence to the discourse of one social construction of reality, posited as *the* truth. This adherence to a totalizing discourse lowers moral inhibitions.

Giskin's research into studies of the Holocaust and its survivors shows that a threefold process allowed the Nazi discourse to control the self: authorization (Violence was authorized by superiors.), routinization (Violent actions were routinized.), and dehumanization (Victims were dehumanized through ideological indoctrination.). Giskin concludes that "the reestablishment of an autonomous self tied to humanity through a common sympathetic bond is the final goal of Semprun's narrative."

Some would argue that this "common sympathetic bond" is nurtured through education in the "liberal arts." In "Piracquo's Missing Finger, Or, The Utility of the Liberal Arts," Dan Latimer deconstructs this assumption. He notes that Albert Speer's devotion to the works of Schiller and other artists did not prevent him from becoming a willing collaborator with the Nazis. He reminds us that Hitler himself was an artist with certain aesthetic proclivities. In short, Latimer affirms that "there are enough examples of diabolism, bloodlust, and madness among people who deal in the 'liberal' arts to cause us to reconsider the terms in which we are recommending them to the young."

If the "liberal arts" become another suspect discourse in the shaping of the self, then what discourses become acceptable? This essay reflects the tension between emphasis placed on the self's mind or its body. Enlightenment concepts of subjectivity and the educational discourses which shape it, nurtured by texts such as Friedrich Schiller's *Essays Aesthetical and Philosophical*, Matthew Arnold's *Culture and Anarchy*, Herbert Marcuse's *The Aesthetic Dimension*, and Ernst Bloch's *The Principle of Hope*, emphasize the life of the mind, reason, spirit, or aesthetic sensibility. Latimer, via his discussion of Georges Bataille's ideas, focuses the discussion of the self on its embodiment, including its materiality and eventual putrefaction.

"We must find in art that which proper bourgeois life denies us," Latimer declares. Art, for example, is about DeFlores, in Thomas Middleton's *The Changeling*, cutting off the just murdered Piracquo's finger to get his engagement ring off and later to become the virgin Beatrice-Joanna's lover. Real poetry reveals sacred wastage, the divine intoxication of "expenditure" and "sacrifice." It communicates convulsively what is ordinarily stifled. Citing Bataille, Latimer affirms that literature is the "dream of sacred violence which no settlement with organized society can attenuate."

"Organized society" tries to shape a self useful for its purposes—bored, reasonable, submissive, communicating banally, and producing useful goods. The belief is fostered that materiality and physical needs degrade and circumscribe the self's freedom. Schiller, for example, writes that aesthetics help man to become rational and liberated from passion and bestiality. This conception of the role of art and the liberal arts in society is founded on "a massive repression of materiality." Latimer believes that "what art is unable to face, indeed, what art conceals, lies about, are its origins in materiality, its birth from the primal slime."

If Silk and Giskin recall for us how linguistic discourse either decenters or centers the self perceived as a verbal construct, then Latimer eloquently forces us to remember that a disembodied self is illusionary and that the discourses which shape the self will always have to reckon with that fact.

The embodied self must live interdependently with others and thus to some degree share its beliefs, skills, and goods with those others. Kent Brudney, in "The Making of the Postmodern Minimal Self: Rousseau and the Denial of Dialogical Politics," believes that "Rousseau's minimal self represents the bridge between modern and postmodern notions of the self." The "minimal self," ambiguous, fluid, frail, and non-integrated, survives from moment to moment only by remaining on guard against the external, imposing discourses which threaten it. It can try to escape and to transcend these discourses through the imagination in an effort to integrate its multiple, fluid selves. As evidenced in Rousseau's autobiographical texts, *The Confessions* and *The Reveries of a Solitary Walker*, the integration sought for is impossible because no independent standard exists for a unified self. This minimal self thus becomes incapable of participating in the dialogical politics necessary for a democratic community. The decentered self has no sense of identity strong enough to share with others.

Reflecting on the postmodern, decentered self, Brudney notes that "the much heralded coming of postmodern fluid, multiple selves conveniently posits an individual who is too playful and too slippery to be pinned down by the myriad forces of social, economic, and political control." In reality, he finds that these minimal selves gravitate to a community of others similar to themselves; thus all are protected from real otherness and difference. This unity with others who mirror the fragile self can prevent the dialogical politics on which pluralistic democracy depends. Freedom becomes "the right to be left alone," and language no longer promotes understanding and political agency.

W. Jay Reedy, in "Rousseau and Communitarian Individualism in

'Late Modern' America: The Interpretation of Benjamin Barber," zeroes in on American communitarian views which warn against the atomized individualism and "interest-group" politics that result in a "vacuous 'moral' content." Communitarians question the Lockean, laissez-fairist bases of liberalism, the self-centered "privatism" which threatens cohesion, economic production, fulfilling communities and successful schools. Reedy focuses on several of Benjamin Barber's texts as they relate to the political and educational theories of Rousseau.

Reedy states that Rousseau's overriding objective was to determine "how people can achieve a diverse but just community made up of autonomous and different but responsible and caring individuals." One of the few Communitarians to use Rousseau's theories, since most rely only on the limited heritage of ideas and attitudes peculiar to the United States, Barber promotes Rousseau's concept of imaginative, creative empathy, or *pitié*, as a means of correcting extreme autonomy. If one is allowed to feel sympathetically for the other, particularly the victimized other, one may desire to construct a community that will minimize injustice and suffering.

Along with *pitié*, education and mandatory community service also have the potential to transform "me language" into "we language" for Barber. He strongly favors "the pragmatics of democratic dialogue," but Reedy notes that "Barber's faith in dialogue *per se* is not Rousseauist and by itself seems untenable as the route to a democratic society." Historically, citizens' discussions with each other have not always been "undistorted" nor resulted in humane, inclusionary policies. Reedy questions how Americans, raised in a society where success thrives on such deception and divisiveness, can conduct open and authentic debates leading to the construction of sound communities.

Barber, like many other Communitarians, refuses to profoundly criticize the contemporary social and economic practices which classical liberalism, in tandem with contemporary capitalism, has produced. He does not fully utilize Rousseau's political insights both because of this reluctance to confront American values and institutions and because of his refusal to theorize in order to make normative and objective judgments about the entire public realm according to a standard external to that realm's present-day conditions. Reedy states that Rousseau "realized that eschewing critical theorizing redounds by default to the established 'facts' and persons in power." People are seduced by an ideology of illusory and undemocratic individualism and remain deceived by it too often. Barber combines some of Rousseau's insights with his own "uncritical pragmatism" so that "the pursuit of 'truth' and ethics and equity" is exchanged "for pragmatic pliability." The result of this lack of theorizing is that Barber's reformist recommendations are diluted to "arbitrary preferences." Barber could have used Rousseau for a fertile if "un-American" theoretical ground, but he stops short of achieving that.

The essays in this volume are, we hope, revealing and suggestive, rather than definitive and conclusive. They are intended to raise important questions rather than to provide all of the answers about identity. They present exemplary analyses of selected texts which may help the reader to think more deeply about the complex issue of subjectivity. They are offered as one contribution to the ongoing, necessarily interdisciplinary discussion of the place of modern identity in a postmodern world.

Notes

1. Martin E. Gloege, "The American Origins of the Postmodern Self," in *Constructions of the Self*, ed. George Levine (New Brunswick: Rutgers Univ. Press, 1992), 59.
2. Irving Howe lists these and other reasons for "the demotion of the idea of the self" in "The Self in Literature," in *Constructions of the Self*, 264–266.
3. Jean-Jacques Rousseau, *Emile: or On Education*, trans. Allan Bloom (New York: Basic Books, 1979), 267. All subsequent quotations from this book are taken from this edition.
4. William Wordsworth, *The Prelude, 1799, 1805, 1850*, ed. Jonathan Wordsworth, M. H. Abrams, and Stephen Gill (New York: Norton, 1979), 10:791. All citations from *The Prelude* are taken from the 1805 version.
5. William R. Caspary, "The Concept of a Core-Self," in *The Book of the Self: Person, Pretext, and Process*, ed. Polly Young-Eisendrath and James A. Hall (New York: New York Univ. Press, 1987), 369.
6. Ibid., 370.
7. See Carole Lambert's essay in this volume for a detailed discussion of James M. Glass's *Private Terror/Public Life, Psychosis and the Politics of Community* and *Shattered Selves, Multiple Personality in a Postmodern World*.
8. Charles Taylor, *Sources of the Self: The Making of the Modern Identity* (Cambridge: Harvard Univ. Press, 1989), 3.
9. Taylor, 27–28.
10. See William A. Galston, "Clinton and the Promise of Communitarianism (Point of View)," *The Chronicle of Higher Education* 39, 25 (December 2, 1992): A52, and Karen J. Winkler, "Communitarians Move Their Ideas Outside Academic Arena," *The Chronicle of Higher Education* 39, 33 (April 21, 1993): A11–A13.

11. See Jean-Jacques Rousseau, *On Social Contract*, in *Rousseau's Political Writings*, ed. Alan Ritter and Julia Conaway Bondanella, trans. Julia Conaway Bondanella (New York: Norton, 1988), 123.

12. Galston, A52.

13. Patricia Waugh, *Practising Postmodernism Reading Modernism* (London: Edward Arnold, 1992), 3.

14. Waugh, 5.

15. Waugh, 8.

16. Waugh, 12.

17. Waugh, 121.

18. Arnold H. Modell, *The Private Self* (Cambridge: Harvard Univ. Press, 1993), 3.

19. Modell, 7–8.

20. Luiz Costa Lima, *Control of the Imaginary: Reason and Imagination in Modern Times*, trans. Ronald W. Sousa (Minneapolis: Univ. of Minnesota Press, 1988), 5.

21. Jane Flax, *Disputed Subjects: Essays on Psychoanalysis, Politics, and Philosophy* (New York: Routledge, 1993), 109.

22. Flax, 118.

**Early Modern
Self-Understanding**

Self and Other in Rousseau:
Love, Equality, and Equity in a World of Flux
by Mira Morgenstern

From the vantage point of the 20th century, Rousseau's literary works can appear to be mindless romantic drivel, prototypical of the sentimentalized Victorian family. Moreover, Rousseau's discussions of love in his more theoretical writings have been castigated as both paternalistic and misogynistic (along with much of traditional political theory). This essay demonstrates first, that Rousseau's writings on love are inextricably tied to the political questions treated throughout his oeuvre and are not romantic musings external to his intellectual enterprise. This is evident in Rousseau's conceptualization of the phenomenon and process of love as an extended discourse between the Self and the Other that can ideally lead to the establishment of both political and personal authenticity, which Rousseau presents as a central goal in all of his works.[1] Second, this essay shows that Rousseau's writings on love, despite their traditional cast and language, in many ways anticipate contemporary philosophic concerns in their portrayal of love as a more complex and ambiguous notion than it is commonly understood to be.

Rousseau first introduces the concept of love as love of Self. This is consonant with his view of Natural Man as an asocial being, lacking much feeling and empathy towards his fellow human. While love is at first conceived only as a reflexive sentiment, however, this feeling is quickly revealed to be quite complex. In *Discourse on Inequality*, Rousseau separates love of Self into the "bad" and "good" types of Self-love. Amour-propre is described as "a relative, false sentiment, born in society, which leads each individual to make more of himself than of anyone else."[2] Amour-propre is clearly a product of the imagination: it is based on the comparison of Self with Others in the human desire to be more favorably considered by the Other, in other words, to distinguish one's Self. Amour de soi, on the other hand, is portrayed by Rousseau as a basic, natural sentiment, which is "anterior to all reflection."[3] Rousseau understands amour de soi simply as the instinct for self-preservation.[4]

The anteriority of amour de soi is emphasized by the contrast that he draws between amour-propre as a sentiment born out of comparison, and amour de soi as a feeling evinced by Natural Man who, aware only of himself, is therefore by definition incapable of making any comparison.[5] However, the definition of amour de soi does not remain merely instinctual and therefore benignly good. By extension, and also as a result of Rousseau's further analysis, amour-propre in its turn comes to be portrayed as not inherently evil, and even, at times, as redeemable. The path that Rousseau takes to arrive at these more complex, nuanced readings of amour de soi and amour-propre bears important implications for his understanding of the underpinnings of a stable and authentic social and political community.

Already in *Discourse on Inequality*, a note of dissonance creeps into Rousseau's portrayal of amour de soi as simply instinctual. In his description of Natural Man's patterns of action in the State of Nature, Rousseau opposes pity to the survival instinct, suggesting that pity restrains amour de soi from turning into a sense of self-preservation so highly developed that it culminates in homicide. This indicates that amour de soi contains within itself some form of Self-regarding and even selfish passion. Far from being merely a benign survival instinct, amour de soi in its operational mode reveals itself to be highly willful, disregarding everything except what it desires in order to attain its goal. Possessing only amour de soi, Natural Man may not yet have a highly developed sense of imagination or even comparison. However, he clearly already has enough imagination to be able to think about himself as a separate entity: Rousseau describes Natural Man who possesses amour de soi as "looking at himself as the only spectator."[6] The ability to think about oneself not only requires a certain amount of metaphoric imagination, but also implies the recognition of other creatures in contrast to whom one distinguishes an idea of Self. Once that is accomplished, one's own sense of Self acquires a priority over others. Whether that is a matter of survival or, as Rousseau points out in the case of the hunt, a question of convenience, it becomes clear that the survival instinct, or amour de soi, easily shades into selfish preference, or amour-propre.

Rousseau hints at the continuum linking amour de soi and amour-propre when describing their embryonic stages. Overtly, however, he takes great care to distinguish both their essential natures and their long-term effects. Throughout his work, Rousseau insists that the outgrowths of amour de soi are positive. First among its benefits is the ability to love someone else. Second is the establishment of justice in society as a whole. Rousseau links these outgrowths to amour de soi by developing an in-depth understanding of the nature of this love.

The kind of love for another human being that develops out of amour de soi forms an important link in Rousseau's social and political theory, for it is that sentiment which will serve as the affective basis for the stability of human society. The essential characteristic of that love is its reciprocity.[7] To be complete, love must be an exchange of feelings. Rousseau specifically distinguishes this type of love from unrequited, i.e. one-sided, passion. Instead, this reciprocal love is reminiscent of a dynamic friendship, which he describes as "an exchange, a contract like the others...the most sacred of all."[8] It is worth noting that Rousseau uses the concept of contract to define his notion of love. In the *Social Contract*, he similarly defines the contract as a "reciprocal engagement."[9] The notion of reciprocity implies the equality and mutuality of giving, and serves as the guarantee of the essential justice and righteousness of the act. In other words, the authenticity of this love is proven by the fact that both participants give and receive love. Unlike amour-propre, which values Self above all others, there is no attempt here to cheat anybody out of anything. On the contrary, equality is strived for precisely because that is the only condition under which this authentic love can flourish.

From this description alone, it is easy to understand why this notion of love, developing out of amour de soi, can serve as a basis for an emotionally cohesive society. By engendering caring relationships between people, this type of love can, if extended on a society-wide basis, achieve similar results for the entire community. The outcome of such a situation would be a cohesiveness based not just on selfish rationality, but on an emotional identification with the community as a whole. Unlike the transitional foundations of cooperation based on rationally perceived needs, as exemplified by the hunt in *Discourse on Inequality*, the cohesiveness grounded in affective identification promotes both a more authentic society, as well as a more stable one.

This view of the development of amour de soi also explains why Rousseau sees justice as an outgrowth of amour de soi and not, as commonly supposed, of reason. He prefers to predicate justice on sentiment because he views sentiment as a more solid operational basis than reason for justice. Analysis of the rationalistic aspect of pity demonstrates that rationalism can easily slide into selfishness: after all, if we are sure that we will never be in the Other's situation (which logical probability underlies our ability to rationally grasp the advantages of treating other people justly), why should we treat him with justice? Why, indeed, would we care about him at all? Therefore, Rousseau relies on "the force of an expansive soul identify[ing] me with my fellow" to establish justice.[10] Rousseau understands this "force" to be a highly developed intuitive understanding leading to perfect empathy. One feels the pain of one's fellow and will therefore treat him fairly.

Along with love's contribution of an expanded sense of justice in the transformation of the foundations of social unity, love also brings with it other positive developments resulting from amour de soi. These are seen in three categories: moral, aesthetic, and philosophical. These categories operate mainly on the individual level, but can contain social implications as well. First, love betokens the entry of man into the moral sphere.[11] This is because love is man's first foray into a realm not entirely governed by reason. Like love, moral concepts are not products of reason alone, but emanate from an enlightened soul.[12] Because love heralds as well the beginning of man's social life,[13] Rousseau emphasizes the inextricable ties between morality and politics,[14] and the central role that love plays in both arenas. Love's contribution to man's moral understanding thus underlines not just love's own importance in man's private life, but in addition its significance for the foundation of an authentic and stable political order.

Aside from its moral and political contributions, love also heightens man's aesthetic sense. Even if love disappoints in a particular case, it bestows the gift of appreciation of the beautiful and sublime. Love makes man aware of perfection, even if, in a specific instance, that perfection remains unattainable, or is only falsely achieved.[15] In that sense, love makes man more human by awakening him to the greater perfection of which he is capable. Love arouses man to his own human perfectibility.

Finally, love encapsulates both the limits and possibilities of human happiness. Love and happiness stand in a paradoxical relationship to each other. Love limits human happiness, because it makes that happiness dependent on another human being. At the same time, however, love enables human happiness to exist because, without love, there is no human happiness at all. Our need for society makes love our pathway to happiness, but our happiness by Rousseau's definition is therefore never complete,[16] since Rousseau defines happiness as a balance between one's desires and one's forces.[17] Clearly, that balance is most easily achieved by someone who needs nobody else, because, in that situation, he can control both his desires and his forces. The minute a need or desire is dependent on someone else for fulfillment, the maintenance of the balance is no longer in one's own control. Rousseau's conclusion is that only God knows absolute happiness, for only He has need of no one else. However, Rousseau emphasizes that such a happiness is not within the purview of human beings. Imperfect creatures must seek their completion and therefore their happiness through other people. Thus, love defines the ambiguity of the human condition by simultaneously delimiting the area of man's happiness and of his imperfection.

According to Rousseau, love introduces us to both morality and aesthetics and allows us to confront our own humanity through the nature of our happiness, but he also incorporates a sinister element into his analysis of love. This is manifest most obviously in the course of Rousseau's *Émile* when that book's protagonist, deliberately educated according to a perfected tutorial system, is introduced to love. In order to prevent Émile from being attracted by the facile charm of society courtesans, the Tutor paints for Émile a picture of his true love, who will later turn out to be Sophie. At this point, however, it is not clear that this creature of the Tutor's imagination exists at all. Nevertheless, the Tutor shrugs off any suggestions of duplicity in his presentation to Émile. He defends himself by arguing that love itself is anyway only an illusory lie.[18] Like the fantasy of Sophie, the chimera of love has a purpose to fulfill. The purpose of love is to set the seal on Émile's socialization, a process that had begun with the development of pity and benevolence in him. One could argue that love need not be an illusion to accomplish the goal of socialization: a love based on reality could complete the process just as well. In fact, Rousseau does not deny this proposition. What he does argue, however, is even more difficult to understand within the general context of his social and political theory. It is Rousseau's contention that the concept of love is *necessarily* an illusion. For Rousseau, love is, by definition, a chimera.

In view of the importance that Rousseau places on love as the affective basis of social cohesion, this new depiction of love as a mirage clearly has negative implications for the possibility of the achievement of an authentic, cohesive community. It is hard to understand why Rousseau would sabotage his own theoretical construct in this way. Furthermore, it is difficult to see from where he could derive this disparagement of love as illusory. In his conception of amour de soi, on which his entire notion of the development of love is based, amour de soi is understood as an entirely natural and authentic sentiment, resulting in many positive and laudable characteristics, of which justice is only one.

A closer look, however, at the way Rousseau introduces the development of love for Émile, as well as at Rousseau's original presentation of love, reveals the early presence of a dark underside to his conception of love. Already in *Discourse on Inequality*, love is presented as the result of a series of comparisons made by various people. Comparisons include preferences, which give rise to love.[19] Love is understood here in the aesthetic sense: the attachment to what is the most beautiful or sublime. Rousseau recognizes, however, that the definition of what is the most beautiful—or at least, what appears to be the most beautiful—is a matter of subjective interpretation and even manipulation. He does not directly comment on the issue of the subjective interpretation of beauty, but it appears clear that this generally had to be the case. Otherwise, if one standard of absolute beauty were to prevail, all people would desire the same person. To be sure, simultaneous desire of the same person does occur at times, which is why Rousseau names jealousy as love's counterpart.[20] In the main, however, he considers the development of standards of beauty and merit as a method enabling each man to choose a specific woman to love, rather than be attracted generally to the entire female sex.[21]

It is the manipulation of the appearance of who is the most beautiful and meritorious that causes Rousseau to condemn love as the harbinger of falsehood and inauthenticity on both the personal and political levels. Establishing a standard of excellence to recognize whom one loves can turn into a method for duping the person making the choice. In other words, it is possible to manipulate the process of choice so as to become the chosen partner. The line between the active chooser and the passive chosen becomes increasingly blurred. More important, however, is the fact that categories of truth and falsehood, reality and appearance, are made to substitute for one another, while they remain in actuality distinct entities. If one cannot really be the best, one has to fool the spectator into believing that one is.[22] As a result, love becomes a process of marketing a product—oneself—rather than an opportunity to expand one's being to enter someone else's soul. The aim of love, as depicted in *Discourse on Inequality*, is to gain one's own advantage, rather than to achieve greater happiness for all concerned. The result is that man becomes a fictive being, recreating himself as a chimera in order to attract someone else. His existence becomes entirely relative, a function of his estimate of the Other's perception. Instead of carrying his own being entirely with himself,[23] as did the authentic Natural Man, man is now reduced to being the slave of someone else's perception of him.[24] This is seen not so much in terms of actual physical strength, as in terms of the power of the imagination to define and recreate reality. By altering man's reactions, imagination changes the effect of man's environment on himself which, Rousseau argues, is just about the same thing as effecting the actual physical metamorphosis itself. In this case, the attempt to manipulate the Other's imagination results in being enslaved to that same imagination. Being chosen depends on how well the other imagination accedes to being manipulated. By attempting to control the Other's imagination, man is paradoxically at its mercy, for the image he wants to propagate hinges upon this Other. The result is that love becomes a series of manipulated images rather than a truly felt emotion.

The emphasis that this depiction of love places on imagery and appearance recalls the definition of amour-propre as a selfish love, born out of comparison, and characterized by a desire for personal advancement and advantage.[25] Amour-propre is not, however, the only type of love characterized by appearances. Hints of it are evident in Rousseau's definition of amour de soi as well. This is most obvious in *Émile*, where Rousseau remarks that comparison—a function of amour-propre—is a fundamental part of any type of loving: "One loves only after having judged, one prefers only after having compared."[26] Rather than being polar opposites, amour de soi and amour-propre are revealed to be linked on the same continuum. This is further emphasized by Rousseau's analysis of reciprocity, another hallmark of amour de soi. He points out that reciprocity means not just wanting to give what you get, but wanting to get what you give. In other words, it is because people want to be loved that they make themselves lovable and desirable.[27] Rousseau seems prepared to regard even amour de soi in a light similar to that in which he views amour-propre: less as a spontaneous emotion than as a method calculatingly used to acquire something for oneself. In fact, amour-propre seems to be incorporated into the very essence of Rousseau's notion of positive love—i.e., amour de soi. Rousseau appears to accede to that notion when he concludes his analysis of amour de soi with the remark that "[a]mour de soi, ceasing to be an absolute feeling, becomes pride in grand souls, vanity in small ones, and in all [souls] nourishes itself endlessly at the expense of their [the souls'] neighbors."[28] This point is further emphasized in the *Letter to Christophe de Beaumont*: "Amour de soi put into fermentation becomes amour-propre."[29] To be sure, the continuum between amour de soi and amour-propre runs both ways. This is seen when Émile's sense of pride is utilized to keep him from falling prey to the vices of youth.[30] Rousseau does admit, however, that the likelihood of transforming amour-propre into an unmitigated good remains slim.

It would seem, then, that the theoretical problems posed by the dark underside of amour de soi prevail. If amour-propre is an inherent part of amour de soi, the implication is that truly authentic love is doomed. The Other-directed aspect of love becomes a mere mask for its selfish Self-referentiality. The claim of amour de soi to be the integral adhesive element of an authentic political community is similarly jeopardized, if its notion of community can at most encompass just one other member. This conflict is encapsulated in the remarks made by the Tutor on the subject of love and passion during Émile's adolescence. On the one hand, the Tutor hails the ability to love as the consummation of Émile's entire education.[31] In the next breath, however, the Tutor reveals his intention to use Émile's ability to love not just to tame Émile's sexuality—which can be viewed as a noble exercise in self-discipline— but, more importantly, to increase the Tutor's personal power over Émile.[32] In other words, the ability to love is used to manipulate.

But can manipulation really be the goal of Émile's education? Is Rousseau's entire theory of love a sham? He certainly recognized love's many theoretical difficulties. His two literary works, *Émile* and *La Nouvelle Héloïse*, can be read in large part as further attempts to work out in practical terms the theoretical problems inherent in this conception of love. While each of these books contains wide ranging deliberations on the subject, each settles on one or two particular complexities to explore. *La Nouvelle Héloïse* focuses to a large extent on the categories of Self and Other. Using these concepts, *La Nouvelle Héloïse* examines the possibility of union with the Other while still maintaining an identity of Self. *La Nouvelle Héloïse* also treats the tension between the private community of lovers and the larger surrounding community with regard to the social responsibility of the preoccupied lovers. *Émile*, on the other hand, presents us with a study of the inner workings of what is supposed to be an ideal, authentic relationship between a man and a woman. Unlike Julie in *La Nouvelle Héloïse*, Émile and Sophie will not have to deal with conflict between Self and Other because they are the perfect mates for each other. In order to establish that ideal relationship with each other, they must incorporate equality and reciprocity into their partnership. As we shall later see, this is precisely what gives Rousseau difficulty in his depiction of Sophie, her education, and her subsequent relationship with Émile. Because Rousseau's literary works present his attempt to work out these major theoretical difficulties in his conception of love—to render man, as Rousseau puts it, both happy (in personal love) and good (loving others and being a responsible citizen)[33]—it is to these works that we now turn our attention.

La Nouvelle Héloïse has been called a "meditation on love."[34] Rousseau himself considered it to be an evocative fantasy of love and friendship.[35] In addition, *La Nouvelle Héloïse* can also be viewed as an extended discourse on the difficulties and pitfalls of love. We will confine our analysis here to a discussion of these pitfalls as they represent Rousseau's further conjectures on the complexities of his own theory of love. Specifically, we will focus on the tension between Self and Other that is manifest in the love relationship. This tension will be examined on the individual level, as it impacts upon the two people in love, and in terms of its effect on the social level, where the hermetic notion of an exclusive couple relationship is challenged by the moral and physical counter-demands of society at large. The extent to which these contradictions can be resolved will indicate the possibility of establishing two different kinds of authenticity. On the individual level, what is at stake is the possibility of maintaining a fully functioning personal identity while participating in a union with another person. The issue at the social level is the possibility of establishing an area of personal choice and action that is outside of communal influence. In other works, the question on the social level is whether the private "we" can exist apart from the communal "us," whether, in fact, there are areas of life apart from the political sphere, properly defined. Rousseau will fully answer this second question only in his political works. However, because he views personal authenticity as an inextricable prerequisite to political authenticity, defusing the tension between the Self and the Other on the personal level as well is crucial to the resolution of Rousseau's political theory.

In a novel that purports to be about love, it is remarkable that so few of its characters seem to believe in love at all. Neither Julie's father nor her husband take any account of this emotion: the Baron d'Étanges marries Julie off to M. de Wolmar in recognition of Wolmar's having saved his life in battle. Even Julie's young cousin Claire finds no place in her life for (heterosexual) love. While remaining deeply attached to Julie, she feels herself incapable of falling in love.

Julie's and Saint-Preux's feelings for each other are in direct contrast to this rational, somewhat cynical attitude towards romantic love. The worldly and world-weary Lord Edward Bomston expresses this when he notes, "It is just this that distinguishes you, that it is impossible to distinguish between you."[36] Bomston's perception of Julie and Saint-Preux being the "unique model of true lovers"[37] leads him to offer them one of his estates as an asylum. Julie, however, rejects the offer, citing the honor and duty she owes her family as reasons for her refusal.[38] Julie's deliberate declining of the opportunity to make a life with Saint-Preux certainly owes something to her inability to overcome the class distinctions between them: Julie is a member of the nobility while Saint-Preux can at best aspire to be called middle-class. In essence, however, Julie's denial of her own happiness can best be understood as the result of her inability to cope with the complexities and ambiguities of loving another human being. It would seem that Bomston has touched upon a sore point with his remarks on the lovers' indistinguishability from each other. As we shall see, it is possible to trace, throughout the exchange of letters between Julie and Saint-Preux, Julie's own growing awareness of and discomfort with these perils of falling in love.

Both Julie and Saint-Preux are aware of the transformation wrought within them by the development of their feelings for each other.[39] Their reactions to it differ, however. Saint-Preux appears wholeheartedly happy to dissolve himself, as it were, into Julie's being.[40] For Saint-Preux, inextricably intertwining his existence with that of Julie serves to ennoble his life,[41] and he wishes that enterprise to be mutually fulfilling.[42] Julie, on the other hand, views the process of falling in love and loving another person with much foreboding. For her, the expansion of soul that accompanies love brings with it as much terror as triumph. Recounting how she fell in love with Saint-Preux, she remarks to her cousin Claire, "It is pity that was my ruin [me perdit]."[43] The pity that Julie speaks of is the developed form of pity that allows one to enter into another's soul, to "feel oneself in another."[44] What is significant here is Julie's characterization of this sentiment. For her, this expansion of her soul is equivalent to the loss of her Self: "la pitié…me perdit."

It might be argued that Julie's trepidation of being in love is due to her selfishness. However, such a conclusion is difficult to sustain. For one thing, fear of losing one's Self is not the same thing as the selfish desire to affirm one's Self at all cost. Moreover, throughout the novel, Julie is portrayed as a person who cares deeply for other people's feelings and welfare (even if, as our analysis of Clarens will subsequently show, she can be sincerely wrongheaded at times). Given Rousseau's own analysis of love, Julie's fear becomes quite understandable. Love based on the expansion of Self necessarily means the alteration of that Self from its previous form. The salient question is whether that alteration means the destruction of the Self, or its reconstitution in another configuration. Julie's attitude indicates that she believes in the first possibility. Her struggle against falling in love with Saint-Preux—and when that fails, from realizing the practical consequences of that love—reveals her efforts to preserve her sense of that Self and the fixed boundaries of her own being.

To a certain extent, Julie is aware of her fear and of the limits it imposes on her ability to love. She reveals this by emphasizing the Self-validation that she attempts to achieve through love. Thus, for example, Julie says that she seeks in Saint-Preux the qualities that complement her own characteristics.[45] Julie loves Saint-Preux for the way he reflects her own feelings.[46] In each of these statements, love is understood not as Other-directed but as Self-referential. Love is valued for what it brings to oneself. This sentiment certainly contradicts the stated purpose of love, which is to reach out to another human being. On the other hand, it does reflect the way that love develops as described in the account of *Discourse on Inequality*. There, as we recall, love becomes a commodity whose aim is to maximize profit in an atmosphere of subterfuge and deceit.

Rousseau does not make it clear in *La Nouvelle Héloïse* whether Julie is fully aware of the connections between love and Self-referentiality. In *Discourse on Inequality*, however, he does analyze just why love can develop in such a selfish and destructive manner. The culprit, he says, is not love but (erotic) passion.[47] Passion, born of amour-propre and the tendency to compare, corrupts the pure sentiment of loving another person derived from amour de soi. Elsewhere, however, we have seen that Rousseau suggests that there is a little of amour-propre present even in amour de soi. The implication, therefore, is that passion is an inextricable part of love. But the characters in *La Nouvelle Héloïse* do not appear to be aware of this subtlety. On the contrary, they seem quite taken by the distinction between love and passion, which they subsequently range along the lines of good and evil. For them, love is bad when it is tainted by passion, and it can be redeemed only when that passion is exorcised.

Influenced by this approach, Julie will try to form relationships that partake of love but not of passion. Her rationalization is twofold. First, passion is held to be selfish and ephemeral. As a result, it can accomplish no real and lasting good. Second, runs this argument, only love that is chaste—without passion—can hope to have positive effects and attain real happiness. After Julie's and Saint-Preux's relationship is discovered and they are forcibly separated, this reasoning dominates the consideration of every relationship in the novel.

A major example of this reasoning occurs at a turning point in the novel: Claire's successful attempt to dissuade Saint-Preux from persisting in his pursuit of Julie. Claire accomplishes this by reinterpreting Saint-Preux's love for Julie as fundamentally passion-driven. Since passion is selfish and based solely on physical attractions, it cannot last. Thus, reasons Claire, Saint-Preux will really be better off if he gives up Julie. That way, he can preserve the untainted memory of her physical perfection, which is held to be the raison d'être of his love for her in the first place.[48] Claire's words fall on fertile soil, for Saint-Preux himself had already expressed similar sentiments in the beginning of his love affair with Julie. At that point, he had urged Julie to make the most of their time together, for her beauty, like all things, is bound to fade and pass away.[49] Perhaps in deference to Saint-Preux's status as a teacher of philosophy, Claire even attempts to state this point as a general rule: due to the impossibility of maintaining the fervor of love in real life, love can exist most perfectly in memory. In a narrative footnote, Rousseau likewise remarks on the illusion of constancy in love in the face of life's eternal flux.[50]

It is perhaps ironic that the means to maintain a purer and more perfect love are found in an appeal to a selfish interest. Saint-Preux is prevailed upon to give up Julie the better to maintain an illusion that could not withstand the rigors of real life. Saint-Preux is persuaded that the life of the imagination is more real than the actual occurrences transpiring in the concrete world. His own happiness, it is argued, is more secure if it is entrusted to his imagination, which is more subject to his control than outside events. The fact that Saint-Preux follows this advice serves to underline Rousseau's contention regarding the centrality of amour-propre even in a love that flows out of amour de soi.

Julie, too, retains this element of Self-referentiality, even as she abjures what she considers to be the selfish aspect of love. Passion is not the embodiment of selfishness for Julie as it is for Saint-Preux, because Julie essentially has no need of passion.[51] For Julie, passion is a metaphor for exclusivity, and it is this sense of passion, rather than its physical manifestation, that she attacks as selfish. Thus, Julie openly claims to feel little passionate love for her husband, and she finds that to be good. For Julie, this absence of love for Wolmar is beneficial in two ways, both personally and socially. First, on a personal level, she no longer has to fight against being absorbed by the adored Other.[52] Not being in love means firmly preserving the delineation between Self and Other that Julie so eagerly defends. She does not appear to be consciously aware of this rationalization, but hints of it are evident in the way she describes her marriage to Wolmar. Writing to Saint-Preux of her marriage, Julie's formulation of its major effect is that she no longer *belongs* to Saint-Preux.[53] Second, Julie's need to lay down the limits of Self and Other leads her to see her relationship with Wolmar as a neatly mapped-out partnership, with each participant awarded his or her particular job or area of expertise. This stands in direct contrast to the threatening fusion that Julie had formerly felt with Saint-Preux. A partnership geared to furnishing a sense of balance will not permit the partners to dissolve into each other.[54] Indeed, the clearly delineated areas of responsibility are characteristic not only of Julie's and Wolmar's own relationship, but form the key to the organization of Clarens as well. The self-sufficiency of Clarens is to a large extent based on a system of individual workers scrupulously kept apart in the performance of their separate tasks, in the name of the greater harmony of the entire enterprise.

In addition to Julie's personal need of the demarcation of Self from Other, the fact that she does not love Wolmar yields another benefit that is more social in nature. The lack of exclusivity in Julie's love also, according to Julie, prevents her from falling into the trap of selfishness by caring for just one other person, the other half of an exclusive couple. Julie writes that the goal of marriage is to reach beyond just one other person to benefit society as a whole. Romantic love, which is by nature exclusive and thereby selfish, has no place in the moral order of things. Julie argues that the primary focus of the married couple should be not on their own uniqueness as a romantic dyad, but on their united contribution to the establishment of an uplifting civil life for all of society.[55]

Although Julie claims to give up love because of its Self-referential nature, it is precisely her own Self-concern that motivates her denial of love. This is not just due to Julie's possibly unconscious need to keep her identity of Self strictly separate from the Other. There is also a more consciously felt drive that directs her actions. Julie wants to be happy. She equates that happiness with a state of repose, or rest. That is why, in the final analysis, she rejects Bomston's offer of asylum for her and Saint-Preux in England. Julie feels that her lack of inner peace, resulting from guilt over the grief to her parents, would also destroy her own happiness.[56] Julie's peace of mind is also invoked by Claire in her appeal to Saint-Preux to give Julie up, and it is a major reason that influences Saint-Preux to obey her.[57] Notwithstanding Julie's avowed purpose in espousing a love without selfishness, it is still Julie's own Self that predominates as the basis on which love, or any other relationship for that matter, is either accepted or rejected.

Nearly all of the characters in *La Nouvelle Héloïse* attempt to respond theoretically to the problem of the Self-referentiality that appears to exist in any type of love relationship. While exorcising passion from love by itself does not necessarily get rid of its selfishness, the characters in *La Nouvelle Héloïse* also attempt to attack the problem from the other direction. They do this by reconstituting selfless love as friendship. In this understanding of friendship, they try to unite the positive aspects of love, with none of their negative accompaniments. Unlike love as it is usually understood, this type of friendship is to be truly mutual and reciprocal. It is supposed to see things as they really are and to have no need of selfish illusion.[58] Consequently, all of the participants in this relationship are to be rendered authentic and truly happy.

As Rousseau portrays it, the epitome of this type of relationship would appear to be found at Clarens. There, people seem to live in total harmony with each other, in friendship untainted by passion or jealousy. Starobinski has characterized the society at Clarens as one where hearts are transparent to each other.[59] Perfect unity reigns because no one has anything to hide.

Unfortunately, as the denouement of *La Nouvelle Héloïse* demonstrates, this situation never really does exist, not even at Clarens. Friendship does not always bring with it true honesty or happiness. This is seen in the lives of both the servants and the masters at Clarens. The estate at Clarens is ostensibly run on the principles of openness and honesty: everyone at Clarens is supposed to feel part of one big happy family. In reality, however, Clarens is neither open nor honest. The friendly air of the estate masks a strongly centralized system of authority, devised by Wolmar and executed by Julie. The camaraderie of the servants is belied by the spying they practice upon each other to curry favor with their masters. As for the masters themselves, their well-ordered and seemingly trouble free existence masks a deep unhappiness that ironically only Julie, at the end, has the courage to express. Since the organizational system at Clarens cannot openly admit to its own shortcomings, an effective method is devised for coping with unhappy people who don't "fit in." One way or another, they are made to leave.[60]

Why is it that friendship, which seems by nature a pure and mature emotion, cannot succeed in actually establishing a society of authenticity and happiness at Clarens? The answer may be found in the nature of friendship itself. Events in *La Nouvelle Héloïse* demonstrate that the existence of friendship in and of itself does not guarantee the purity of its intentions. Many critics have noted, for example, Claire's somewhat suspect motives for working so hard to keep Julie and Saint-Preux apart.[61] Also, and perhaps most important, friendship is not always an adequate substitute for the love that it is supposed to replace. This is seen most clearly when Julie, feeling the lack of love in her life, invites the now widowed Claire to join her at Clarens. It is even more poignantly evident later in the novel, when Julie, surrounded by friends, confesses that she is still unhappy.

Friendship fails to establish a purified love bereft of the negative aspects of the passion and selfishness associated with love, but the presentation of this alternative does fill an important theoretical function in the novel. It lays the basis for the discussion of the relationship between happiness and love, which will also serve as a major catalyst for the events in the denouement of the novel. While Julie may feel unsatisfied without love at Clarens, she is unable to fully express what is bothering her. Claire, who does not feel the need for love, is indeed capable of enunciating the theoretical connections between love and happiness. The reason that Claire gives for the impossibility of happiness in love is that there are flaws inherent in love itself. In the final analysis, it is this unhappiness that condemns love as an unworthy emotion, for surely a worthy emotion would have a happier result.

The rationale that Claire brings to bear in her analysis of love is important, for it colors the attitude of many of the other characters to the events in their lives. Judging the moral worth of an emotion or enterprise by the happiness or unhappiness that results from it means that happiness becomes a moral barometer for the measure of virtue and justice. In this sense, it is possible to view Julie's pronouncements regarding her love of Saint-Preux, and her subsequent refusal to run away with him, in a new light. Being happy is a way of ascertaining that one has indeed made the right choice. Conversely, any emotion other than the placidity of repose would indicate that the selection had not been validated. Thus, in her postnuptial reinterpretation of her experience with Saint-Preux, Julie may be understood as rereading her previous actions in the light of a new philosophical approach to love and happiness.

In view of the philosophical underpinning attributed to the rejection of love and the election of happiness as the validation of moral worth, it marks a crucial turning point when, after several years as wife to Wolmar and mistress of Clarens, Julie declares that she is not happy.[62] Julie thereby emphasizes two important points. First, she proclaims that Wolmar's philosophy of Clarens—the spirit of ostensibly authentic and passionless friendship—fails on its own terms because the terms of its validation—ensuring the happiness of everybody on the estate—are not fulfilled. The recognition of this omission is particularly striking with regard to Julie, because, as the mistress of Clarens, she serves as the transmitter of its values. When these values fail her, they call into question the validity of the entire system. Julie's announcement of her unhappiness marks the end of her existence at Clarens. Like all unhappy people, she no longer fits in and therefore must leave.

Julie's second statement has to do with the nature of happiness. At the same time that she rejects Wolmar's road to happiness as embodied in the philosophy of Clarens, she also attempts to define for herself what love is. Certainly Julie recognizes what for her, at least, love is not: it is not the calm unchanging stasis of the repose that is valued by Wolmar and that she herself had once so eagerly sought.[63] Living in a state of equilibrium means that nothing need ever be changed, that desire is unnecessary. But Julie also comes to realize that a human being without needs or desires is not, as Wolmar may have thought, a divine being. Rather, he remains simply a loveless human being whose life is essentially empty. God may be characterized by His lack of desire; human beings, on the other hand, are defined by their need for love. In spite of the difficulties of living with the unfulfillable desires that love, and through it the imagination, evoke, Julie understands that life without these is tantamount to death.[64]

As with her previous statements on love, Julie herself does not realize the full theoretical implications of her statements. She only expresses what she intuitively feels. She can no longer deny her love for Saint-Preux and that, for her, a life without love is a living death. Julie's thoughts find further elaboration in *Émile*, where Rousseau tells us that human happiness can be only partially achieved at best and that what portion of it can be grasped is attainable only through human love.[65] This makes the essence of human happiness ambiguous at best, but it still remains the only happiness that we have.

In terms of its makeup and its purpose, love can be seen as doubly ambiguous. It is constructed of seemingly contradictory elements that are both Self-regarding and Other-directed. It may or may not achieve a happiness that is only partial. Reaching out to the Other, which is supposed to promote our happiness, may wind up destroying our own Selves. On the other hand, not even trying to love is, as Julie discovers, to condemn that same Self to death. It is ironic and sad that, in a novel dedicated to love, no one character in *La Nouvelle Héloïse* appears to arrive at a practical realization and understanding of love's fundamental ambiguity. Saint-Preux opts out of its difficulties by professing to dedicate his life to virtue, which he understands to be opposed to passion of any sort. Claire and Wolmar do not feel the need to love at all. Julie only partially grasps the major issues involved. She comes to see the basic contradictions of her own life: she has fled from love in order to preserve her sense of Self, only to find her Self immolated on the altar of loveless sacrifice and unhappiness. However, Julie can only articulate her findings in a negative way. She knows that she is not happy, but she has no practical idea of how to actually achieve happiness in love. Still, this realization is potentially the first step to the construction of a dynamic, authentic, and mutual loving relationship.

La Nouvelle Héloïse does not present us with a positive theory of love, but, in its exploration of the internal contradictions of love, the novel makes several important contributions. First, it establishes the nature of love's ambiguity, with the recognition that a total solution to the tensions between Self and Other may never be found, least of all in love. A perfect synthesis between Self and Other—a Hegelian-type Aufhebung—may not exist. Indeed, we find that Hegel himself expresses similar sentiments regarding the nature of love. Hegel notes that the very fact that the beloved Other is capable of having an autonomous existence, and of participating in relationships apart from his partner, makes real Aufhebung in a love relationship elusive at best.[66] As far as Rousseau is concerned, however, living a full and mature life means accepting the necessity of partial solutions together with the ambiguous methods for their achievement. Working out a loving relationship can abide by no set formula.

This leads us to a second important contribution of *La Nouvelle Héloïse*: its strongly implied conclusion that the ability to love authentically presupposes a free and authentic existence. Hints of this are evident in Julie's use and eventual rejection of repose as a standard by which to evaluate happiness and to disparage love. The term "repose" carries salient overtones for Rousseau. In *Considerations on Poland*, he specifically contrasts it with liberty and warns that one cannot have both: a choice must be made.[67] As Julie finds out, repose does not bring happiness. The implication is that only liberty can achieve that. This indicates that loving authentically not only influences the personal issue of happiness, but also has important political consequences. Both liberty and love are essential prerequisites to authentic personal and political existence.

In the end, *La Nouvelle Héloïse* may offer us no practical solutions to the complexities of love, but by openly proclaiming the necessity of love, it attests to love as an integral part of individual and social life, despite all the attempts in the novel to denigrate and purge love. It remains for *Émile*, Rousseau's work on education, to explore the practical methods of implementing between two people a relationship of authentic love based on freedom, which would in turn serve as the basis for an authentic and honest social community.

Throughout *Émile*, Rousseau's stated goal is to develop a system of education that will allow man to function in an imperfect world while remaining true to his natural character, untainted by outside corruption. Rousseau's hope is that if enough people are educated in that way, they will be able to effect a sort of "revolution from below" and transform the corrupt political and social institutions of their day into structures that will promote greater individual and social authenticity for everyone. He does recognize, however, that this kind of change cannot be achieved by individuals working separately. Neither will this transformation have any lasting effect if it cannot be transmitted to future generations. In order to ensure the success and continuity of his proposed moral and political revolution, he realizes that he must include women in his scheme.

Women have two roles to play in the facilitation and continued duration of this proposed transformation from corruption to authenticity. As spouses, they socialize their husbands and teach them to function within society. As mothers, they protect their children from the dangers of a corrupt world and transmit to them the ethic of honesty and authenticity. Rousseau pays great attention to woman's role in facilitating man's transformation of the world, presumably because his concern is to get this revolution started. His analysis of woman's role occurs at the stage of adolescence when Émile, now developing a sense of humanity and benevolence, is preparing to study society and politics. Émile is ready to be socialized at the hands of a woman.

While Émile's entire education may be said to be characterized by careful forethought on the part of the Tutor, the level of planning at this point of Émile's life reaches the height of detailed complexity. Nothing is left to chance; even the most seemingly innocent and spontaneous of occurrences appear to have been planned years ahead of time. This is understandable, because there is a great deal at stake. The whole success of Émile's education depends on how he weathers this late- and post-adolescent period. Making matters more complicated is the fact that there are great natural forces at work within Émile, threatening the successful completion of his education. These forces are the passions that develop during adolescence. Of all the passions, sexuality poses the greatest threat to Émile's (and the Tutor's) stated goals, since sexuality can easily lead Émile into a life of vice and degradation. Consequently, the Tutor constantly monitors Émile's sexuality. At the same time, he allows all of Émile's energies to mature to their potential. True to Rousseau's method of "extracting the remedy from the evil itself,"[68] the Tutor uses love not merely as an outlet for Émile's natural sexuality, but also as a means of controlling Émile. This occurs because love, dangerous since it exposes Émile to forces that his Tutor cannot govern, also gives Émile, for the first time, an experience in common with the rest of humanity. Love, in a sense, makes Émile more human, for it opens him up to human concerns in general. The Tutor, in his turn, makes use of this to awaken Émile to his social and political duties towards the rest of mankind.

In keeping with Émile's movement during adolescence from a solitary to a more community oriented existence, the Tutor no longer operates alone or directly upon Émile. Much of what is accomplished during this period of Émile's life hinges on the influence that his helpmate, Sophie, has upon him. Consequently, the education of Sophie herself becomes crucial to the accomplishment of Émile's own goals, both as an individual and as a man taking his place within society. Sophie will therefore be educated for her specific role as Émile's helpmate, and her education will bear a double responsibility. It must enable Sophie to socialize and humanize Émile, which in its turn will determine how successfully Émile will be able to promote authentic personal and social relationships within the world at large. In addition, Sophie's education will also allow us to evaluate the tenor of her own relationship with Émile.

For Émile and Sophie, love has more than just personal consequences. If their love fails, it is not just a romantic story gone sour. Rather, it will point to the flaws that had already existed within their respective prior educations. On the other hand, the success of their love will herald not only their own personal fulfillment, but also the onset of a more authentic social and political existence for all of mankind. Love remains the cornerstone of both the individual unit of the couple and the community as a whole. In *Émile*, Rousseau wants to demonstrate the connection between education, love, and liberty. It is Rousseau's contention, to be proven by the lives of Émile and Sophie, that one can be educated to love well, that is, to maximize personal and political authenticity.

The problem is that the success of Émile's and Sophie's life together is only superficial. The façade of achievement comes apart in the denouement to *Émile* called *Les solitaires*. The questions left for us to consider are twofold. First, how can we explain the failure of an enterprise of love whose participants were educated expressly for each other in pursuit of a common goal? Second, faced with that failure of love, must we then conclude that love is a chimera on both the personal and political fronts and is therefore unable to serve as a basis for political community?

We will start by answering the first question in order to achieve a theoretical perspective that will allow us to respond to the larger concerns of the second question. We will begin by exploring the education of Sophie, the woman made expressly to Émile's measure.

One of the major difficulties in understanding the education of Sophie is that Rousseau seems to be presenting us with two visions of Émile's helpmate. On the one hand, Sophie is portrayed as a brilliant prodigy, with more sympathy for theoretical excellence than practical imperfections. This Sophie is so taken by the story of Telemachus that she refuses to have anything to do with the real life suitors surrounding her. Eventually, this Sophie dies. On the other hand, Rousseau also describes another Sophie, who possesses very average abilities, but is distinguished by her good heart and modest, virtuous behavior. This second Sophie is said to epitomize "Woman." Since Émile is basically just an average fellow whose faculties have been developed to the utmost by his Tutor, Rousseau decides to shape Sophie along similar lines. Ostensibly, then, the story of Émile's and Sophie's love and marriage will be a very ordinary one, in spite of the clearly extraordinary task set for the young couple of redeeming the world—or at least, their surrounding environment—from corruption.

However, the large amount of planning and contrived happenstance belies the supposed ordinariness of the tale. Rousseau even admits, through the offices of the Tutor, that Sophie is a contrived fiction created during Émile's adolescence primarily to keep Émile's burgeoning sexual passion in check. When, after a long introduction, the reader, together with Émile, finally meets Sophie, it is clear that Rousseau has found new uses for her. Aside from being a convenient stopgap during adolescence, Sophie can also be utilized to direct Émile's general feeling of benevolence towards one person, thus socializing Émile through love. Looking further into the future, Rousseau also decides that Sophie can help Émile fulfill his task by being a loving background supporter of his efforts and by transmitting his beliefs to their children.

This vision of Sophie's role in Émile's life has considerable implications for the type of personality that Sophie will have. Clearly, genius is out of the question for Sophie. Her role is to be a passive enabler, not an active participant on her own. If Sophie possesses her own brand of genius, she will create her own agenda. Rousseau therefore determines to deprive Sophie of her imagination, claiming (citing the experience of the first Sophie) that it only makes her unhappy.[69] However, that contention would be true only if Sophie's own agenda were to radically contradict that of Émile. Judging from Rousseau's statements about Sophie and about women in general, it would appear that Rousseau feels that Émile's task could be more certainly and easily accomplished if Sophie were to serve primarily as a means for Émile to achieve his own goals, rather than as a fully developed person with ideas of her own.[70] By identifying Sophie with the prototypical "Woman," Rousseau is further able to support the statements he makes about Sophie by claiming that they are generally true for women as a whole. In this way, Rousseau can bolster the endeavor he undertakes in *Émile*, of writing not for the extraordinary individual, but of inspiring ordinary men and women to take action against the corruption of their age and thereby to take control of their own lives.

Depriving Sophie of her imagination has two important results. One is that Sophie has no ideas of her own. She becomes mere potentiality, "prepared ground," to receive and perpetuate Émile's own ideas.[71] The second result becomes apparent only gradually in the lives of Émile and Sophie. The deliberate absence of imagination in Sophie not only results in intellectual inferiority for her, but also, more crucially, leaves Sophie morally and psychologically incomplete. The deprivation of Sophie's imagination renders Sophie less human and even, possibly, incapable of fully loving. The irony lies in the fact that while Sophie's capabilities are restricted in the name of better serving Émile's aims, it is precisely these limitations that effectively undermine those very goals. In the process, Émile's and Sophie's personal happiness is also destroyed.

The perpetuation of inauthenticity in women's lives is manifest not just in their relationships with their husbands, but at other junctures in their lives as well. Even the young girl is described as being "all in her doll...she awaits the moment when she will be her own doll."[72] Rousseau views this incident of childhood play as characteristic of women's childhoods, which serve to prepare them for a lifetime of manipulation and living outside of themselves. Significantly, this type of existence is elsewhere deplored by Rousseau as incomplete and unsatisfactory.[73] However, women are brought up to lead that kind of life. Another example of the inauthenticity that continually reasserts itself throughout women's lives is the standard by which women are taught to judge themselves. This yardstick is "opinion," a criterion that for men is condemned as immoral.[74] Interestingly, Rousseau demands that women be both subject to and set the standard of opinion.[75] His rationale is that women's existence, being relative to that of men, must constantly justify itself in the eyes of the world at large, especially with regard to the legitimacy of their children.[76] In that sense, women are subject to opinion. But since women are also the guardians of domestic morality and responsible for the proper education of their children, they must also know when to disregard public opinion. Consequently, they must be able to set the proper standard for public opinion in order to know how to judge.

The link that Rousseau sets up between women and opinion

symbolizes the conflicts within his notion of the association between men and women in general. In the paradoxical relationship that he has established between women and opinion, Rousseau fails to see that he has given women a task that is impossible to fulfill. One cannot be both subject to and controller of a particular standard. On the individual level, regarding the relationship between Sophie and Émile, one can conclude that it is likewise impossible to be both a man's disciple and his mistress (taken in either the sexual or the directorial sense of the word). In the attempt to theoretically bridge the gap between two very different notions of women, the entire issue threatens to blow up from the overwhelming force of its internal contradictions.

Rousseau makes one more attempt to defuse the incipient explosion by suggesting a practical method by which this can be avoided. He proposes a division between power and authority. In this view, men would have the official right to exercise power, while women would retain actual control from behind the scenes. Thus, women could appear to be the submissive disciples, while actually directing the course of events. This approach would seem to dissolve the internal contradictions mentioned above that threaten to tear women apart. This strategy does not work, however, because the exercise of authority, deemed to be women's job, is impossible without possession of full knowledge of the situation, but knowledge is precisely what is denied to Sophie in her education. She is commanded to accept her husband's tastes and her father's religion.[77] She is not given reasons for the code of ethics she must follow.[78] While Sophie loves virtue, she does so primarily because it makes other people happy with her.[79] She herself has no deep comprehension of the philosophy that governs her life. Unlike Émile, Sophie is not taught to develop the power that is both etymologically and logically the guarantee of virtue's continued existence.[80]

The result is that Sophie's existence is irretrievably torn between two moralities. Her tragedy is that she lacks the intellectual skills that would permit her to make a reasoned choice between them. Sophie is trained from the start to lead a life of constraint, in perpetual battle with herself. Therefore, she is unsure, when confronted by two moral alternatives, which path to take. Does she follow her own conscience or abide by conventional wisdom? Does she listen to herself or fight her instinct, as she has been taught to do? If Émile were there to guide her, all might be well. He would take the burden of decision from her shoulders. As real life demonstrates, however, that situation does not always obtain. Sophie is forced to make a choice, but she has no Self, or inner voice of conscience, to fall back on as a guide. In fact, one sign of the success of her education is the destruction of the Self that Sophie has been trained to combat. Her complaisance before Émile easily extends itself to an acceptance of alternate moralities. With no innate moral sense to direct her, Sophie can fall prey to the vices from which she was originally supposed to protect her own family.

It is not at all surprising, then, that the sequel to *Émile*, *Les solitaires*, presents us with the spectacle of a Sophie who cannot withstand the enticing vices of Paris with which she is confronted. What may be more shocking is that Sophie's fall from grace precipitates Émile's furious rejection of her and his decision to end their marriage. This is unexpected because true love, as defined by Rousseau, is supposed to be able to withstand the excesses of jealousy.[81] According to Rousseau, true love would evince concern at such a turn of events rather than the anger that Émile displays towards Sophie. Émile's actual reaction raises the question of how true his love for Sophie ever really was. His rejection of Sophie would seem to indicate that Émile's love for Sophie was more Self-referential than Other-directed, emphasizing amour-propre over amour de soi. The denouement of *Les solitaires* leaves Émile forswearing not only love, but also freedom and citizenship.

The collapse of Émile's and Sophie's marriage may lead us to conclude, however reluctantly, that Rousseau is disappointed in his hope that love serve as the personal, and by extension, the political nexus of the human community. This would seem to be a logical deduction, especially in light of Émile's rejection of the status of citizen.[82] Further examination, however, reveals that this obvious conclusion is not necessarily the correct one.

In being Émile's helpmeet, Sophie's avowed task—and the main reason Émile is drawn to her and loves her—is that she makes Émile all the more himself.[83] In other words, Sophie sets the seal on Émile's authenticity as a human being and guarantees the fulfillment of his future task as the founder of an authentic society. There seems to be no struggle within Émile or within Sophie regarding the dissolution of Self into the Other that appears to accompany the process of loving in *La Nouvelle Héloïse*. Our critical analysis of *Émile* reveals why. Émile does not have to worry about being subsumed by Sophie when he loves her, precisely because Sophie is not allowed to have a distinctive Self. As a result, harmony reigns, but this lack of struggle also reveals why their love cannot survive. In loving Sophie, Émile is actually loving only an extension of himself inasmuch as it continues to reflect him. For all the talk of mutuality, no real reciprocity can exist in a relationship between two people, only one of whom is truly autonomous. Sophie's education makes her receptive to the outward mechanisms of love, but no dynamic relationship between her and Émile is really possible. As a result, both of Émile's enterprises—the political and the personal—fail.

In his own way, Émile echoes the choice made by Julie in *La Nouvelle Héloïse*. Like Julie, Émile cannot handle love's ambiguities. Chief among these is the ability to accept that love is not a stable, restful achievement but an ever changing continuum. Love is a gamble on both liberty and happiness: it thrives on obstacles and does not fear them.[84] Loving another person means being willing to risk one's own identity in the hope of enriching two lives. Neither Émile nor Julie succeed in rising to this challenge. Julie refuses to commit herself to love for fear of jeopardizing her sense of Self. Émile, on the other hand, can "love" only his mirror image. When that shatters, his love disappears. In the end, as the slave of the bey of Algiers, Émile follows Julie by rejecting love altogether in favor of repose. In so doing, Émile chooses not to discover the true meaning of interactive, reciprocal love. At the same time, on the political level, Émile refuses freedom, along with the struggles and challenges that accompany it.

We can now understand the denouement of *Émile* and the relegation of Sophie to a subservient role, less as a misogynistic exercise on Rousseau's part than as an attempt to demonstrate the price of trying to achieve, at all costs, a life that perfectly conforms to the demands of a theory of ideal human development. The conclusion of *Émile*, like that of *La Nouvelle Héloïse*, demonstrates the pitfalls of constraining human growth to fit a preexisting notion of the ideal human relationship, either in terms of filial or class duty (*La Nouvelle Héloïse*) or marital bliss (*Émile*). Regarding the specific project of *Émile*, Rousseau may be said to have failed. He does not succeed in achieving his avowed purpose as he stated it at the beginning of *Émile*: to resolve the contradictions between the individual and social identities existing in modern man.[85] Neither does Rousseau manage to clearly resolve the dilemmas raised by his own theory of authentic love. Like *La Nouvelle Héloïse*, *Émile* does not offer a prescription for loving authentically. Émile ends by refusing any personal or political reciprocity altogether. He solves his dilemma by ignoring it: Émile opts out of authenticity.

In spite of this impasse, however, Rousseau does not give up on the idea of love as the basis for achieving both personal and political authenticity. In his political writings, he experiments with various notions of what sort of love might fulfill man on both levels. For Rousseau, the family is the medium through which love authentically experienced on the personal level could be transformed into the cohesive glue that bonds society together in the search for the communal good life. To be sure, Rousseau does not consider it inevitable that the family and the State must share a positive relationship. At times, he seems to suggest that there is a substantial opposition between the "private we," as exemplified by the family, and the "communal us," as embodied in the State. We recall that it is precisely this opposition, on the personal level, that Julie struggles with in her letters to Saint-Preux, and we know that her attempted resolution of this issue at Clarens is to dissolve the "private we"—and even the "individual I"—into the "communal us." At different points in his theoretical works as well, Rousseau seems to suggest that the concerns of the private family and of the communal State are at odds.[86] However, Rousseau at various times also insists that the State and the family are both different forms of the same essence,[87] and therefore that the existence of an authentic family life is the best guarantee for the development of the authentic political State.[88] This point of view emphasizes the role of the family as a socializing agent for the State. In this understanding of the relationship between the family and the State, the family socializes each individual to be a good citizen by accustoming the individual to living with others. Furthermore, by nurturing the ability to love other people, the family also lays the foundation for love of one's country.[89] In other words, love, which influences the behavior of members of the same family towards each other, also accounts for the actions of the citizens of the State towards each other.[90] Emotionally, the other citizens are viewed as one's siblings, and the State itself as one's parent.[91] As a result, that love is the surest guarantee of a citizen's loyalty to the State.[92]

Rousseau gives this point a mutually reciprocal and practical dimension when he speaks of the need for the State in its turn to physically nurture its citizens in order to be fully deserving of their loyalty.[93] The emphasis on nurture and love deliberately invokes the structure and operation of the family for the private citizen as well as for the public State. In his evocation of the State in that mode, Rousseau seems to be making the point that the State will be just and thereby successful only inasmuch as it imitates the family's organizing principle. In other words, Rousseau claims that the artificial structure of the State can morally justify itself by seeking to closely identify with the family which is the most natural of all organizations.[94] By utilizing the natural emotion of love, the State can negate the pleasure of command that motivates most rulers and which serves to guarantee their corruption.[95]

Given Rousseau's high hopes for the family as the guardian of the authentic spirit in inauthentic times, as well as the family's incarnation as the socializing agent for political authenticity, the seeming inevitability of the family's self-destructive collapse, as shown in both *La Nouvelle Héloïse* and *Émile*, would appear to set the final seal of doom on the possibility of ever transcending an existence of inauthenticity, whether personal or political. The evidence can also be read, however, not as a prophecy of doom, but rather as a handbook for the options that can be actualized in inauthentic times. *La Nouvelle Héloïse* is particularly instructive in this regard, through the personage of Julie's cousin Claire. In many ways, Claire remains a cipher throughout the novel: she is married, with a child, and once she is widowed agrees readily to live with Julie and her family at Clarens. Yet Claire's apparent conventionality is a carefully maintained pose. She admits to Julie that it is only when widowed that she feels she has the control necessary to indulge her own interests, and she describes her life frankly as a series of roles, of which the "coquette" and the "merry widow" are just two examples. To be sure, living one's life deliberately wearing the masks necessary to play chosen roles is certainly far from leading a life of authenticity that Rousseau envisages as the goal of his political and social theory, and to which Julie so desperately aspires. On the other hand, Claire is able to use the inauthentic methodology of wearing masks to create enough space for a sense of Self to emerge. Although it is possible to argue that Claire's resultant sense of Self is not much in evidence, since it does not seem that Claire ever had much of a Self to begin with, it is evident that at the end of the novel, the realistic and cynical Claire is in a much better position than the moribund Julie who has nothing but dashed ideals to show for a lifetime of constraint. Of the two women, it is Claire who manages to survive the crushing society of Clarens. In addition to the psychological contrast that Claire presents to Julie, Claire's opinions and structuring of her life reflect another theoretical option for surviving in an inauthentic world and establishing the beginnings of a more authentic society. The character of Claire gives the reader the opportunity to pose a different question: what if a person with a stronger, more moral notion of Self—like Julie, for example, but better able to weather the world of inauthenticity—were to make use of Claire's survival techniques? One could then envision a host of possibilities that would allow an authentic Self to flourish—albeit with difficulty—in an inauthentic world. This, in turn, could be the beginning of the authentic transformation that Rousseau was trying to achieve. In this case, moral sensitivity and the desire for authenticity would not have to preclude survival.

Rousseau's analysis of the possibilities of authentic transformation in an inauthentic world underlines an important source of hope for the future realization of his theory. His sense is that the root of transformation and revolution lies not with philosophical theories or political power, but rather in the concrete minutiae of everyday life. Moreover, his emphasis on the practical achievements of daily life in attaining authenticity highlights the liberating notion that there are many pathways to authenticity.

The fact that there are many ways to achieve authenticity—and not just one ordained path to that goal—differentiates Rousseau not only from traditional utopian/religious thinkers, but also highlights his essential modernity. The term "modernity" here does not only indicate that Rousseau's writings heralded the eigtheenth-century French Revolution, nineteenth-century Weltschmerz, or even twentieth- century angoisse and existential futility. Certainly, Rousseau did all of these things. The point here, however, is that basing his theory of revolutionary change on everyday life gives him a certain practical freedom in determining how his ultimate goals would be achieved. If attaining authenticity is not restricted to one approved method, then the variety of mechanisms used for coping with the exigencies of daily living are also revealed as strategies that allow for the slow, albeit inevitable, consolidation of authenticity. Ultimately, this approach allows for a great deal of optimism with regard to the human condition in an imperfect world.

This analysis of the human condition is based on Rousseau's unique view of reality: that nothing is made up of unadulterated components but is often, instead, a mixture of opposites, and that categories conventionally understood as exclusionary (such as Rousseau's understanding of amour de soi and amour-propre) are often interpenetrating and porous. Interestingly, an analysis of the implications of Rousseau's unique perception of reality reveals also the extent to which he partakes of our own postmodern skepticism about normally accepted verities: that truth is uniform and stable and that life consists of choosing between alternate versions of battling dualisms.

Rousseau's analysis of love and its effect on the sense of Self strongly prefigures many of the concerns raised by postmodernism. This is apparent in many ways. First, there is the refusal to accept any concept on its own terms as an unalloyed essence. This is evident in Rousseau's analysis of both private and public issues. In his analysis of love, as we know, the apparent exclusive dualities of amour de soi and amour-propre are revealed to be linked on a continuum where the elements of Self-referentiality and Other-directedness are manifest in varying mixtures. Rousseau keeps to this approach as well when examining issues in the public arena. In his analysis of political systems, for example, he remarks that there is no single essence that defines the perfect polity: the quality of a political system is judged not on its achievement of generalized philosophical goals, but on its fit to the particular country, people, and era in which it operates.[96] This anti-systemic element in his writings is echoed by contemporary postmodernist thought in its call for "non-totalizing theories."[97] Postmodernism insists that no one theory can capture all of reality in its myriad forms: human diversity will not yield to rigid theoretical encapsulation.

The second convergence between Rousseau's thought and the postmodern critique is in fact inferred from Rousseau's demonstration that major concepts (like love, Self and Other, public and private) resist dualism and oppositional categorization. The ensuing implication, which we have already seen in his analysis of the Self-referential and Other-directed aspects of love, is that these categories are also porous and interpenetrating.

Finally, Rousseau's valorization of everyday life on its own terms prefigures the appreciation of daily life on the part of postmodernist critics who likewise have come to understand that theoretical thinking must take quotidian reality into account if that theory is to describe the actualities of real life and consequently be able to effect changes in the human condition. It is interesting to note that Rousseau places women at the critical juncture of all of these movements. In particular, Rousseau sees them as central to evoking the transformative potential of everyday life. By lactating infants, by teaching their children the authentic way to live, women would transform the banal quotidian into an arena that is overtly active and liberating. Thus, in both practical and cognitive terms, women would challenge the heretofore accepted division of private and public, everyday and heroic. This would seem to be a potent argument for evaluating Rousseau's approach to women as empowering, innovating, and transforming rather than misogynistic, paternalistic, and patriarchal.

To that extent, of course, his approach is sympathetic to the focus of much contemporary feminist critical theory as well. Feminist scholarship has particularly singled out the tendency of modern liberal political theory to valorize the political over the private and to exclude women from those public areas of life where power was exercised. The consequences—that women have been relegated to the back benches of history—have been the ironic result of those very liberal writings that purported to liberate all of humanity from the hierarchical notions inherent in feudalism and absolute monarchy. In that context, Rousseau's focus on women and everyday life as dynamic sources of political change fits in well with the postmodernist contention that totalizing theories, however attractive, have based their generalizations on an understanding of human life that ignored those groups that did not fit in with the values propounded by the party in power.[98]

All of this, however, is not to say that Rousseau is really a perfect feminist, or that there exists a perfect understanding between the aims of feminism and postmodernism. Neither is it possible to maintain that his statements make him into the perfect postmodernist. In fact, one area where he parts company from the more radical postmodernists is the concept of the Self. Postmodernism casts doubt on the traditional notion of the Self: for the more radical amongst these theorists, no unified sense of Self can be said to exist. Rousseau, by contrast, insists that an integrated sense of Self is central to one's existence as a human being. At the same time, Rousseau also differs from many of his own contemporaries in their conventional understanding of the Self. Needless to say, for Rousseau, the Self is not a fixed essence. It is not a finished product of Divine provenance. By the same token, however, since the Self gives meaning to human existence, it cannot function as a destabilized morass. To grasp the essence of Rousseau's sense of Self, it is useful to use a metaphor to which he himself often has recourse: that of Nature. Predictably, Rousseau has a unique understanding of this concept. For him, Nature is not an unchanging, fixed notion against which one could critically evaluate philosophical phenomena. Instead, he sees Nature as combining the qualities of stability and change, much as the face of Nature alters itself over the seasons. Similarly, the Self for Rousseau does have a stable core and identity, although, over time, these manifestations may change. For Rousseau, this does not point so much to a decentered (postmodernist) Self as to the existence of a dynamic core that retains a sense of identity.

Rousseau's ability to view reality as a unity of disparate elements normally seen as contradictory—his emphasis on fusion rather than duality—marks his sensibility as unique for his time as it is for our own. One should beware, however, of forcing his writings to "fit" the category of postmodernism exactly: paradoxically, that would render him time bound and potentially obsolete. Instead, we must focus on his sense of Self that gives us a basis to start to transform our world while still retaining a measure of skepticism about the entire enterprise. The sense of irony that Rousseau brings to his understanding of life—the fact that nothing is what it appears to be and that the key to authentic development lies in our ability to perceive and work with the continuum of opposing qualities that together make up our reality—enables us to maintain our distance and judgment. In this way, our critical faculties remain alive, impervious to the seductions of totalizing theories. Rousseau's theoretical accomplishment is no mean feat. It allows us to think about our own existence in a way that does not stultify actions (as in the "perfect" arrangement at Clarens) and that enables fundamental change to take place. In the end, Rousseau's writings continue to stand as a challenge to all of us to maximize our sense of Self: to strive for personal and communal authenticity.

Notes

Citations of Rousseau's works are taken from the Pléiade edition of the *Oeuvres complètes*, with the following exceptions:

a) *Lettre à d'Alembert sur les spectacles*, Fuchs edition (cited hereafter as *Letter to d'Alembert*)

b) *Essai sur l'origine des langues*, Porset edition (cited hereafter as *Essay*)

1. Throughout this essay, the word "Self" is capitalized when referring to the unique moral and psychological worth of an individual that must be taken seriously if personal and political authenticity is to be achieved. Similarly, the word "Other" is capitalized when it is used as a psychological and political construct that stands in contradistinction to this sense of Self. In this context, "authenticity" signifies the full

realization of human potential, in both the personal and political arenas, whose achievement is portrayed as a constant goal in the works of Jean-Jacques Rousseau.

2. *Discourse on Inequality*, Note XV, 219.
3. *Discourse on Inequality*, 155.
4. *Discourse on Inequality*, Note XV, 219.
5. *Discourse on Inequality*, Note XV, 219.
6. *Discourse on Inequality*, Note XV, 219.
7. "L'amour doit être réciproque" (*Émile*, Book IV, 494; *Emile,* trans. Allan Bloom [New York: Basic Books, 1979], 214, cited hereafter as Bloom).
8. *Émile*, Book IV, 520 note; Bloom, 233 note.
9. *Social Contract*, I.7, 362.
10. *Émile*, Book IV, 523 note; Bloom, 235 note.
11. *Émile,* Book IV, 522; Bloom, 235.
12. *Émile*, Book IV, 522–523; Bloom, 235.
13. *Émile*, Book IV, 524; Bloom, 236.
14. *Émile*, Book IV, 534; Bloom, 235.
15. *Émile*, Book IV, 494; Bloom, 214.
16. *Émile*, Book IV, 503; Bloom, 221.
17. *Émile*, Book II, 304; Bloom, 80.
18. *Émile*, Book IV, 656; Bloom, 329.
19. *Discourse on Inequality*, 169.
20. *Discourse on Inequality*, 169.
21. *Émile*, Book IV, 493; Bloom, 214.
22. *Discourse on Inequality*, 174.
23. *Discourse on Inequality*, 136.
24. *Discourse on Inequality*, 174–175.
25. *Discourse on Inequality*, Note XV, 219.
26. *Émile*, Book IV, 493; Bloom, 214.
27. *Émile*, Book IV, 494; Bloom, 214.
28. *Émile*, Book IV, 494; Bloom, 215.
29. *Lettre à Christophe de Beaumont*, OC, IV, 937.
30. *Émile*, Book IV, 536; Bloom, 244–245.
31. *Émile*, Book IV, 520; Bloom, 283.
32. *Émile*, Book IV, 520–521; Bloom, 233.
33. *Lettre à Christophe de Beaumont*, OC, IV, 937.
34. Guyon, notes to the Pléiade edition of *La Nouvelle Héloïse*, 1357.
35. "Je me figurai l'amour, l'amitié, les deux idoles de mon coeur sous les plus ravissantes images" (*Confessions*, IX, 430).
36. *La Nouvelle Héloïse*, II.3, 197.
37. *La Nouvelle Héloïse*, II.3, 199.
38. *La Nouvelle Héloïse*, II.4, 201.
39. "Nous ne sommes plus les mêmes" (*La Nouvelle Héloïse*, II.1, 189). Saint-Preux speaks of "ce premier regard qui me fit une autre âme" (II.1, 190).
40. Saint-Preux even calls on her soul to be the guide for them both (*La Nouvelle Héloïse*, I.26, 93).
41. *La Nouvelle Héloïse*, I.5, 42.

42. *La Nouvelle Héloïse*, I.23, 83.
43. *La Nouvelle Héloïse*, I.29, 96.
44. *Émile*, Book IV, 504; Bloom, 222.
45. *La Nouvelle Héloïse*, III.18, 340.
46. *La Nouvelle Héloïse*, III.18, 340.
47. *Discourse on Inequality*, 158.
48. *La Nouvelle Héloïse*, III.7, 320–321.
49. *La Nouvelle Héloïse*, I.27, 92–93.
50. *La Nouvelle Héloïse*, III.7, 320.
51. *La Nouvelle Héloïse*, I.9, 51.
52. *La Nouvelle Héloïse*, VI.7, 675–676.
53. *La Nouvelle Héloïse*, III.18, 363.
54. *La Nouvelle Héloïse*, III.20, 373.
55. *La Nouvelle Héloïse*, III.20, 372.
56. *La Nouvelle Héloïse*, II.6, 208.
57. *La Nouvelle Héloïse*, III.6, 318.
58. *La Nouvelle Héloïse*, II.11, 225. Also see ibid., I.65, 188; VI.3, 653; and I.46, 128–129.
59. See Starobinski, *Jean-Jacques Rousseau: Transparency and Obstruction*, trans. Arthur Goldhammer (Chicago: Chicago University Press, 1988), 102–110, especially 107 ff.
60. *La Nouvelle Héloïse*, IV.10, 455.
61. See, for example, Hans Wolpe, "Psychological Ambiguity in *La Nouvelle Héloïse*," *University of Toronto Quarterly* 28:3 (April 1959); also see Jane Todd, *Women's Friendship in Literature* (New York: Columbia University Press, 1980), especially the chapter on "Manipulative Friendship."
62. *La Nouvelle Héloïse*, V.5, 513.
63. *La Nouvelle Héloïse*, VI.8, 694.
64. *La Nouvelle Héloïse*, VI.8, 693 and 689.
65. *Émile*, Book IV, 503; Bloom, 221.
66. In an early essay on the subject, Hegel notes that only discrete manifestations of the synthetic union between lovers exist: he points to children and jointly held property as such examples (see G.W.F. Hegel, *Early Theological Writings*, trans. T.M. Knox [Chicago: University of Chicago Press, 1948], 308).
67. *Considerations on Poland*, 955.
68. *Social Contract*, 1st version, 288; my translation.
69. *Émile*, Book V, 763; Bloom, 405.
70. *Émile*, Book V, 766; Bloom, 407.
71. *Émile*, Book V, 769; Bloom, 410.
72. *Émile*, Book V, 707; Bloom, 367.
73. In *Discourse on Inequality*, Rousseau says that inauthentic social man "ne sait vivre que dans l'opinion des autres" (193; also see *Émile*, Book IV, 515; Bloom, 230).
74. *Émile*, Book V, 702–703; Bloom, 365.
75. *Émile*, Book V, 731; Bloom, 383.
76. *Émile*, Book V, 697; Bloom, 361.
77. *Émile*, Book V, 721; Bloom, 377.

78. *Émile*, Book V, 721; Bloom, 377–378.
79. *Émile*, Book V, 751; Bloom, 397.
80. *Émile*, Book V, 817; Bloom, 444.
81. *Émile*, Book V, 798–799; Bloom, 430–431.
82. *Les solitaires*, Lettre 2ème, 912, 916.
83. *Émile*, Book V, 801; Bloom, 433.
84. *Letter to d'Alembert*, 113.
85. *Émile*, Book I, 251; Bloom, 41.
86. *Du bonheur public*; OC, III, 510.
87. *Social Contract*, first version, 330.
88. *Political Economy*, 241. See also *Émile*, Book V, 700; Bloom, 363.
89. *Political Economy*, 259.
90. *Political Economy*, 254.
91. *Political Economy*, 258.
92. *Political Economy*, 255.
93. *Political Economy*, 262.
94. *Social Contract*, I.2, 352.
95. *Social Contract*, I.2, 352.
96. *Social Contract*, 419.
97. See Seyla Benhabib, "Epistemologies of Postmodernism" (in Linda J. Nicholson, ed., *Feminism/Postmodernism* [New York: Routledge, 1990]); and Louise D. Derkson, "The Ambiguous Relationship Between Feminism and Post-Modernism" (in Magda Pelikaan-Engel, ed., *Against Patriarchal Thinking* [Amsterdam: VU University Press, 1992]).
98. Jane Flax makes this point in "Postmodernism and Gender Relations in Feminist Theory" (in Linda J. Nicholson, ed., *Feminism/Postmodernism* [New York: Routledge, 1990]).

Rousseau's Beautiful Soul:
A Hegelian Reading
by Ronnie Littlejohn

Introduction

My intention is not to argue a contentious thesis about who is right regarding the formation of the self, Jean-Jacques Rousseau or G.W.F. Hegel. I want to place them in dialogue with each other and try to indicate why I think they take the positions they do and what this means for drawing our own conclusions about self-formation within the limits of their projects. I hope to make their views accessible, and this is especially important when writing about Hegel, for I think there are few philosophers so often misunderstood as he. This is partly because the great demarcations between his major works are sometimes not given enough attention, and often it is simply owing to the fact that his writing is opaque and repetitious. I have not located any new texts, and I doubt that I will raise any new details from the texts I will discuss for persons who are scholars in the thought of either of these men. But I do think that the dialogue itself will show their respective claims and comments in a different light than before.

The choice of this topic is fairly easy to explain. It has become increasingly obvious that the understanding one has of what it means to be a person casts in relief the very shape of one's epistemology, as well as one's moral and social theory.[1] Selfhood turns out to be intertwined inextricably with these other interests. Here is just one example of the relationship between the concept of the self and morality.

The topology of the moral world is defined by urgent and powerful demands that we recognize to be connected to the respect for the life, integrity, and well-being, even flourishing, of others. But of which sort of others? Obviously, persons are different from animals in moral grammar, and one way in which this is true is that persons are not only given moral consideration, but they are also appraised by how they conduct themselves toward other persons. Animals may be beneficiaries of moral consideration, but they are not subject to nearly the same sort of moral evaluation which we make of persons. This difference is owing to the unexposed concept of the person which is nested in the moral practices by which our community lives.

Of course, showing that the understanding of the person is of interest in this way does not really justify the choice of Rousseau and Hegel as subject theorists. Certainly I am not claiming that they are the only thinkers who should be studied on this subject, nor even that they represent the most definitive alternatives for the construction of an understanding of the self. I can, however, offer a few reasons for choosing to analyze some of their texts. 1) Rousseau and Hegel both belong to the early modern period which has left its mark on our own understandings of what it means to be a person in ways that no previous era had done before. The more we can know about the key figures who rattled Western civilization from its slumbers the better. 2) Coming to comprehend the momentous ways our own culture and society have departed from their mode of seeing things helps us appreciate the tasks which yet lie before us. 3) Each of these men considered himself to be a prophetic voice, standing at a pivotal point in history. Each tried to map the way forward as his own lights directed him, and his understanding of what it means to be a person is crucial to following the way he charted. 4) Finally, both of these thinkers wrote complex and intricate texts the nature of which is to invite continued conversation and engagement. In their texts are the familiar sounds of the early modern period, but also the discords of the postmodern disturbance whose waves we still ride.

Biography

There is a way, too, in which the biographies of these men provide an interesting reflection of the understanding of the person which they advocate. Rousseau, for example, was born in Geneva and had absolutely none of the advantages Hegel enjoyed. His mother died when he was only a newborn. He was raised for a short time by his father, and then he was sent to live with a minister and the minister's sister. He spent most of his young adulthood, certainly through his teenage years, bouncing around trying to find a family and a place to belong. This required him virtually to be self-taught both in respect to his formal academic gains and to his ability to relate to other persons in the common situations of life. By his own testimony, he had virtually no sustained relationship during this period of his life. Later, as both the *Confessions* and *Reveries of the Solitary Walker* amply illustrate, he reached his senior years having severed the friendships which had come his way as an adult. Rousseau's radical understanding of what it meant to be a person spun him like a dervish, attracting and repelling friends and enemies alike. Many of his bitterest enemies were, in an earlier day, numbered among his dearest friends.

In contrast, Hegel led a vastly different life. He enjoyed a highly stable family interaction. Although his mother died when he was eleven, she had been a warm and loving companion, as well as his teacher, throughout his early childhood. He received a solid education in the classics at the Stuttgart gymnasium and was at the top of his class from the age of ten until his matriculation at Tübingen eight years later. While at Tübingen he made intense and longlasting friendships with, among others, the remarkable young poet Friedrich Hölderlin and the brilliant philosopher, Friedrich Schelling. Hegel found a community with these young men who were filled with passion and zeal for a new world aborning in Germany.

At the age at which Rousseau was a lackey and footman, in his best days living off the graces of wealthy benefactors, and in other times moving from town to town in a gypsy-like existence, Hegel was in a prestigious university, surrounded by admiring peers and respectful professors. In fact, it would be fair to say that it was not until his graduation from Tübingen that Hegel encountered any serious impediment to anything he wanted to accomplish or possess. It seems certain that he had experienced no crisis of confidence or self-assurance until then.[2] For any reader of Rousseau's *Confessions*, this, in itself, is a striking difference between the two men.

Sources

Unlike Rousseau, Hegel left no truly introspective texts aside from his letters. It is true that he kept a Tagebuch at Stuttgart, but it mainly contains his responses and reflections about intellectual and philosophical questions arising from his assignments and rather extensive personal reading program. My own interpretation of Hegel's lack of preoccupation with himself is that he seems to have been so comfortable with his own identity and relations to others as to have felt no compelling need to narrate his story or probe his intimacies.

Hegel was very familiar with Rousseau's writings, and various sources show that these were quite influential on him. The Stuttgart Tagebuch reveals his sympathies with Rousseau's doctrine of the natural goodness and nobility of man and discloses his agreement with the view that we shall not go wrong if we do what our conscience tells us. Both of these sentiments are well-known themes from Rousseau's key texts: *The Discourse on the Origin of Inequality, The Social Contract*, and *Emile*. It is probable that Hegel had read all of these works before his years at Tübingen, but it is certain that he read them while he was there. Hegel was familiar as well with Rousseau's *Confessions*. Passages from this work were included in his *Excerpts*. His essay "On the Religion of Greece and Rome" dated in August of 1787 (the Stuttgart period) is a thoroughgoing defense of folk-religion, which he distinguishes from all institutional forms and to which he attributes the development of the moral sentiments which are in human nature. The main lines of his argument are reminiscent of Rousseau's discussions of religion in *The Social Contract* and *Emile*.

In one of Hegel's four sermons that survive from the years at Tübingen, he preached on the subject of the justification of God in reward and punishment (10 January 1792). In this sermon, he tried to show, by means of reasoning similar to that of Rousseau's Savoyard Vicar in *Emile*, that the voice of conscience is the voice of God's revelation to every man, leaving each without excuse.[3]

Hegel's political views during his years as a Tübingen student were shaped by Voltaire and Rousseau. Under the eyes of the professors, Hegel donned his cassock, studied the appointed books, completed his essays, preached the required sermons, and rehearsed arguments supporting approved doctrines. But on his own time, he joined a small group of fellow students reading Rousseau's *Discourses* and *The Social Contract*, as well as French newspapers and journals. They marched for "Liberty, Equality and Fraternity," planted a "Liberty Tree," and organized a concert at which the new anthem of the Revolution was sung, much to the scandal of Tübingen conservatives.

While I think the evidence is just too skimpy to know for sure, my hypothesis is that after his graduation from Tübingen (1793–1796), Hegel modeled his service as Hofmeister to the von Steiger family in Berne after the governor in Rousseau's *Emile*. I base this conclusion on the fact that *Emile* had been his frequent reading in the year preceding the assignment, and he often comments on the need for a revision in the education of the next generation in his letters and early papers. During his years in the sleepy town of Berne, while revolution was in the air elsewhere, he wrote on the subject of education and the role of individual teachers in the reformation of corrupt society during this period, themes quite in harmony with *Emile*. I also consider this to be a plausible explanation for why the Berne experience was such an unpleasant one for him as well as for the von Steiger family. Those familiar with the methods and plan of *Emile* will find it quite believable that Karl von Steiger might object to his promising young aristocratic children being tutored as Emile was. Likewise, trying to follow the rule of Emile's governor would have probably been quite difficult for one educated as Hegel had been, and we see in his letters to Hölderlin and others such frustrations as one would expect to find if this were true.

It was also while working at Berne that Hegel became interested in the philosophy of the self, and he made notes on this subject under the imposing title, "Materials for a Philosophy of Subjective Psychology." From this period we should probably date the beginnings of his departure from Rousseau's way of conceiving the formation of the person, and I do not think that we should underestimate the influence of Hegel's failure as a Hofmeister in Berne on his decision to reconsider Rousseau's theory of the self in *Emile* and the *Confessions*. Though he was not discharged from this position, and actually left it to take a similar job, nevertheless von Steiger was anxious to release him, and Hegel arrived in Frankfurt discouraged about what seems to have been his first serious failure in life. So, I believe that lurking behind the discussion of the formation of the self in *Phenomenology* is Hegel's conviction, based on personal experience, that Rousseau's notions of the self and how it is to be formed were unsatisfactory.

Through Hölderlin's arrangement, Hegel took a Hofmeister position in Frankfurt from 1797–1800. This was a significant move in his development because it meant he was no longer working in virtual isolation, as had been the case while he lived in Berne. Many of his views on the self, which would eventually find their way into the *Phenomenology of Spirit*, were first put forth tentatively in this period. So, in "In the Religion of Greece and Rome" and the "Materials for a Philosophy of Subjective Psychology," we witness Hegel moving away from Rousseau at a theoretical level, completing the change which had already occurred for more practical reasons. We see that he regarded the formation of the self as irreducibly dialectical. Being a person is understood to involve the unification of subject and object, freedom and nature, independence and dependence, and equality and reciprocity.

In essay fragments from 1798 on the subject of love, Hegel said love for another is the sense of one's own life as doubled. In the completed unity of love, the separation between beings actually continues to exist, but the opposition is not absolute. Among intimates this separation is most completely superseded: "What is most private to oneself [*das Eigenste*] is united in mutual contact and shared feeling to the point of unconsciousness, of the transcending (*Aufhebung*) of all distinction."[4] In 1799, Hegel was working on the development of his views regarding opposition and individuality in consciousness.

> The concept of individuality includes opposition to infinite manifoldness and juncture with it; a man is an individual life, inasmuch as he is distinct from [*ein anderes ist*] all elements, and from the infinity of individual lives external to him, but he is only an individual life inasmuch as he is one with all elements, with all the infinity of lives external to him.[5]

In 1800, Hegel anticipated the beginning of hostilities with France and looked forward to the creation of a new state and society. He wrote about the way in which an individual needed to recreate limiting cultures in order to realize his own flourishing.

In January of 1801, he received a long desired appointment to a philosophy faculty at the University of Jena. There his lecture schedule provided him an opportunity to work on his "new science," and thus we are led to the *Phenomenology of Spirit,* a work whose most compelling descriptions are concerned with what it means to be a person. In 1806, the year that Hegel wrote most of the *Phenomenology,* the European theater was in a state of total change. The English Revolution had undermined the divine right of kings, and the French Revolution had eliminated the monarch himself. Hegel saw this as a time of promise, and the *Phenomenology* was meant to be a tract for understanding what it meant to be a person in such times.

> Besides, it is not difficult to see that ours is a birth-time and a period of transition to a new era. Spirit has broken with the world it has hitherto inhabited and imagined, and is of a mind to submerge it in the past, and in the labour of its own transformation. Spirit is indeed never at rest but always engaged in moving forward. The frivolity and boredom which unsettle the established order, the vague foreboding of something unknown, these are the heralds of approaching change. The gradual crumbling that left unaltered the face of the whole is cut short by a sunburst which, in one flash, illuminates the features of the new world.[6]

It is clear that Hegel was quite familiar with Rousseau's work on the self, but that he went his own way on the subject. In the process of doing so, he offered a sustained analysis and critique of Rousseau's understanding of the self, without ever mentioning him by name. I wish to proceed by offering an exposition of the key ideas of each thinker on the self. Then, I want to use my own summary and evaluation to place these men in conversation on the very specific issue of how independence and dependence is integrated into the self. This approach to the subject should provide the reader with ample opportunity to enter into dialogue with me at various levels throughout.

Rousseau on the Self

If one considers the theories of the self put forward by Descartes, Leibniz, and Kant on the continent, and Locke and Hume in Britain, a single fact stands out rather strikingly: other persons do not figure prominently in their philosophical explanations about personal identity. The self is understood as isolated and self-forming. In Germany, this view was so deeply ingrained that J.G. Fichte could say, "I am indeed conscious of myself as an independent being;...I have immediate knowledge of myself alone....I am wholly my own creation and whatever has an existence for me has it through myself."[7]

Not only is the self formulated in isolation, but also it is regarded as fixed. That is, it has a certain natural substance which does not change. This natural self includes internal directives of various sorts. There were different ways to construct this theory. The Continental Rationalists conceived of the fixed structure of the self as innate ideas, and, although empiricism turned from this view, even Locke retained a notion of natural law, and Hume continued to speak of moral sentiments common to all men. Kant likewise continued to find some modification of it necessary by his transcendental deduction of synthetic a priori knowledge.

Locke was the first to give us cause to question the stability of the self in his discussion of memory. Nonetheless, his view of substance suggests that he wanted to hold on to some essential nature in the self which he thought was unchangeable throughout time. Although Hume discarded the view that the self has an abiding nature or substance which remains constant, even he did not do so in order to acknowledge the role that others play in the formation of a person. In fact, it seems clear that the reason he could not find the self is that he was looking for the sort of isolated and fixed phenomenon for which he had been taught to look. The contributions of others to our self-understanding is not a part of his objection to the reality of the self.

This view of personal identity, as by nature discrete and fixed, lies behind the search for the "inner self," or "real self," which drove Rousseau's autobiographical quest, as well as his political theory. When he undertook to explain the origin of inequality, this view of the self determined his approach to the problem.

I consider the subject of this discourse to be one of the most interesting that philosophy can propose, and, unhappily for us, one of the thorniest that philosophers can try to resolve, for how can the source of inequality among men be known, unless we begin by knowing men themselves? And how will man succeed in seeing himself as nature created him,...and in separating what he owes to his own essence from what circumstances and his advances have added.[8]

Rousseau believed that the essential self can be known completely because it is fixed, but it can never be known in this way by others. Only we can *know* our true selves, and only when we free ourselves from others can we *be* the persons we truly are. Rousseau often said that he could see from the way in which others interpreted his actions that they did not know the person he really was. He boldly affirmed that "nobody in the world knows me but myself."[9] This belief underlies his conviction that he can set the story straight, correcting all of his detractors, and tell what he was really like in his autobiographical works: *Confessions, Rousseau Judge of Jean-Jacques: Dialogues*, and the *Reveries of the Solitary Walker*.[10]

In the *Discourse on the Origins of Inequality*, Rousseau spoke fondly of man in the state of nature because persons in this condition enjoyed isolation. In fact, he took the natural man as his model of the most real self, because in the state of nature man was strong, self-loving, absolutely independent, and without need for society or speech. In the natural state, indifference reigned between humans; there was neither mutual dependency, interdependency, nor hostility. Procreation was based on temporary biological desire; it was no social affair and required no caring between the partners. Sex was a chance coupling without need for speech, and male and female afterward left each other with ease. Children were left by their mothers as soon as they were old enough to survive on their own. In short, in the state of nature, according to Rousseau, there was no society or dependency, and no war or violence, because there was no concept of property to define what was "mine" or "yours." Rousseau considered this idyllic:

> Such is the melancholy evidence that we might have avoided almost all the ills we suffer from, if we had kept to the simple, uniform, solitary existence prescribed to us by nature. If she intended us to be healthy, I venture almost to affirm that the state of reflection is a state contrary to nature, and the man who thinks is a depraved animal. (*Discourse on Inequality*, 13)

Understanding this makes it clear why Rousseau was interested in proposing an educational project in which a person would be raised from infancy as though he were in the state of nature, without the influence of other people. He wrote about this project in detail in *Emile*. In this work, the first book Emile is assigned to read by his governor (teacher) is *Robinson Crusoe*. Crusoe was attractive to Rousseau because on his island Crusoe was alone and isolated from both the assistance and opinions of others. Rousseau said, "it is on the basis of this very state that he [Emile] ought to appraise all the others. The surest means of raising oneself above prejudices and ordering one's judgments about the true relations of things is to put oneself in the place of an isolated man and to judge everything as this man himself ought to judge of it with respect to his own utility."[11] Unfortunately for Rousseau's project, it is all too obvious upon reading about Emile's education that he was not reared in a Crusoe-like situation. He depended on his governor for all sorts of things, and the governor intentionally engineered Emile's experiences, giving him some and preventing him from having others.

Apparently, what Rousseau expected such isolation to yield was a person who would know the truth in knowledge and morality. He intended for Emile to use the Crusoe situation as the "surest means of raising oneself above prejudices and ordering one's judgments about the true relations of things" (185). When faced with making a choice later in his societal life, Emile was told that he would be guided best if he judged everything as Crusoe would, that is, without regard for others. In providing such advice, Rousseau did not mean that Emile should be selfish in any petty sense, but that he could only be true to his real self by detachment from the opinions of others. This helps us understand what Rousseau meant when he said that he did not want to make Emile a savage and send him back to the woods, but rather that he wanted to teach him to live in the whirl of social life and not to be carried away by the passions and prejudices of men. Rousseau had no doubt that whenever Emile placed himself in this imaginative situation, the resulting decision would be the right one.

It is legitimate to wonder why Rousseau thought isolation from others would yield persons of this sort. In order to understand this, we need to look beyond *Emile* to another work. In the "Preface" to the *Discourse on the Origins of Inequality*, Rousseau contrasted the socially warped and unjust man who is in a state of "delirium" with "a being which always acts according to certain and invariable principles,...that celestial and majestic simplicity which its author imprinted on it" (*Discourse on Inequality*, 4). Rousseau praised the person who acted according to his own conscience. This does not mean, however, that he was necessarily suggesting a self-interest ethic to Emile. He was saying that the fixed natural self is in touch with certain, invariable principles imprinted by its creator and that, if one can remove the opinions of others and function in a solitary way, these will manifest themselves. In the educational treatise, Emile will know what is right because of a "divine instinct" and "immortal celestial voice."

I still must investigate what manner of conduct I ought to draw from these truths and what rules I ought to prescribe for myself in order to fulfill my destiny on earth according to the intention of Him who put me there. In continuing to follow my method, I do not draw these rules from the principles of a high philosophy, but find them written by nature with ineffaceable characters in the depth of my heart,…The best of all casuists is the conscience…Conscience is the voice of the soul; the passions are the voice of the body.

It is not my design here to enter into metaphysical discussions which are out of my reach and yours,…I have already told you that I wanted not to philosophize with you but to help you consult your heart…For that purpose I need only to make you distinguish our acquired ideas from our natural sentiments…The acts of the conscience are not judgments but sentiments…and we had sentiments before ideas. Whatever the cause of our being, it has provided for our preservation by giving us sentiments suitable to our nature, and it could not be denied that these at least, are innate. These sentiments, as far as the individual is concerned, are the love of self, the fear of pain, the horror of death, the desire of well being…(*Emile*, 286, 288, 289, 290).

In *Reveries of the Solitary Walker*, when he commented on deciding difficult ethical questions, Rousseau said, "I have always found it best to be guided by the voice of conscience rather than the light of reason. My moral instinct has never deceived me."[12] It is clear that he thought that the inner true self is equipped with natural moral sentiments which are innate and certain guides (*Confessions*, 585). For him, conscience was the only reliable source for the moral life: "Whether the command comes from other people, duty or even necessity, when my heart is silent, my will remains deaf and I cannot obey" (*Reveries*, 96).

Rousseau called pity and compassion natural sentiments. He did not believe they were derived from civil society or culture: "It appears at first that men in that state [the natural state], lacking among themselves any kind of moral relationship or any known duties, could be neither good nor evil and had neither vices nor virtues" (*Discourse on Inequality*, 26). The presence of natural compassion, much like the reluctance of horses to trample a living body underfoot, is what Rousseau called "the pure movement of nature," and he considered it to be nature's preparation for the move from the natural relation of indifference between persons to that which employs the moral categories necessary for relationships between an individual and others.[13]

Rousseau not only thought that the inner natural self was a source of absolute moral guidance, but that it also remained pure, even when the social self was corrupt.

> I drew this great maxim of morality, perhaps the only one of practical use, to avoid situations which put our deities in opposition with our interests and which show us our good in the hurts of others, sure that in such situations, however sincere our love of virtue, we weaken sooner or later without realizing it, and become unjust and wicked in our actions, without having stopped being just and good at heart. (*The Confessions*, 8. This seems also to have been a characteristic of Mme. de Warens; see 219–220).
>
> If I had remained free, unknown and isolated, as nature meant me to be, I should have done nothing but good, for my heart does not contain the seeds of any harmful passion. If I had been invisible and powerful like God, I should have been good and beneficent like him (*Reveries*, 101).

Alas, for Rousseau, living with others meant that "[t]here are times when I am so unlike myself that I might be taken for someone else of an entirely opposite character" (*Confessions*, 126).

Rousseau considered life in society a disaster because it presents so many opportunities for the natural self to be overtaken and lost under the veil of the social self.

> The most unfortunate effect of formal politeness is to teach the art of getting along without the virtues it imitates. Let humanity and beneficence be inspired in us by education [as Emile is educated], and we shall have politeness, or we shall no longer need it. If we do not possess the politeness heralded by the graces,...we shall not need to resort to falseness. Instead of being artificial in order to please, it will suffice to be good (*Confessions*, 338).

Rousseau decided not to allow society to corrupt him. Along with his resolution not to undertake moral action, he wanted to be true to his inner pure nature by resisting the influences of society and culture: the opinions of men.

> I quitted the world and its vanities, I gave up all finery—no more sword, no more watch, no more white stocking, gilt trimmings and powder, but a simple wig and a good solid coat of broadcloth—and what is more than all the rest, I uprooted from my heart the greed and covetousness which give value to all I was leaving behind...I did not confine my reformation to outward things. Indeed I became aware that this change called for a revision of my opinions...which was to order my inner life for the rest of my days as I would wish it to be at the time of my death (*Reveries*, 51. See also, *Confessions*, 343–344).

Rousseau seems rarely to have felt at home with others, but this is not just the result of oppressive law or government. It is a deep discomfort with others which extends from his passing acquaintances down to his most fundamental human intimacies: conversation, family relations, and love.

The *Confessions* narrate several desperate attempts to win the acceptance of others. In some, Rousseau resorted to bizarre forms of role playing, such as pretending to be a musician/composer and an English gentleman, in order to win the attention and companionship of others. His relationships with women were particularly strange. I do not think I am exaggerating when I say that he believed that any woman who spoke to him cordially was really in love with him and desired him sexually. Of course, this created significant problems for him. If the liaison did not come to fruition, he explained it as the woman's fickleness or fault, or blamed it on a third party, but he never thought of this failure as a result of either his own miscue or overactive fantasies.[14]

When he wrote about those persons with whom he had relationships, Rousseau typically framed his description under the concept of the "use" they were to him or to which he put them (Cf. *Confessions*, 201, 266, 464, 466, 558). He seemed not to think of the mutuality which one often considers to be fundamental to relationships. He thought that others *had no real contribution to make* to his own personhood and indeed that they *should not be allowed to shape* who he was. He made no secret about doing what was expedient for his own interest in any situation, no matter what the consequences (*Confessions*, 53).

In the episode which Rousseau himself says "tells all about Jean-Jacques Rousseau," what we have is another encounter in which he not only finds a flaw in someone, but in which he felt that he *must* do so (see *Confessions* 300–302. Cf. also 57, 83, 95, 267, 276, 281, 552, 568, 569, 571, 583, 584). Rousseau sought, searched, probed, and exposed, until a flaw in another person became apparent. This meant that virtually everyone wanted to get away from him. He preferred imaginary to real people.

> My reader has already guessed, if he has paid the least attention to my progress so far. The impossibility of attaining the real persons precipitated me into the land of chimeras; and seeing nothing that existed worthy of my exalted feelings, I foster them in an ideal world which my creative imagination soon peopled with beings after my own heart (*Confessions*, 64).

After the banning of *Emile* and *The Social Contract*, Rousseau sought refuge from the persecutions of his critics. He found what to him was an idyllic place to inhabit: the island of Saint-Pierre.

This choice was so much in keeping with my peaceful tastes and with my solitary, indolent disposition, that I think of it as one of these sweet dreams for which I have felt the most enthusiasm. It seemed to me that on that island I should be further removed from men, safer from their insults, and more forgotten by them; freer, in a word, to surrender to the pleasures of idleness and the contemplative life (*Confessions*, 589).

But even the island was flawed. There was a better place. "The moment I left the bank I almost leapt for joy. The cause of this I cannot tell, nor can I really understand it, unless it was perhaps some secret self-congratulation at being thus out of reach of the wicked. Then I rowed alone all about the lake, sometimes approaching the shore but never landing" (*Confessions*, 594).

While musing about the self's relationship to others, Rousseau wrote a very disturbing passage in the *Reveries*.

It is strength and freedom which make really good men; weakness and slavery have never produced anything but evil-doers. If I had possessed the ring of Gyges, it would have made me independent of men and made them dependent on me. I have often wondered, in my castles in the air, how I should have used this ring,...Always impartially just and unfalteringly good, I should have guarded myself equally against blind mistrust and implacable hate, I should have found few who were likable enough to deserve my full affection and few who were odious enough to deserve my hate (*Reveries*, 102).

Perhaps pride has a part in these judgments. I feel too much above them to hate them (*Reveries*, 100).

Independence from and dependence on others was also a major theme in *Emile*. Although Rousseau valued independence and indifference as the most natural states of man, he also recognized that all persons have some dependencies. In *Emile*, he spoke of two sorts of dependencies: dependence only on things and dependence on others. In his project of educating Emile, his goal was to eradicate dependence on others, because it is artificial, and leave only dependence on things, which he considered to be a natural form of dependency and therefore harmless. According to Rousseau, if dependence was shifted in this way, then all the contradictions of the social system would be resolved.

There are two sorts of dependence: dependence on things, which is from nature; dependence on men, which is from society. Dependence on things, since it has no morality, is in no way detrimental to freedom and engenders no vices. Dependence on men, since it is without order, engenders all the vices, and by it, master and slave are mutually corrupted (*Emile*, 85).

In *Emile*, Rousseau was not interested in teaching Emile how to play the dependence/independence game and win. He wanted Emile to know how to be indifferent to the opinions of others, to break the dependence cycle by choosing only to be dependent on things.

> From these contradictions is born the one we constantly experience within ourselves. Swept along in contrary routes by nature and by men, forced to divide ourselves between these different impulses, we follow a composite impulse which leads us to neither one goal nor the other. Thus in conflict and floating during the whole course of our life, we end it without having been able to put ourselves in harmony with ourselves and without having been good either to ourselves or for others...if perchance the double object we set for ourselves could be joined in a single one by removing the contradictions of man, a great obstacle to his happiness would be removed (*Emile*, 41).

Rousseau deplored dialectic, and he did not believe the true self is found in the struggle between individual assertiveness and dependence on others, but only by escaping this conflict.

It is sad and shocking to read about this understanding of the relationship between himself and others during his last years:

> So now I am alone in the world, with no brother, neighbour or friend, nor any company left me but my own. The most sociable and loving of men has with one accord been cast out by all the rest. With all the ingenuity of hate they have sought out the cruelest torture for my sensitive soul, and have violently broken all the threads that bound me to them. I would have loved my fellow-men in spite of themselves. It was only by ceasing to be human that they could forfeit my affection. So now they are strangers and foreigners to me (*Reveries*, 27).

The final years were spent in fear of and alienation from others.

> The accumulation of so many chance circumstances, the elevation of all my cruelest enemies, as if chosen by fortune, the way in which all those who govern the nation or control public opinion, all those who occupy places of credit and authority seem to have been hand-picked from among those who harbour some secret animosity towards me to take part in the universal conspiracy, all this is too extraordinary to be a mere coincidence (*Reveries*, 44).

Rousseau damned the society that made him feel this way. He spoke of others as though they were dangerous and vicious, as if they would inevitably distort his real and morally pure self, a self whose pristine character would have been preserved inviolate otherwise. He went so far as to say that men love to create monsters, to disfigure everything (*Emile*, 37).

According to Ann Hartle, Rousseau ceased admiring the men in Plutarch's *Lives* because they were "living in the opinions of others."[15] They were considered noble because others said so, not because they were so in themselves. On Rousseau's terms, this was the most damning condemnation possible.

> [Civilized man] pays court to men in power whom he hates, and to rich men whom he despises;...proud of his slavery, he speaks with disdain of those who have not the honor of sharing it...the savage lives within himself, whereas social man, constantly outside himself, knows only how to live in the opinion of others; and it is, if I may say so, merely from their judgment of him that he derives the consciousness of his own existence (*Confessions*, 261).

Hegel on the Self

Let us move now into a very different form of writing and a totally different source of ideas. Whereas, for his views of the self, I often relied on Rousseau's autobiographical reflections and ideas about how to educate a person, my exposition of Hegel will be quite different. The principal difference will be that I intend to confine my remarks about Hegel's views to one source: *The Phenomenology of Spirit*. This work is not in any straightforward sense an autobiographical account. It is a critique of the history of philosophy. Those sections we will be analyzing provide a careful criticism of several views of self-formation.

"With Self-Consciousness," Hegel informs us, "we have entered the native realm of truth" (*PS*, 160). We have also entered the realm of the most famous part of the *Phenomenology*, the parable of the "Master and Slave." This parable is usually the first point where a beginning reader feels as though he or she knows what Hegel is trying to say. The parable falls into two parts. The first (*PS*, 178–189) is the battle for recognition, with each individual trying to assert independence, culminating in the victory of one over the other. In the second section of the parable (*PS*, 190–196), we find that the victory was both tentative and relative. The second section describes the turnabout in which the master becomes dependent on the slave and the slave independent of the master. For Hegel, to be a person is to be a consciousness in this dialectical process with another consciousness.

It is this struggle that turns consciousness into self-consciousness, and without it, self-consciousness or personhood would not emerge. Viewed in this manner, the parable is a corrective to the view of the self that dominated Hegel's philosophical world and which I have been attributing to Rousseau, that view which holds that the self is essentially an entity known through immediate intuition, without the need for others. More especially, in Rousseau's case, this view believes that the interference of others in self-formation and self-understanding is necessarily harmful and to be avoided whenever possible. The real self is fixed, not in flux.

Hegel's strategy is to break down this way of seeing in much the same manner as he attacks the received understanding of knowledge as some relation between the self (as "knower/subject") and the world (as "known/object") earlier in the *Phenomenology*, and the key entry into his deconstruction of this understanding is the lord-bondsman (master-slave) parable.

Nested in the title of this section we find Hegel's sense of the point at which previous views of self-formation go wrong. The actual title of the section is "Independence and Dependence of Self-Consciousness: Lordship and Bondage." Hegel thought that how we think about independence and dependence would determine our philosophy of the person and thus our ability to possess a sense of happiness and fulfillment. To put his idea bluntly, Hegel believed that the entire idea of considering oneself to be either independent or dependent upon others is poor philosophy. In the *Phenomenology*, such antinomies are regarded as moments in the dialectical process of existence, abstractions from the flow of experience or the life process itself, remarks made after the autopsy of the cadaver of a once living thing (Spirit). Accordingly, for Hegel, to seek full independence and isolation would be as dreadfully destructive to one's self-identity as it would be to turn over determination and description of the self completely to others, and both are equally impossible.

As a construct of abstract thinking, Hegel knew how such dichotomies worked, but he thought they were systematically misleading. Life does not come to us in this well analyzed and dissected manner. Only by murdering it and performing an autopsy on the corpse could one come up with the idea that a self should be totally independent or dependent: "Both moments are essential. Since to begin with they are unequal and opposed, and their reflection into a unity has not yet been achieved, they exist as two opposed shapes of consciousness; one is the independent consciousness whose essential nature is to be *for itself*, the other is the dependent consciousness whose essential nature is simply to live or to be *for another*" (*PS*, 189). "Its [the self's] moments [independence/dependence], then, must on the one hand be held strictly apart, and on the other hand must in this differentiation at the same time also be taken and known as not distinct" (*PS*, 178). "The twofold significance of the distinct moments has in the nature of self-consciousness to be infinite, or directly opposite of the determinateness in which it is posited" (*PS*, 178).

The Master-Slave parable then is an ontology of self-formation meant to overcome a fixation on either independence or dependence. It describes the reciprocity between selves, whose complexity frightening. There can be no master without a slave, and no slave without a master. Likewise, no one is always master or always slave, completely independent or completely dependent on someone else. Even if someone could make another person over into exactly what he or she wanted him or her to be, this would not mean that he or she had become absolutely independent and master of his or her own self, and the other totally dependent on him or her. By the very process of coming to dominate some other person, the master actually becomes dependent on that person to preserve his or her own identity as master, and he or she thus finds himself or herself a slave. Commenting on this rather strange turn of events, Hegel said, "Just as lordship showed that its essential nature is the reverse of what it wants to be, so too servitude in its consummation will really turn it into the opposite of what it immediately is" (*PS*, 193). The more one tries to take away the independence of another and assert oneself as dominant, the more one actually becomes dependent on the other at the same time (*PS*, 190).

Furthermore, persons are at one and the same time, under different descriptions, masters and slaves, independent and dependent, relative to the context. A son may be dependent on (slave to) his father for financial resources to go to college, and his father, then, may seem independent (master). But, of course, his father is dependent on his job (thus a slave) for the funds needed. Likewise, the father may be emotionally dependent upon (slave to) his son, who thereby is relatively independent emotionally from his father (and thus, master).

Hegel pictured the master/slave struggle as a "life and death" encounter because of its seriousness. Since the struggle with others is ontologically necessary in order for self-consciousness to exist, then there can be no lasting or fundamental indifference between individuals and others without the destruction of selfhood, just as there is no escape from the struggle without death.

Hegel knew his enemy well. He understood that if one believes that the self is isolated, discrete and wholly self-defining, then any mutuality will appear to be intrusive and destructive. He argued that the more one believes oneself to be wholly self-defining, the more difficult it will be to belong with and relate to others, because the fear of dependency will manifest itself in all kinds of bizarre ways. Hegel's discussion of the ways persons try to escape the dialectic of individual and other is found in his remarks on the forms of self-consciousness entitled "Stoicism, Skepticism and Unhappy Consciousness." Hegel called these strategies of self-formation "rationalistic fantasies" (*PS*, 197). He believed that history shows increasingly more desperate strategies, culminating in the Unhappy Consciousness he associated with Christianity.[16]

These attempts to overcome the master-slave struggle express themselves in various shapes of self-consciousness, or styles of life, which Hegel thought to be self-defeating and self-destructive (*PS*, 357–359). They are Hedonism, "The law of the heart and the frenzy of self-deceit," Pietism, and Radicalized Individuality.

I do not plan to describe his views on all the shapes of self-consciousness. However, one section is of particular interest to a comparison between Rousseau and Hegel. In "The law of the heart and the frenzy of self-deceit" Hegel's argument seems to be directed at Rousseau, especially at *Emile* and *The Confessions*. His argument is that the move from Hedonism turns into a form of self-righteous self-denial, which appeals to the "inner goodness" of the self, irrespective of its outward deeds. He called this "the law of the heart." Hegel said that persons who have such a self-consciousness find that they must resort to hypocrisy and to a rigid fault-finding judgmental attitude, which leads them eventually to find themselves cut off from others because they live always solely by their own lights. "This individuality therefore directs its energies to getting rid of this necessity [others, culture, law, morality] which contradicts the law of the heart" (*PS*, 369).

Hegel held that such persons experience their relationships with others as a form of oppression, "a violent ordering of the world which contradicts the law of the heart" (*PS*, 369). Because they follow only their own wisdom and way, these individuals will, in fact, find themselves punished and oppressed, actually desiring community, but being unable to have it because of the law of others' hearts. Hegel said of those who live by the law of their own hearts, "others do not find in this content the fulfillment of the law of *their* hearts, but rather that of someone else;…Thus, just as the individual at first finds only the rigid law, now he finds the hearts of men themselves, opposed to his excellent intentions and detestable" (*PS*, 373).

The result is that the individuality which it so very much valued is thereby warped.

> The heart-throb for the welfare of humanity therefore passes into the ravings of an

insane self-conceit, into the fury of consciousness to preserve itself from destruction; and it does this by expelling from itself the perversion which it is itself, and by striving to look on it and express it as something else. It therefore speaks of the universal order as a perversion of the law of the heart and of its happiness, a perversion invented by fanatical priests, gluttonous despots and their minions, who compensate themselves for their own degradation by degrading and oppressing others, a perversion which has led to the nameless misery of deluded humanity (*PS*, 377).

With these comments in mind, we can appreciate why Hegel is so deliberate in his attack on radical individuality's trust in conscience as the only certain moral guide, a key component in Rousseau's theory of the person. "The declaration of this assurance in itself rides the form of its particularity. It thereby acknowledges *the necessary universality of the self*...i.e. it calls itself a universal knowing" (*PS*, 654). "Conscience, then, in the majesty of its elevation above specific law and every content of duty, puts whatever content it pleases into its knowing and willing. It is the moral genius which knows the inner voice of what it immediately knows to be a divine voice; and since, in knowing this, it has an equally immediate knowledge of existence, it is the divine creative power...it is in its own self divine worship, for its action is the contemplation of its own divinity" (*PS*, 655). Hegel believed that this form of self-consciousness is self-defeating and destroys what it is trying to create. "Here, then, we see self-consciousness withdrawn into its innermost being, for which all externality as such has vanished—Refined into this purity, consciousness exists in its poorest form, and the poverty which constitutes its sole possession is itself a vanishing" (*PS*, 657).

The law of the heart, which elevates the individual conscience to moral supremacy, culminates in a so-called "beautiful soul." Seeking to keep itself pure, the beautiful soul abstains from moral action. "It does well to preserve itself in its purity, for *it does not act*; it is the hypocrisy which wants its judging to be taken for an *actual* deed, and instead of proving its rectitude by actions, does so by uttering fine sentiments. Its nature, then, is altogether the same as that which is reproached with making duty a mere matter of words" (*PS*, 664).

Eventually, the beautiful soul vanishes away:

It [the beautiful soul] lives in dread of besmirching the splendour of its inner being by action and an existence; and in order to preserve the purity of its heart, it flees from contact with the actual world, and persists in its self-willed impotence to renounce its self which is reduced to the extreme of ultimate abstraction...The hollow object which it has produced for itself now fills it, therefore, with a sense of emptiness. Its activity is a yearning which merely loses itself as consciousness becomes an object devoid of substance, and rising above this loss, and falling back on itself, finds itself only as a lost soul. In this transparent purity of its moments, an unhappy, so-called "beautiful soul," its light dies away within it, and it vanishes like a shapeless vapour that dissolves into thin air (*PS*, 658).

With his description of the "beautiful soul" Hegel's discussion of the bankrupt ways of self-creation draws to a conclusion. What he has to say about the beautiful soul seems to me to fit the life of Rousseau very well. It appears to be a philosophical commentary on a man whose autobiography had become his obsession. In his culminating remarks about the "beautiful soul" Hegel provides us with a sad epitaph for Rousseau. "The 'beautiful soul', lacking an actual existence, entangled in the contradiction between its pure self and the necessity of that self to externalize itself and change itself into an actual existence, and dwelling in the immediacy of this firmly held antithesis—this 'beautiful soul', then, being conscious of this contradiction in its unreconciled immediacy, is disordered to the point of madness, wastes itself in yearning and pines away in consumption" (*PS*, 668). These strains remind us of the Rousseau of the *Confessions*, alone on Saint-Pierre, solitary, rowing about the lake, sometimes approaching the shore where those who might help him untangle his individuality and self-for-others live, but he never lands (*Confessions*, 589, 594).

If these are approaches to the master-slave conflict which are undesirable, one may ask whether or not Hegel held any more hopeful view. The answer to this is maybe. Hegel offered no absolute way of synthesizing the dialectic of independence and dependence. In fact, his view was that there is no one right way of relating all our relationships with others. Neither is any individual synthesis final. There is always the on-going process of life. "It is *this very flux* as a self-identical independence which is itself an enduring existence,...*Being* no longer has the significance of *abstract being*; on the contrary, *being* is precisely that simply fluid substance of pure movement within itself" (*PS*, 169).

Hegel recognized only limited value in what he called the "laws of Psychology." He did not think that psychology or philosophy could prescribe the way others shape our personhood into any formal laws. "Psychological observation discovers no law for the relation of self-consciousness to actuality, or to the world over against it;...it is forced to fall back on the *peculiar determinateness* of real individuality which exists *in and for itself*, or contains the antithesis of being *for itself* and being *in itself* effaced within its own absolute mediation" (*PS*, 309).

Hegel's advice to us is not to probe psychological laws. Instead, he chooses to call attention to how the community in which we live provides structure to the way we become persons. Hegel had a very different view of community and culture than did Rousseau. He indicated that the community's law and moral practice proves itself to be a law of all hearts. He valued the ways in which the community has come to provide for public order and human flourishing. With the French Revolution as his backdrop, he argued that if the public order is not preserved by law and moral practice, then the frenzy of the law of the heart will either turn individuals against each other and lead to a state of perpetual war or create vapid and empty persons who tear at the webbing of the community from the inside (*PS*, 379).

With what has been said thus far, it is not surprising to find that the very idea of a social contract, where atomistic individuals gather together to form society, is totally incoherent for the Hegel of the *Phenomenology*. He rejected this entire picture. Indeed, the belief that individuals are what is truly actual occupied his attention in the central section of the *Phenomenology*: "Individuality Which Takes Itself to be Real In and For Itself" (*PS*, 394–437). For Hegel, society is not what is created by a set of rules agreed to by isolated individuals. It is that webbing of shared practices born of innumerable master-slave struggles which make possible not only human flourishing but the very emergence of persons themselves. Sometimes, these practices become codified into law, but the practice always comes first, then the rule, if one is needed. The justification for these rules, the search for reasons which legitimate them, arrives still later if at all (*PS*, 439).

Hegel's affirmation is somewhat analogous to what occurs when one plays a new table game. In playing, one discovers what practices and procedures are followed and basically what the yield of these is. One learns the rules by playing the game. In human society, this means that laws are codifications of the ways we have found productive for self-formation and personhood over many generations.[17]

> The spiritual being [humanity as community] thus exists first of all for self-consciousness as law which has an *intrinsic* being;…The law is equally an eternal law which is grounded not in the will of a particular individual, but is valid in and for itself; it is the absolute *pure will of all* which has the form of immediate being. Also, it is not a *commandment*, which only *ought* to be: it *is* and is *valid*; it is the universal "I"…laws are the thoughts of its own absolute consciousness (*PS*, 436)… In this determination, therefore, the ethical substance is actual substance, absolute

> Spirit realized in the plurality of existent consciousnesses; this spirit is the
> community...As *actual substance*, it is a nation, as *actual consciousness*, it is the
> citizens of that nation (*PS*, 447).
> They [laws, morals] *are*. If I inquire after their origin and confine them to the point
> whence they arose, then I have transcended them; for now it is I who am the
> universal, and they are the conditioned and limited...It is not, therefore, because I
> find something is not self-contradictory that it is right; on the contrary, it is right
> because it is what is right; I have not to argue about it, or hunt around for or entertain
> thoughts, connections, aspects, or various kinds; I have to think neither of making
> laws nor of testing them (*PS*, 437).

Hegel believed that once pre-reflective acceptance of law or moral
tradition is broken, the existence of the shared practices which have
developed selves and created community are threatened. He showed that,
using rationality alone, it is not difficult, as the Sophists demonstrated so
long ago, to reduce all maxims and laws to pointlessness, to show that any
ultimate law must appeal to another law for its justification, and so forth (*PS*,
747). But according to Hegel, there is not some supreme law or moral
principle which has an independent justification. There is only the nest of
laws and moral practices which interlock dialectically in such a way as to
make possible the formation of personhood.

In the final analysis, Hegel's description of the self marks the end of
those modern views which conceived of self-formation as isolated and
discrete, and also the beginning of the postmodernist understanding of the
self as always in process, a state of perpetual vanishing and recreation. Hegel
learned much from Rousseau. Perhaps he did not learn the lessons Rousseau
wished to teach explicitly, but he was certainly taught by Rousseau's self-
reflections and justifications. Hegel came to believe that the self is much
more accurately described in Rousseau's autobiographical works than it is
in his theoretical writings. Hegel's theoretical understanding of the self
captures what Rousseau describes.

Both Rousseau and Hegel can teach us about the move from the modern
to postmodern self. Hegel does so through explicit philosophical reflection,
devoid of autobiographical narrative. Rousseau does so through
autobiographical narratives, which are seriously discontinuous with his own
explicit theory of the self.

Notes

1.   I like this image very much, and I am grateful to Charles Taylor for suggesting it to me.

See *Sources of the Self: The Making of Modern Identity* (Cambridge, MA: Harvard University Press, 1989), ix.

2. Of course, Harris tells us about his wanting to shift from theology to law at Tübingen, but his father insisted that he stay the course, and also we know about his being ranked fourth in his class, rather than first (the position to which he was so accustomed). These really are, however, fairly unremarkable experiences for students, and neither seems to have made any lasting mark. In fact, the change in his class rank only spurred him to work harder the following term to regain his preeminent position, the response for which his professors had probably hoped. For the biographical and source information which follows in the text I want to thank H.S. Harris. See H.S. Harris, *Hegel's Development: Toward the Sunlight, 1770–1801* (Oxford: The Clarendon Press, 1972).

3. Although I am unaware of Rousseau ever using conscience to make this sort of point, it does not seem to be inconsistent with what a Calvinist might argue. But I am not suggesting that conscience functioned in this way for Rousseau at all, simply because conscience normally appears to be a form of positive directive. I simply note that these need not be mutually exclusive interpretations. As to whether Rousseau would have approved of this use, I do not know. In fact, I do not know how seriously we should take Hegel's sermon anyway. It was required of those studying under the theological faculty that they preach, and Hegel was under this faculty, partially at least, in order to receive a state supported education. He had no intention of going into the ministry, and his early theological writings are moralistic reinterpretations of Christianity in a Kantian fashion, showing disgust for orthodox and popular Christian belief alike.

4. Harris, 309.

5. Ibid., 385.

6. G.W.F. Hegel, *Phenomenology of Spirit*, trans. A. V. Miller (Oxford: Oxford Univ. Press, 1977), 11. All future quotations from *Phenomenology* are taken from this translation and will be cited parenthetically.

7. Johann Gottlieb Fichte, *The Vocation of Man* (New York: Macmillan, 1985), 103.

8. Jean-Jacques Rousseau, "Discourse on the Origin and Foundations of Inequality Among Men," in *Rousseau's Political Writings*, translated by Julia Conaway Bondanella (New York: W.W. Norton, 1988), 4. All future references to this text will be made parenthetically.

9. Jean-Jacques Rousseau, "First Letter to Malesherbes," cited in Jean Starobinski, *Jean-Jacques Rousseau: Transparency and Obstruction*, translated by Arthur Goldhammer (Chicago: University of Chicago Press, 1988), 181.

10. See, for example, Jean-Jacques Rousseau, *The Confessions*, translated by J. M. Cohen (London: Penguin Books, 1953), 262. All future references to this text will be made parenthetically.

11. Jean-Jacques Rousseau, *Emile or On Education*, translated by Allan Bloom (New York: Basic Books, 1979), 185. All future references to this text will be made parenthetically.

12. Jean-Jacques Rousseau, *Reveries of the Solitary Walker*, translated by Peter France (London: Penguin Books, 1979), 68. All future references to this text will be made parenthetically.

13. *Discourse on Inequality*, 28–29. It may seem that Rousseau is following a line very similar to that taken by Hume in *An Enquiry Concerning Human Morals*. But in the *Confessions*, he states unequivocally that he had read only one of Hume's books and

that was one of his works on English history. We should not forget that Rousseau was working on a book on the moral sentiments which he never completed, so I think we need not look outside of his own reflections for the origins of these ideas.

14. I do not think fixation is too strong a word. Rousseau desired married women, wealthy benefactoresses, young girls, mistresses of his friends, and his music pupils. Cf. also *Confessions*, 141.

15. Quoted in Ann Hartle, *The Modern Self in Rousseau's Confessions: A Reply to St. Augustine* (Notre Dame, Ind.: University of Notre Dame Press, 1983), 4.

16. I do not think it is necessary to accept Hegel's need to fit the attempts to gain independence on a historical model in order to value what he has to say.

17. Naturally, once someone has codified the rules, then these can be taught before playing, or even without ever playing at all one may study and criticize the rules.

Goya and the Duchess of Alba:
A Pictorial Confession Revealed
by Ann Glenn Crowe

This essay provides a close examination of five disparate images by Goya, all dating from the close of the eighteenth century. They are disconnected in chronological time by their media and by the nature of their primary intentions. I submit that the images are linked, nonetheless, by the repetition of items of clothing worn by their five respective female figures. Scrutiny of these images reveals that these items of clothing function as visual signs and link these disparate images together as a highly personal, psychic narrative. These images of clothing reveal their artist's subversive confession whose shifting focus takes place over time.

The images constitute a testament to the unfortunate progress of Goya's amorous and illicit infatuation with the Duchess of Alba. The lower caste *hildago* Goya was fifty years old in 1796. He had been married to Josefa Bayeu, the sister of Goya's early mentor, the professionally well-connected painter Francisco Bayeu, for twenty-five years. Goya had been totally deaf for four years, yet was, by the closing years of the eighteenth century, the most sought after portraitist in Madrid. The aristocratic Duchess of Alba was thirty-five, recently widowed (1797), and considered the most illustrious beauty of her day. It can be demonstrated that the subversive nature of each of Goya's images to be discussed is increased when they are treated together as a sequence. I suggest, as well, that these images also provide concrete evidence of the evolution of Goya's romantic modernity, that is, of this artist's tendency at the turn of the new century to allow purely private references and personal feelings to appear in works of art intended for public viewing.

One aspect of the genesis of the modern self is hermeneutics, the explanation of that self.[1] Unlike Rousseau's *Confessions*, however, Goya's images of confession are oblique and disjunctive. By virtue of a difference in their individual temperaments, perhaps by a difference in nationality, but certainly by virtue of a difference in the demands of the differing social worlds in which they moved, Goya's confessions lack the directness of Rousseau's straightforward narrative. His visual hermeneutics are tempered by the political and social realities of his position in the Court of Carlos IV, where in 1800 this ambitious provincial painter advanced from the rank of Court Painter to First Court Painter to the King.

As Michel Foucault reminds us, Christianity is a confessional religion.[2] And, while Goya's art demonstrates his anti-clerical bias, there is no indication that this artist was anti-religious. It can be plausibly hypothesized that the strongly confessional mode of Spanish Catholicism is the ground from which Goya's secular and modern hermeneutics of the self develops. Paraphrasing his earlier book *The History of Sexuality* (1976), Foucault wrote in 1988 that "confession has traditionally played an important part in penal and religious institutions for all offenses," and of Enlightenment culture he wrote,

> Sexual behavior more than any other was submitted to very strict rules of secrecy, decency and modesty, so that sexuality is related in a strange and complex way both to verbal prohibition *and* to the obligation to tell the truth; of hiding what one does, and of deciphering who one is."[3]

Throughout Christianity, as Foucault convincingly argues, there is a correlation between the confession, or disclosure of the self, and penance, which is a renunciation of the self. From the eighteenth century forward, however, this disclosure of the self gives rise to a positive reconstitution of the self, or, as Foucault says, a new, autonomous self.[4] This, he argues, constitutes the eighteenth century's decisive break with both the classical as well as the Christian past. I suggest that the disjunctive narrative that connects the five images by Goya to be discussed provides both a record and an example of a subjective modern self, as it deciphers and/or explains that self in regard to what was forbidden and taboo.

Connected by the common thread of repeated items of clothing, these visual signs of Goya's disjunctive narrative begin with his well-known portrait of the *Duchess of Alba in Black* (1797, Hispanic Society of America, NYC, Plate 1). The Duchess is not dressed as a *maja* as is frequently claimed. The popular dress of urban lower class women, the *majas*, often imitated by aristocrats like the Duchess, was far more colorful than the somber black seen here. Instead, the Duchess wears the traditional national costume preferred for morning wear at this time by aristocratic Spanish women, in spite of their dual infatuations with both *majismo* and French fashion. This generic Spanish costume consisted of a heavy overskirt, the *basquina,* and a *mantilla* or shawl.[5] For street wear only, this overskirt or *basquina* was usually removed upon entering the house, exposing one or two petticoats, called the *camisa.* The *camisa* was considered appropriate for informal, indoor wear, particularly in the boudoir. The serious impropriety of wearing the *basquina* in any color other than black has been discussed by social historians.[6] The *mantilla* could be either black or white, usually depending upon the season. This is the same costume in which Goya painted other aristocrats and royalty at this time, such as, for example, the *Marquesa de la Solana* (1795, Louvre, Paris, Plate 2) and *Queen Maria Luisa* (1799, Prado, Madrid, Plate 3), the arch-rival to the Duchess at Court.[7]

We know from one of Goya's early biographers of the Duchess's passion both for the bullfight and for specific matadors,[8] and that red and gold were her favorite colors.[9] A wide, red satin sash and the close-fitting, fancy gold tufted sleeves of the bull fighter's bolero jacket, the *traje de luces* or "jacket of lights," can be seen to extend from the Duchess's mantilla. The sash and bolero are not part of the native Spanish costume preferred by aristocrats, but they *are* part of the professional attire of the bullfighters for whom the Duchess had a special fondness. For example, Goya's *Portrait of the Matador José Romero* (c. 1795–98, Philadelphia Museum of Art, Plate 4) has an inscription on the back of the canvas which notes that José is shown wearing a *traje de luces* given him by the Duchess of Alba. Like the Duchess, José also wears the wide satin sash customary for matadors. The Duchess of Alba was the only aristocrat on whom Goya painted either the wide satin sash or the *traje de luces.*

Also different from Goya's portraits of Queen Maria Luisa and the Marquesa cited above is the presence on the Duchess's right temple of a black circular "beauty spot" worn in the specific position on the face known as "the passionate."[10] And very different from the preceding two portraits are the very prominent rings on the Duchess's right hand inscribed "Goya" and "Alba." The emotionally cool, imperious gaze of the Duchess is subverted, not only by the possessiveness expressed by the rings, but also by the gesture of the Duchess herself, who points directly to Goya's signature in the sand before her bright golden shoes. Goya's signature is preceded by the word "Solo," which was revealed only in 1960 by a restorer at the Hispanic Society of America.[11] While the date of the portrait (1797) is painted right side up for the benefit of the viewer, the signature "Solo Goya" ("Only Goya") was inverted by the artist, as though painted for the Duchess's eyes alone.

Because of the presence of the umbrella palm tree to the right of the Duchess, it has been argued that she stands very specifically in the countryside near Sanlucar in Andalusia, where she owned a country estate.[12] Goya visited there with the very recently widowed Duchess for several months in 1796–7.[13] He began this journey without official leave from the Court of Carlos IV, where at the time he held both the rank of Painter to the King and the post of Director of Painting at the Royal Academy of San Fernando. It was most certainly on that visit that this signed and dated portrait of the Duchess of Alba was painted. At the death of Goya's wife Josefa in 1812, Goya officially willed this portrait to his son Javier. But the Duchess's portrait did not leave Goya's possession until he left Spain for Bordeaux, France in 1824,[14] a self-imposed exile from the repressive monarchy of Ferdinand VII.

In this portrait, and in each of Goya's documented images of the Duchess of Alba, the artist established the characteristic features of the lady, as he saw her. In addition to the fact that the Duchess had a small waist and a full bosom, she also had an elegant, proud carriage. Goya takes full note, as well, of her narrow, oval face; her long, straight nose; her small mouth and large, almond-shaped, heavy-lidded eyes, obliquely arched with thick dark eyebrows. These same features can be observed, though less markedly described, in Goya's earlier portrait of the *Duchess of Alba in White* (1795, Liria Palace, Madrid, Plate 5), in which she also wears a red satin sash. In this slightly earlier portrait of the Duchess in white, Goya also foregrounds her plenitude of heavy, dark curly hair, as he does in his small, informal genre scene of *The Duchess of Alba Teasing her Duena, La Beata* (1795, Prado, Madrid, Plate 6) in which she is already sporting a golden *traje de luces*.

Goya's portrait of the Duchess of Alba in Black of 1797 is, then, the first in the sequence of the five disjunctive images which I suggest trace a private narrative of the lower caste Goya's covert feelings for the aristocratic Duchess. Three etchings by Goya, two published, one withheld from publication for over a hundred years after Goya's death, until 1940, contain images considered by major scholars to be references to the Duchess. The images document Goya's growing jealousy, disillusionment, despair and final loss of the capricious and inconstant lady. All three etchings were originally intended for inclusion in his notorious series of eighty prints created for commercial sale and published in 1799, but Goya himself withheld one from publication. He titled the series *Los Caprichos* or "the caprices." They are images of social satire, witchcraft, and fantasy, all three categories sometimes existing in one image.

These etchings, in the sequence that I believe they belong, begin with one of the *Caprichos* published in 1799. It is *Capricho 19*, "All Will Fall" (Figure 1) which depicts a flock of male birds flying around a female decoy-bird precariously balanced atop a barren tree. Below are two young women and an old bawd, procuress, or *celestina*. As the male birds succumb to the decoy-bird and fall to the ground below, their feathers are plucked, and they are eviscerated by beautiful young women, while the old bawd watches, rubbing her hands in anticipation of the next victim. While on a public and general level this image is clearly a satire on the victimization of men by prostitutes, it can also be read, on a specific and particular level, as a quintessential image of the growing anxiety and jealousy of a lover over the recognition that his beloved must be shared with other suitors. For, on a personal level, Goya's etching is also a reference to the Duchess of Alba and to himself.[15] The likeness is clear in each case. The decoy bird is the Duchess, who though seen in profile, nonetheless exhibits her characteristically heavy, slanted eyebrow, large eye, and ample bosom. The Duchess-bird also wears a beauty spot in the "passionate" position identical to its placement in Goya's portrait of the Duchess in black discussed above. In the etching, the bird closest to the Duchess-bird very much resembles an early self-portrait by Goya in the Zurgena Collection, Madrid, painted around 1775 when he was twenty-nine years old. As in *Capricho 19*, "All will Fall," this early self-portrait is of a very young Goya, full-face with his characteristic broad nose and wide, full mouth.

In *Capricho 19* the feet of the Duchess-bird rest precariously upon a pitfall device placed upon a tree branch. This circular device may also be a reference to Fortuna's globe of inconstancy and fickleness, as one scholar has argued.[16] Though the Duchess-bird is surrounded by suitor-birds, the Goya-bird is in the most prominent position, literally hovering around her. The young beauty on the lower right side of the etching wears the same beauty spot as the Duchess. This may indicate a sequential narration in time; that is, Goya's graphic illustration of illicit love's cycle of attraction, seduction and destruction.[17] The artist's sardonic fatalism is apparent in his caption for the etching, that "All will Fall," and also in the commentary on this etching preserved in the Prado Museum thought by many scholars to be Goya's own. The commentary reads: "And those who are about to fall will not take warning from the example of those who have fallen! But nothing can be done about it. All will Fall."

The next etching in my sequence is the unique proof withheld by Goya from the publication in *Los Caprichos*. It still bears its original title, "Dream. Of Lies and Inconstancy" (Figure 2). Most scholars interpret this etching as an image of Goya's increasing chagrin over the inconstancy of the Duchess of Alba since, again, several scholars have recognized the features of both Goya and the Duchess on the left two of the four intertwined figures depicted in the image. Goya's description of his own features in a letter he wrote to his boyhood friend Martin Zapater is useful as we examine both Goya's *Self-Portrait* etching (Figure 3) that he used as Frontispiece for *Los Caprichos* as well as the male figure on the extreme left of the "Dream. Of Lies...," for both are depictions of Goya in profile. Goya wrote to Zapater on 28 November, 1787: "I am now an old man with many wrinkles, you wouldn't know me, but for my snub nose and sunken eyes."[18] The artist was forty-one years old when he wrote that description. He was fifty-three when he etched his *Self-Portrait* for *Los Caprichos*. But his deeply socketed eyes, short, snub nose, broad cheeks and full mouth are as readily apparent in the male figure on the left side of the "Dream. Of Lies and Inconstancy" as they are in his *Self-Portrait* from *Los Caprichos*.

With an architectural motif which has been variously identified as the Chateau d'Amour, as the House of Fortuna, and as the Castle of Hero observable in the background,[19] the Goya figure in the "Dream. Of Lies and Inconstancy" passionately grasps, with both of his hands, one arm of the reclining Duchess. A closer look reveals that she is clad in her *camisa*, a garment for intimate spaces. She is, therefore, not dressed, but half-dressed. The Goya figure is literally trying to hold on to a woman he depicts with the two faces symbolic of deceit and the butterfly wings symbolic of fickleness and inconstancy.

In the etching, the theme of inconstancy is extended to the second partially-clad woman, who reclines across the Duchess and also has two faces of duplicity. One of her faces looks toward the Duchess and Goya figures while the other looks away. Unobserved by the Goya-figure, this second woman joins her hand with the Duchess's free hand, which she would appear to offer to the hand of the male figure on the right side of the etching, a figure who is completely unseen by the Goya-figure. This second male figure does not make a gesture for silence, as many scholars

Figure 1 (top left): *Capricho 19*, "All Will Fall," etching and aquatint (1799).
Courtesy of the Virginia Museum of Fine Arts, Richmond.
Figure 2 (top right): "Dream. Of Lies and Inconstancy," unpublished etching and aquatint
for *Los Caprichos* (1798).
Courtesy of the Biblioteca Nacional, Madrid.
Figure 3 (bottom left): Goya's *Self-Portrait*, etching and aquatint, frontispiece for *Los Caprichos* (1799).
Courtesy of the Virginia Museum of Fine Arts, Richmond.
Figure 4 (bottom right): *Capricho 61*, "They Have Flown," or "Gone for Good," etching
and aquatint (1799).
Courtesy of the Virginia Museum of Fine Arts, Richmond.

Figure 5: "Pedro Romero Slaying a Bull," Plate 30 from *La Tauromaquia*, etching and aquatint (1815). Courtesy of the Virginia Museum of Fine Arts, Richmond.

have claimed. Rather, his forefinger, so clearly pressed to the side of his nose, represented, in eighteenth-century Spain, a gesture of challenge, insult and arrogance.[20] The two figures to the right have been variously identified as Queen Maria Luisa and the Prime Minister, Manual Godoy, who served as the Queen's *cortejo*, or gallant, and reported lover.[21] The Duchess, too, was on very friendly terms with the Prime Minister, presenting him, about this time, with Velazquez's mysterious *Venus with a Mirror*, a painting long in the Alba collection.[22] The second pair of figures has been identified by others as the personal maid servant of the Duchess who, unseen by the Goya figure, welcomes a new suitor for the Duchess.[23] The identity of this secondary couple is not, however, of primary concern to our subject, except as it adds to the general theme of duplicity and deceit.

The theme of inconstancy is represented a third and fourth time in this image, the third in the form of the grinning foreground mask supported by two saddle bags. They are very likely a reference to an old Spanish expression, "to change over to another saddle bag"—meaning to take undue liberties and thus to switch loyalties.[24] The predatory gestures of the snake and two frogs, undoubtedly symbols for the Duchess and her two suitors, adds a fourth and final note of tension and conflict.[25] Folke Nordstrom has convincingly suggested that the Duchess figure is not so much lying on what appear to be cushions resting on the ground, as she is levitating in a space just above them, anchored by the gestures of both Goya and the secondary female figure.[26] After all, this is a dreamscape, as Goya's title tells us, and therefore outside the confines of earthly time and space.

The last of the five images to be placed together as documents of Goya's personal narrative is an image of his final loss of the Duchess. It is to be found in *Capricho 61*, "Volaverunt" ("They have flown," or "Gone for Good" [Figure 4]). In this image, the female figure almost universally considered to be Goya's reference to the Duchess of Alba is again represented with the butterfly wings of fickleness on her head. She appears to have hastily donned her *basquina* for outdoor wear. Her bullfighter's *bolero* jacket with its characteristic tight sleeves puffed at the shoulder appears to have been hastily donned, for both the sleeves and the front closure of this bolero are only half-buttoned. The Duchess utilizes her *mantilla* as a kind of sail and is partially borne aloft through indeterminate space by three figures variously identified as witches, as bullfighters, and as Fortune, Time and the Fates.[27] I would add to previous discussions of this image that the visual evidence of their sleeves clearly indicates that these figures at the Duchess's feet are bullfighters. Like the Duchess they wear bolero jackets identical to those worn by matadors in Goya's series of etchings on bullfighting, *La Tauromaquia*, published in 1815. Number 30 from that series is "Pedro Romero slaying a bull" (Figure 5). Pedro Romero was a brother to José, seen in the earlier portrait by Goya noted above. Pedro was yet another matador favored by the Duchess of Alba, and the design of his jacket sleeves is identical to that worn both by the Duchess figure in *Capricho 61* and by the figures who make up her pedestal of support.

Folke Nordstrom also rightly argued, I suggest, that the subject matter of *Capricho 61* is connected to, and follows sequentially, the "Dream. Of Lies and Inconstancy,"[28] for what is seen in *Capricho 61* is an image of the Duchess having flown free of Goya's two grasping arms depicted in "Dream. Of Lies and Inconstancy." The Duchess is, now, for Goya, as his caption proclaims, "Volaverunt" or "Gone for Good."

We are now ready to contemplate a final problematic image by Goya. I suggest that Nordstrom's connection of *Capricho 61* with the "Dream. Of Lies and Inconstancy" should be extended further, to include Goya's mysterious *Maja Vestida* or "Dressed Maja" (c. 1800–05, Prado, Madrid, Plate 7). I make this extension by virtue of the items of clothing which, again, act as visual signs repeated in this most personal narrative. The *Maja Vestida* was neither titled nor dated by Goya, and there is no record of a commission for this painting. The identity of the model has not been established. It has been noted that her facial features are perhaps purposefully generalized,[29] like those of her even more notorious pendant painting, the *Maja Desnuda*, or Nude Maja (Prado, Madrid, Plate 8), considered on stylistic grounds alone to have been painted a few years earlier.

Clearly there is no similarity between the facial features of the Duchess of Alba and either of these *Majas*, though both the full bosom and small waist clearly recall those of the Duchess. Even more compelling are the repeated items of clothing which function as signs, linking the *Maja Vestida* to the sequence of images discussed above. Like the Duchess figure in the "Dream. Of Lies and Inconstancy," the *Maja Vestida* reclines, wearing a clinging *camisa*, and so is in fact not fully dressed, but half-dressed. Moreover, like the Duchess figure in *Capricho 61*, the *Dressed Maja* also wears a bullfighter's *traje de luces* with fancy golden sleeves,[30] puffed just below the shoulder, though this time it is wholly unbuttoned and thrown back against the pillows. As noted above, a similar yellow jacket is to be seen under the black *mantilla* in Goya's *Portrait of the Duchess of Alba in Black* of 1797 and is nearly identical to the *traje de luces* worn by the Duchess in the small genre painting of 1795 (Plate 6). Also, the *Maja's* wide, rosy red sash is of the same fabric as that worn by matadors, not only in *La Tauromaquia*, but also in Goya's "cabinet paintings" of 1793, for example, *Pass with a Cape* (Private Collection, Madrid). It is very like the more vivid red sash worn by the Duchess in her portrait in Black. Moreover, the *Maja's* shoes of gold also recall the shoes of gold in that same portrait. I suggest that the *Dressed Maja* is also, then, his allusion to the Duchess of Alba. I argue that she should take her place, sequentially, sometime *before* the hovering, *camisa*-clad Duchess in the "Dream. Of Lies and Inconstancy"—which itself belongs chronologically, as Nordstrom suggested, just *before* the lady donned her *basquina* and *traje des luces* to become the airborne Duchess in *Capricho 61*, "Gone for Good," for that is the image which ends this narrative sequence as well as Goya's infatuation with the Duchess of Alba.

Critical to my argument is the fact that Goya's *Dressed Maja* wears a conjoining of items of clothing that this artist painted together on no other female aristocratic figure except the Duchess of Alba. By the repeated visual signs of the bullfighter's bolero, the Duchess's favored rosy red sash, a clinging *camisa*, and a pair of golden shoes, Goya connects his *Maja Vestida* to the shifting narrative traced above. Considered in the sequence I have presented herein, these images produce an accretion of meanings, an accumulative content. However veiled and oblique, Goya's confession is one of taboos broken and scandal revealed. His confession is disjunctive and therefore covert. He nonetheless provides the viewer with a series of visual signs, or clues, which demonstrate that the depth of his illicit passion for the aristocratic Duchess was considerable, even obsessive, however non-sequential the narrative by which he reveals it.[31]

The advent of Goya's essentially modern identity discussed herein suggests that like Rousseau, Goya, out of a powerful personal need, either consciously or unconsciously devised a secular form for the religious practice of confession. But Goya did not confess unreservedly in the manner of Rousseau's *Confessions*; he did not directly reveal the thoughts and feelings of his innermost self in his art. These were revealed verbally, though still obliquely, only in Goya's letters to his boyhood friend, Martin Zapater, who, unlike Goya, remained in the northern provincial city of Saragossa in Aragon, the site of their youth. It is noteworthy, I suggest, that Goya's letters to Zapater diminished, then disappeared completely, about the time of the beginning of the disjunctive narrative traced and revealed above.[32]

The realities of Goya's social, political and personal worlds temper the confessions of his innermost self as an autonomous arbiter of value, order and meaning. The disclosure of his modern self occurs within the discourse of the signs and symbols examined above. This discourse was to become the pattern and strategy of Goya's confessions throughout the remaining thirty years of his long life and abundant, multifaceted *oeuvre*.

Notes

1. Michel Foucault traced this hermeneutics of the self through both pagan and early Christian practice. Though Foucault saw this "technology of the self" as being diffused throughout the history of the West, he examined the radical shift to the modern autonomous self as a late eighteenth-century phenomenon. See Foucault, "Technologies of the Self," in *Technologies of the Self*, ed. Luther H. Martin, Huck Gutman, and Patrick H. Hutton (Amherst: University of Massachusetts Press, 1988), 16–49.
2. Foucault, "Technologies of the Self," 40.
3. Ibid., 16.
4. Ibid., 49.
5. See Frederick Augustus Fischer, *Travels in Spain in 1797 and 1798* (London, 1902), 180–181.
6. See in particular Charles E. Kany, *Life and Manners in Madrid, 1750–1800* (Berkeley: University of California, 1932; reprint, New York, 1970), 188-89. Page references are to the reprint edition.
7. Aureliano de Beruete y Moret wrote of the rivalries of the Duchess of Alba with the Duchess of Osuna and Queen Maria Luisa, and that the Duchess of Alba "equaled in extravagance and excelled in beauty" both of these ladies. See Beruete y Moret, *Goya as Portrait Painter*, trans. Selwyn Brinton (London, 1922), 70. (*Goya, pintor de retratos* [Madrid, 1916]).
8. Joaquin Ezquerra del Bayo, *La Duquesa de Alba y Goya* (Madrid: 1928, reprint Madrid: Aguilar, 1959), Chapter X. Page or chapter references are to the reprint edition. Ezquerra del Bayo discusses the specific pursuits of the Duke and Duchess of Alba.
9. Ezquerra del Bayo, 203.
10. Elizabeth de Gue Trapier, *Goya. A Study of His Portraits 1797–99* (New York, 1955), 5. This "passionate" beauty spot appears on several female figures in *Los Caprichos*.

11. See Trapier, "Only Goya," *Burlington Magazine* 685 (April 1960), 159. The restorer reported that the word "Solo" had been covered with pigment of the same tone, hue, and approximate date as the pigment used in the rest of the painting. Trapier hypothesized that Goya covered the "Solo" sometime after his disillusionment with the Duchess.

12. Trapier, *Goya. A Study of His Portraits*, 5.

13. Pierre Gassier and Juliet Wilson, *The Life and Complete Works of Francisco Goya* (New York: Reynal & Co., 1971), 114–5. The Duke of Alba died in Seville on 9 June, 1796. See also Eleanor Sayre, "Eight Books of Drawings by Goya—I," *Burlington Magazine* 106 (1964): 21, for a discussion of the probable dates of Goya's visit(s) with the Duchess.

14. See F. J. Sanchez-Canton, "Como Vivia Goya," *Archivo Espanol de Arte*, 18 (1946): 88 for a discussion of how this portrait came to be the property of Javier Goya. It apparently remained with Javier when his father went to Bordeaux.

15. Most scholars consider this etching to contain visual references to Goya and the Duchess of Alba.

16. Victor Chan, "Goya the Duchess of Alba and Fortuna," *Arts Magazine* 56 (1981), 133.

17. This is Chan's suggestion; see "Goya, the Duchess of Alba and Fortuna," 134.

18. Goya's letter to Zapater was first published in Francisco Zapater y Gomez, *Coleccion de 449 reproducciones* (Madrid, 1924), 45.

19. See, respectively, José Lopez-Rey, *Goya's Caprichos: Beauty, Reason, and Caricature* (Princeton: Princeton University Press, 1953), vol. 1, 169–70; Folke Nordstrom, *Goya, Saturn and Melancholy. Studies in the Art of Goya* (Stockholm, 1962), 146; and Chan, 135.

20. Gertrude Jobu, *Dictionary of Myth, Folklore and Symbols* (New York, 1962), 569. Among Goya scholars only Eleanor Sayre has recognized that the second male figure in this etching "touches his nose with a mocking gesture"; see Sayre, *The Changing Image: Prints by Francisco Goya* (Boston, 1974), 121.

21. For a discussion of the social institution of the *cortejo*, a gallant who attached himself to a woman of fashion, often performing the function of her lover as well, see Kany, *Life and Manners in Madrid, 1750–1800*, 209–216.

22. *Venus with a Mirror* (c. 1640) was catalogued in Godoy's collection in 1800. See Enrique Pardo Canalis, "Una Visita de la Galeria del Principe de la Paz," *Goya* 9 (January-June, 1979), 302.

23. Pierre Gassier also believes that the Duchess's second suitor in this etching may represent Godoy. See Gassier, *Goya, A Witness to His Time* (Secaucus, New Jersey, 1983), 143–44.

24. Nordstrom, 146.

25. See Nordstrom, "Portraits of the Four Temperaments," 76–94, in *Goya, Saturn and Melancholy*, for a discussion of the ideas of several Spanish scholars on the emblem of the evil woman symbolized by a serpent. See especially page 81. Nordstrom plausibly suggests that the Duchess as snake hypnotizes and prepares to devour Goya, who is symbolized by the snake on the right. The Duchess's second suitor (Godoy) is symbolized by the frog to the left who prepares to devour the snake-Duchess.

26. Nordstrom, 151.

27. Goya's caption for this etching preserved in the Prado Museum (which he may or may not have written himself) refers to the three figures who make up the Duchess's pedestal as witches. Sanchez-Canton reports that Goya's nineteenth-century biographer, the Conde de Munoz y Manzano de la Vinaza, *Goya, su tiempo, su vida y sus obras* (Madrid, 1887), considered the three figures to be bullfighters. See Sanchez-Canton, *Los Caprichos de Goya y sus dibujos preparatorios* (Barcelona, 1944), 95. Chan, 134, believes that the figures are witches and that they signify the threefold aspect of Fortune, Time and the Fates.

28. Nordstrom, 151.

29. The Conde de la Vinaza was the first among many of Goya's biographers to notice this fact. See *Goya...,* 57.

30. Vinaza (1887) is the only scholar that I know of who notes that the *Maja Vestida* wears a bullfighter's jacket. See *Goya...,* 57.

31. Xavier de Salas, "Sur cinq dessins de Goya au Musée du Prado, *Gazette des Beaux-Arts,* LXXV (1970): 29–42, and Sayre, *The Changing Image,* 58–59, are two of the few historians who acknowledge the significance of the image of the Duchess in Goya's art.

32. Francisco Goya, *Cartas a Martin Zapater,* ed. Mercedes Agueda and Xavier de Salas (Madrid: Turner, 1988). Goya's letters to Zapater diminish greatly by the mid-1790s and did not resume.

Plate 2: *Marquesa de la Solana* (1795).
Photograph: Art Resource, N.Y.
Courtesy of the Louvre, Paris.

Plate 1: *Duchess of Alba in Black* (1797).
Courtesy of the Hispanic Society of America, N.Y.

Plate 4: *Portrait of the Matador José Romero* (c. 1795–98).
Courtesy of the Philadelphia Museum of Art:
The Mr. and Mrs. Carroll S. Tyson, Jr. Collection.

Plate 3: *Queen Maria Luisa* (1799).
Photograph: Art Resource, N.Y.
Courtesy of Prado Museum, Madrid.

Plate 5: *Duchess of Alba in White* (1795).
Photograph: Art Resource, N.Y.
Courtesy the Liria Collection, Prado Museum, Madrid.

Plate 6: *The Duchess of Alba Teasing her Duena, La Beata* (1795).
Photograph: Art Resource, N.Y.
Courtesy Prado Museum, Madrid.

Plate 7: *La Maja Vestida* (c. 1800–05).
Photograph: Art Resource, N.Y.
Courtesy of Prado Museum, Madrid.

Plate 8: *La Maja Desnuda* (c. 1798–1800).
Photograph: Art Resource, N.Y.
Courtesy of Prado Museum, Madrid.

The Romantic Subject and the Betrayals of the Text
by Anthony John Harding

Journals and diaries, as opposed to more connected kinds of autobiographical narrative, have attracted relatively little attention from poststructuralist critics, despite the *prima facie* possibility that they might offer rich hunting grounds for readers interested in tracking the fugitive manifestations of decentered selves. This neglect may be in part a reaction against modernist privileging of the authorial consciousness, the mythologizing of the author as hero of her or his own life and of the life, in turn, as *Bildung*, the development of the mature self.[1] For understandable reasons, then, journals and diaries written between 1800 and 1960 have become the peculiar province of modernist commentary and interpretation. Modernist studies, whether emphasizing the connectedness and progress of the subject's life or, as is now more common, the tensions and contradictions that cut across it, read an author's private journal as a text providing special access to that author's subjectivity.

One good example of what I am calling a modernist biography in which tension and contradiction dominate is Anne Stevenson's biography of Sylvia Plath. Stevenson frequently quotes Plath's journals to give the inside story, to reveal a stark contrast between what observers thought Plath was thinking and feeling and what Plath herself thought and felt. "Through her journals," Stevenson comments, "we have been able to follow Sylvia's inward struggles, realizing with every entry just how difficult it was for her, at times, to sustain ordinary existence, even for a day."[2] Stevenson is at pains to point out how often Plath's own record of an event differs from the accounts of others and how this very dissonance, or dissociation, is itself a symptom of Plath's "struggles." Nevertheless, Stevenson's biography is modernist in the sense that it assumes the subject's unitary consciousness and perceptions are directly revealed in the text of her private journal.

Similarly, the recent biography of Coleridge by Richard Holmes claims him as "one of the great English diarists," and, citing the wealth of material in his notebooks, places him in the company of such anxious modernist keepers of journals as Franz Kafka, W.N.D. Barbellion, and

Anaïs Nin.[3] Despite the occasional "postmodernist" interventions that break up Holmes's own narrative, the assumption behind this statement is clearly and perhaps inevitably that the author exists as a unitary subject whose anxieties may be more closely traced in his notebooks than in other texts bearing his name.

The editors of journals, too, are not above claiming a special authority for the text they print, as a more transparent and direct medium for the author's inmost thoughts than other more carefully constructed works could be. The editors of the Princeton edition of Thoreau's journals, for example, appeal to Thoreau's own observation that "thoughts written down thus in a journal might be printed in the same form" to bolster their claim that "the entire original Journal...provides the simple and sincere account of life that he most valued."[4]

What might happen to such claims, and to the reader's reception of such texts, if these texts were exposed to a poststructuralist questioning of the coherence of the unitary authorial subject? The philosophical speculation that individual selfhood may be multiple, not unitary, together with more recent psychological evidence that the subject is not a stable core or structure but rather is constituted by complex processes, are common themes in poststructuralism. Friedrich Nietzsche's notebooks touch on the possibility that the individual consists of a "multiplicity of subjects, whose interaction and struggle is the basis of our thought and consciousness in general."[5] Such a speculation easily affiliates itself with the view that the unitary subject is actually a complex cultural creation of the past three centuries of Western humanism and that its costs—in social and environmental as well as psychological terms—are now all too apparent. Paralleling this ideological argument, critics have begun to investigate the very notion of the author, showing how it is a creation of copyright law, developments in the book trade, religious practices, and the development of a "technology of the self" including the writing of diaries and journals.[6]

Michel Foucault's observation that, in poststructuralism, writing is understood to be about "creating a space into which the writing subject constantly disappears" might suggest that poststructuralism denies journals the special status they had for modernist writers.[7] One consequence of this view could be that the study of a journal can now be considered valid only so far as the text can be an occasional source of information about the conditions of production of other works, showing how the demands of editors and publishing houses, a literary coterie, or a circle of friends and family members might have affected in a material sense the processes of composition. The coherence of such a document would be merely textual and material, owing nothing to any privileged inner revelation, within the text, of the author's subjectivity. The journal forfeits any claim to special consideration as repository of the particular subjective experience or consciousness.

This would seem to be the consequence if the thinking subject is considered as a product of those legitimating metadiscourses whose seriously weakened state Lyotard documents in *The Postmodern Condition*. If one accepts Jean-François Lyotard's claim that the "grand narrative," here meaning any narrative that grounds the legitimated subject in a metadiscourse of transcendence or of Spirit, has "lost its credibility," then there is no unitary consciousness to be extrapolated from the text of a journal. Such a text, instead of granting privileged insight into the mind of its author, becomes a mere "series of seemings" (to adopt the phrase Hardy rather disingenuously used of *Jude the Obscure*).[8] It certainly seems to be the immediate goal of poststructuralist critics like Felicity Nussbaum to push diaries and journals off their modernist pedestal and dismember them. Yet even Nussbaum, after summarizing the postmodern view that "the self is less a reified thing than an ideological construct articulated in the language available to the individual at a particular historical moment," offers a way to salvage the significance of journals, diaries, and daybooks as reflecting an "experienced inner life" in some form.[9] She comments:

> Individuals construct themselves as subjects through language, but the individual—rather than being the source of his or her own meaning—can only adopt positions within the language available at a given moment. The poststructuralist concept of the self redefines a self as a position, a *locus* where discourses intersect. We *believe* that the different positions make an autonomous whole, but that *feeling* that we are constant and consistent occurs because of memory ("Toward Conceptualizing Diary," 131–32).

Following Nussbaum's hint, then, I want to propose a mediating position between what I take to be the modernist position, that the text of a journal somehow comes closer than any more finished work could to revealing the true inwardness of an author's unitary, subjective self, and the pure form of the poststructuralist position: that such subjectivity is itself a product of historical contingency, that the subject position implied by reading Thoreau's or any other writer's diaries or day-books in sequence as a "sincere account of life" is mere fiction, and that journals have therefore only a very limited value, as fragmentary and partial material evidence of historical events or circumstances. This mediating approach might take, as its governing principle, the simple observation that the text of the journal is clearly "other than" the subject which (in Foucault's phrase) "constantly disappears" into it, and we might start from the position that it is exactly this otherness that redeems the journal-text, for the "postmodern" reader, just as its attraction for the writing subject may once have been its otherness.

This is different from saying that journals can simply now be viewed in a fragmenting mirror, so to speak, as reflections of the "fragmented" or "decentered" self, instead of viewing them in a unifying mirror as reflections of a whole self. To consider the subject as "fragmented" is to reify it just as certainly as to consider it as unitary, its unity transcendentally guaranteed. The fragmentary selves of De Quincey experiencing an opium dream or Nietzsche proposing that there may exist a "multiplicity of subjects" appear from this perspective as none other than the ideologically-permitted opposites of the unitary self, the detritus of other subjectivities that have to be "forgotten," or levelled down, in order for the unitary subject to be affirmed, triumphant, a new Troy built on the ruins of several old ones. At least for those who see the rationalist theory of subjectivity as destructive in both the psychological and social dimensions, the task now, as Jane Flax suggests, is rather to "imagine subjectivities whose desires for multiplicity can impel them toward emancipatory action," subjectivities which would be "fluid rather than solid, contextual rather than universal, and process oriented rather than topographical."[10]

Journal literature is peculiarly suited to, and perhaps may be constitutive of, such a way of imagining subjectivities as fluid, contingent, contextual, as interactive with a particular time and space rather than as either simply unitary or simply fragmentary. Rather than abstracting a hypothetical, ideal authorial "consciousness" as we might wish to construct it (out of our own desire to have a stable model of that author's presence to us, or out of a unity provisionally imputed to the text), we would learn to read the text slant, to see in it the trace of a subjectivity momentarily realized (not *revealed*) in the confluence of historical, material, physical, social, linguistic and subjective factors. Recognition would be given to the contingent and contextual as much as to the personal and individual in such a reading.

Since the confluence of the social with the psychological is one of the main themes of feminist analysis, it is in the work of feminist critics, especially in the work written on women writers, that recognition of "fluid" and "process oriented" subjectivities has developed furthest. Rachel Blau DuPlessis, making the point that "Any work is a strategy to resolve, transpose, reweight, dilute, arrange, substitute contradictory material from culture, from society, from personal life," takes as her exemplary case the diary of Anaïs Nin. Duplessis treats it not as a representation of the author's consciousness in any simple sense but as a text through which Nin constructs, "works on," and deploys subjectivity in a particular social context.

> Her diary as form and process is a stratagem to solve a contradiction often present in acute form for women: a contradiction between the desire to please, making woman an object, and the desire to reveal, making her a subject. The culturally sanctioned relationship to art and artists which Nin imagines (ornament, inspiration, sexual and psychic reward) is in conflict with the direct relationship she seeks as artist, colleague, fellow worker.... [T]he diary can be either public or private; Nin will choose to reveal or to conceal what it says based on the balancing of double (sometimes duplicitous) needs to please herself and placate another.[11]

In the culture of modernism, then, the text even of a personal diary borrows from its author's socially constructed self as well as her inwardly self-authenticating subjectivity. For DuPlessis, the doubleness of the subject posited by Nin's diary exemplifies a contradiction most acutely experienced by women, since most men, most of the time, are not forced to consider whether the selves they project in their private writings are pleasing or desirable to others. Without denying the social-cultural reality of this gender difference, I would suggest that the general principle implied in DuPlessis' analysis could be applied to diaries by male writers as well as by female ones. *All* diaries and journals are stratagems that make possible a momentary resolution of contradictions. In the most general terms, these contradictions are those between the "person" demanded by familial, social, and interpersonal relationships, and the "self" produced by inner desires and drives; also recognizing, however, that the division between the social and the psychological is a vexed and shifting one.[12] From this perspective, the claim that a journal or diary provides access to a sincere account of life appears overly invested in the ideology of the transcendentally-guaranteed subject. It seems like a hopeless attempt to seek refuge from the culturally contested public sphere and build knowledge "about" a writer from within an artificially delimited way of reading.

One important and moving example of what I am referring to occurs in the diary which Virginia Woolf kept (intermittently) from 1915. In the 1919 volume, headed by Woolf "Diary VII," there is an entry in which Woolf ironically recognizes the mixture of professional fastidiousness, self-deprecation, and pride with which she reads her own diary:

> I got out this diary, & read as one always does read one's own writing, with a kind of guilty intensity. I confess that the rough & random style of it, often so ungrammatical, & crying for a word altered, afflicted me somewhat. I am trying to tell whichever self it is that reads this hereafter that I can write very much better; & take no time over this; & forbid her to let the eye of man behold it. And now I may add my little compliment to the effect that it has a slapdash & vigour, & sometimes hits an unexpected bulls eye.[13]

Woolf herself was intensely aware of the vulnerability of the conscious self, since in 1913 and 1915 she suffered two separate periods of psychological disorder. Despite the light tone of this passage, it is evident that she ironically credits the text of her diary with having more continuity and coherence than her own self as present and future reader of that text. The self, that is, rather than underwriting the unity of the text, makes the text symbolic of the unity that the self cannot (even, perhaps, should not) hope for. Precisely because Woolf is capable of such reflections which reconfigure the ever shifting relationship between the text and its author's mental life, her diary is a vital point of reference not only for feminist poststructuralism but also for any poststructuralist understanding of subjectivity as it expresses itself, or eludes expression, in diaries and journals.

A premise of the "historicized" way of reading journals I am outlining, then, would be that the various subjectivities that appear in journal literature are themselves products of changing ideas about the place of the text in relation to the subject, as well as of individual consciousnesses, as these have been impinged upon by wider social and cultural forces.

Tilottama Rajan points out that even in writings of the immediate post-Kantian era—an era we associate with the cult of individual genius—the idea that the authorial subject is the sole source of meaning and coherence in the text was already being questioned. In the theory of hermeneutics developed early in the nineteenth century by F. D. E. Schleiermacher, the "Reden" or discourse of a text is "a speech act that is not private property. Discourse is 'the mediation of shareable thought,' a site for the interchange rather than the fixing of meaning..." In the new hermeneutic that Rajan derives from Schleiermacher's theories, the "diacritical nature of the text as part of a network of other writings" would be emphasized, and interpretation would "try to suggest the different and intersecting ways in which the manuscript evidence can be construed."[14] By linking this observation to a specific historical moment, and to the assumptions underlying a particular discourse of the period (Schleiermacher's), Rajan is suggesting that the postmodern disenthronement of the transcendent subject does not put an end to the consideration of subjectivity in relation to textuality but rather places the study of that relationship on quite a new footing. It becomes possible, that is, to historicize (the experience of) subjectivity, for example, to relate it to a contemporary context such as that of "interchange...of meaning" between Schleiermacher's concept of education and von Humboldt's.

This particular "interchange" is the example used by Lyotard himself, in demonstrating the manner in which knowledge came to be legitimated in a number of European and North American jurisdictions, through the appeal to philosophy and philosophical discourse (initially, that of idealism). In other words, the collapse of the metanarrative that according to Lyotard guaranteed the "fully legitimated subject of knowledge and society" does not write off the subjective as a category needing critical, historical investigation.[15] Indeed, it could mark the point where writing a history of subjectivity or of subjectivities becomes for the first time possible. The keeping of a diary or journal can be seen as a practice rooted in a particular historical moment when it becomes vital for the individual to construct her or his feelings and conduct as having both continuity and significance, and to examine feelings and conduct from a certain ethical standpoint.[16] The professional usefulness of keeping a diary as a kind of limbering-up exercise for writers, and subsequently as a good source of material, is increasingly recognized through the nineteenth century, and by 1915, when Virginia Woolf began keeping her diary, the convention has become part of the writer's stock-in-trade.

The theorist's skepticism about the immediate presence of the subject in the text is often supported by the remarks of diarists themselves. In other words, diarists and journal-writers have themselves stumbled on the betrayals of the text, the fact that the text betrays (is false to) the thought. In one of the more self-reflexive passages in the notebooks of Coleridge, after a sentence in which the word "not" has been inserted as a correction, an afterthought, the text continues: "The words, you omit in writing, your *caret*-words, will be generally found to express subjective *Acts*, determining the relation of the Object to your own Being, not objects (i.e. Noun Substantives) themselves. Thus 'not' you will very often have occasion to overline with an Λ." The same notebook, a few pages later, contains this observation, itself an insertion in space left in the margin after the page was filled: "It is curious, how often I find (in reperusing my Mss) the noun put for the verb—ex. gr. expression for expresses, contemplation for contemplate. It seems to fall under the rule, that the *Subjective* is the liable [*sic*] to omission, i.e. to the being taken for granted—Verbs are *acts*."[17]

The subjective, this suggests, is actually *not* present in the text even of a journal or diary, certainly not in any unmediated or unproblematic way, because the act of writing, the very point at which thought and the material world interreact, tends to let the subjective slip away. The subjective is what is "taken for granted" and therefore not written. At the textual level, then, the subjective, the mind's "acts," are rather less likely to leave a trace than are bodily sensations, abstract concepts, perceptions of outward objects, other texts, and so on. In a sense, this is merely to say that, if the subjective is to be found at all in the text of a journal or diary entry, its presence is evanescent, something that leaves traces between the lines and around the margins of the text, even though the text itself may ostensibly be aimed at establishing the continuity of the writing subject.

Still more pertinent to retheorizing the subject of journals and daybooks is the realization that so far as authorial subjectivity can be imagined as subsisting separately from the text at all, it borrows its continuity from the page, and not vice versa. This is an idea which has its origin in the practice of journal writing itself. Coleridge was certainly not the first author to consider his notebooks as "the history of my own mind for my own improvement." Addressing one of them as "dear Book! Sole Confidant of a breaking Heart" he continues, "All minds must think by some *symbols*...every generous mind not already filled...feels its *Halfness*..." This very passage, however, is broken up by a long digression on what "fills" many minds, lesser minds than his own—

namely, among other things, the details of crowded streets and popular chatter about a "rout": "1100 persons present, all of more or less distinction in one House!—The Prince of Wales, Townshend the Thief-catcher, & the Intelligencer from the Morning Post, all present!—what glory!—and the whole Street unpassable..."[18]

The whole entry revealingly alternates between the presumption of the reality of continuous consciousness, implied by the metaphor of possession—"the strongest minds possess the most vivid Symbols"—and the admission that even such "strong" minds are dependent on signs, or symbols, that have "the property of *Outness*," being capable of transmission to the public or inter-subjective sphere, Rajan's "mediation of shareable thought." But Coleridge's scathing comment on "worldly power" and "Vanity" is clearly meant to privilege the peculiar kind of "Outness" that characterises a certain limited class of symbols. He had a considerable stake in establishing the self-conscious, reflective, philosophizing author as the site and source of literary value. This is part of the immediate context for all those writings that were not meant for publication, as well as those that were. As his career continued to meet with only qualified success in the 1810s and 1820s, Coleridge cultivated the reputation of the reclusive sage who would deliver his best thoughts only in the company of a few admiring friends or in the total privacy of notebooks that were meant for the eyes of one or two trusted collaborators, at most. To be involved in public life, whether "in the pursuit of literary Reputation," in well-meaning public bodies such as a Patriotic Fund, or merely in a "rout" at some wealthy friend's house, was to give oneself over to public discourse and therefore to the ephemeral and trivial (*Notebooks*, 2:2368). The point I want to emphasize here is not whether it is good to value public activity less than study and writing; it is that the rejection of this public sphere, and the cultivation of the dmoestic and intimate, is part of the context that formed the particular kinds of subjectivity that are to be glimpsed in this writer's notebooks.

Like desire itself (as analyzed by Jane Flax), the writing subject is "simultaneously constructed yet undetermined."[19] Authorial subjectivity exists at the nodal point where the material, linguistic, and social intersect with what are for psychoanalysis (Freudian, Lacanian, or object-relations) the already conflicted elements of the self. Paradoxically, the fact that Coleridge's private writings represent this intersection so well makes them a promising resource for those interested in theorizing the subject as processual, not as stable and cohesive. There is some irony in the fact that poststructuralists would identify Coleridge as a major British proponent of the stable individual self, as bourgeois humanism defines it, and of inviolable selfhood as the necessary ground of all morality and law,[20] for there is much evidence that Coleridge experienced directly how little stability or inner authority the individual self actually had. His interest in theories of inspiration and possession, his troubled inner life as revealed in the notebooks and poems, and his very insistence on the "I AM" as the ground of self-knowledge, all point to a chronic nervousness about the self. "Self," Coleridge himself writes, "is Definition; but all Boundary implies Neighbourhood—& is knowable only by Neighbourhood, or Relations" (*Notebooks*, 2:3231, f 14). Even though he purports to affirm a *"continuous <& ever continuable> Consciousness,"* the concession implicit in these notes is that relations, not inward integrity, constitute the writing subject, and that this is no less true if the writing subject's only relation is with the blank page, or with the limitless range of linguistic possibilities it represents.

These blank pages—the notebooks themselves—are often anthropomorphized in Coleridge's notebook jottings. In May 1808, for instance, Coleridge addresses them as "passive, yet sole <true &> unkind friends." (In other words he first wrote "sole unkind friends," realized his error, struck out "un-" and added "true &," in the process inadvertently demonstrating once more the slipperiness of subjective thought in its dealings with the "outness" of signs.) Besides casting the notebook into the role of a "friend," the remark implicitly genders it female, perhaps reflecting the fact that he used the notebooks for the "Soother of Absence," a collection of aphorisms, fragments and detached thoughts intended to console him for the loneliness he felt when he could not be with "Asra" (Sara Hutchinson, the woman he fell in love with in 1799 and who frequently acted as his amanuensis).

These particular observations about the notebooks should be viewed in the context of "subjectivity" as a value in journal-writing in the early 1800s, pursuing a point made earlier: that subjectivity as a value in authorship is itself a product of certain historical circumstances. The "context" of such reflections as these includes Coleridge's fight against what he considered to be the debilitating idea of mind as a merely passive thing (and of passive poetic creation), suggested for him by Hartleian associationism and even by the idea of the plenary inspiration of the Bible. These preoccupations were in turn related to his perception of the need—for economic as well as philosophical reasons—to stake out a claim to a particular concept of literary ownership. Sonia Hofkosh summarizes well the economic conditions that lay behind Coleridge's concept of the author: "Drawing on the logic of possessive individualism as well as on evolving theories of copyright from the previous century, Coleridge's account [of authorship] merges work and personality to the point where they become mutually and inextricably definitive...Literary property is in this way crucially distinguished from 'all other property'...in so far as what the author produces is the inalienable stuff of his own subjectivity."[21] For Coleridge, it was especially important to establish the cohesiveness, autonomy, and moral authority of the self-conscious writing subject, in opposition to a literary marketplace he represents as dominated by unprincipled and opportunistic journalists, hack-writers and anonymous reviewers, writing (it seemed to him) for no higher purpose than to make money and too often interposing the reviewer's arrogantly pluralized "we" between the poor marginalized author and the audience he was trying to reach.

In Coleridge's own more "private" writings, however, especially in the notebooks, the unstable and processual nature of authorial subjectivity is tellingly evident, despite the frequency of appeals to the notion of the integrity of the subject. (It might be added that similar evidence for the subject as being perpetually "in process" could be found in the letters, where the tastes and political or religious creed of Coleridge's correspondent invariably dictate the tone and subject matter of his reply.) To read the notebooks this way is of course to read against the grain of Coleridge's own ideology of subjectivity, his post-Kantian struggle to reconceptualize and reconfirm continuity of consciousness as the *sine-qua-non* of rationality and morality. The moral conscience, not the Lockean or Hartleian way of ideas, is the basis of consciousness for Coleridge. "*From* what reasons do I believe a *continuous* <& ever continuable> *Consciousness*? From *Conscience!*" (*Notebooks*, 2:3231, f 14). This program forms the basis of his resistance to Hartleian associationism in *Biographia Literaria*. Without denying the reality of the phenomenon of "association of ideas," Coleridge argues that Hartley, whose theory took as its premise the materiality of the brain and nerve atoms which supposedly enable ideas to associate, had made "contemporaneity" not the condition of laws of association (as it was for Aristotle), but itself the sole law. The result was that the will, the reason, the judgment, and the understanding, instead of being the determining causes of association, must needs be represented as its *creatures*, and among its mechanical *effects*. Conceive, for instance, a broad stream, winding through a mountainous country with an indefinite number of currents, varying and running into each other according as the gusts chance to blow from the opening of the mountains. The temporary union of several currents in one, so as to form the main current of the moment, would present an accurate image of Hartley's theory of the will.[22]

As philosopher and moralist, Coleridge could in no way tolerate this transferring of will, reason, judgment and understanding—the philosophical basis for personal agency—from the category of causes of association to the category of its effects. In a sense, the preservation of personal agency and responsibility as the basis of philosophy, morality, law, literary analysis, and the social state was the chief aim of all Coleridge's public writings from *Biographia* (1817) onward. The "public" writings include both the overtly "political" works, such as the 1818 Addresses in support of Sir Robert Peel's bill to shorten the working hours of child factory workers, and more esoteric writings, such as the "Letters on the Inspiration of the Scriptures" (1825, published posthumously in 1840), written to explode the then widespread view that the Bible was "dictated...by an infallible Intelligence" rather than composed of the words of individual human beings, moved by one Spirit working "diversly."[23]

Now that thinkers such as Foucault and Lacan have pointed out the social, psychological, and physical costs of privileging the inviolable integrity of the individual as the supreme value, we are in a position to reexamine more critically the relationship between subjectivity as a value in authorship and the political and ideological pressures which historically led to this privileging of a certain concept of personal agency.

A careful examination of the text of Coleridge's notebooks would show that the public faith in what Coleridge himself calls the "Philosopher's" consciousness, in which "the Subject by a mysterious Act of self-construction becomes an Object for itself" could be sustained only by the relentless suppression of alternative, more fragmented and fugitive versions of the authorial subject (*Notebooks*, 4:5283). These other versions resemble more a Hartleian flowing-together of many currents than the "transcendental...Will" of the Folio Notebook. In other words, though evidently experiencing, all the time, selfhood as a processual, fugitive, and even disturbingly unstable phenomenon, Coleridge strove even in the notebooks to affirm the doctrine of the primacy of the will, to adhere to the "ethical practice" of positing the originary will of the finite individual as the sole guarantee of personal agency (see *Notebooks*, 4:5286). There is thus a revealing tension in the notebooks between the ideologically-driven affirmations of the transcendental Will, directed against the views of Hartley, Schelling, and others, and the evidence which the notebooks themselves adduce of more fluid and transitory configurations: the "possibility," as Notebook 28 puts it, "that a man may be a Hive, a myriad of men in each man, every one of the Myriad holding himself & held by others, to be *the* man" (*Notebooks*, 4:5177, f 69ᵛ).

It is perhaps not surprising that this tension should exist in the personal notebooks of an author so much identified as Coleridge is with a particular version of the romantic ideology—perhaps the most fully articulated version of that ideology in English. However, the fugitive nature of the private self, and its highly oblique and fitful relationship to the material text, are equally apparent in the journals and notebooks of other writers. The journals of Dorothy Wordsworth, for instance, seldom reveal directly much of their author's thoughts, feelings, or state of mind. It used to be common to credit these journals with an almost uncanny ability to enable a reader to share Dorothy Wordsworth's subjectivity. Helen Darbishire's introduction to the popular Oxford edition which first appeared in 1958 typically claimed that "to meet Dorothy Wordsworth we have only to open her journal and enter her world."[24] It is easier now to see the shortcomings of such statements than to understand why they were made. Darbishire's claim may now seem uncritical or sentimental, but it reflects a pervasive modernist view, a narcissistic desire to feel that the reader of a journal is positioned to enjoy a peculiar intimacy with another consciousness. This sense of intimacy is itself too interesting to be dismissed as a mere illusion. It is a way of reading, a hermeneutic which itself has roots in the romantic period and which, as a by-product of privileging the authorial subjective consciousness, puts the supposedly unstudied and artless text—the letter and the journal—at the top of the scale of intimacy.

A more recent study of the journals, Pamela Woof's *Dorothy Wordsworth, Writer*, formulates in a more guarded way this sense of somehow entering the "world" of Dorothy Wordsworth, which I have argued is a reflection of the romantic and modern wish to see the text as giving privileged access to another unitary consciousness. Having quoted and commented upon two journal entries of 1834, Woof continues: "Dorothy was not a primitive; she learned to write. Like all writers she built on and used other writers."[25] Woof shows in detail, and with considerable critical acumen, how hard Dorothy Wordsworth worked to achieve the effect which Darbishire describes by such terms as "the heart of her experience," "naïveté," "minute observation" (Darbishire, xvii, xiv, xii)—all more or less equivalents of the eighteenth-century term "sensibility." As Woof observes, "Dorothy is entirely at one with her age and time" (25). That in itself is a reminder of the historically determined quality of the Grasmere Journals. They are, quite evidently, the work of a writer trained in a historically specific way of observing and recording natural phenomena. Moreover, the journals achieve the effect of intimacy far more by the judicious use of narrative economy than by full and specific descriptions or expressions of inner states.

On 16 May 1800, for instance, Dorothy Wordsworth writes, "I had many of my saddest thoughts," but the text does not proceed to tell what these thoughts were. On 1 June 1800 the Journals tell us merely, and movingly, "I lay upon the steep of Loughrigg my heart dissolved in what I saw." Even in the later entries, which grow more elaborate and expansive, the narrative more connected, a rule of economy still operates, so that any mention of personal feelings or of a subjective point of view gains its effect far more from the sense of strict controls being exercised than from the explicit analysis or description of a subjective state. There are certainly hints of powerful emotions at work—the best example being the notorious entry of October 1802 which recounts the events of her brother's wedding day; but it would be truer to say that the reader infers Dorothy Wordsworth's state of mind than that she or he reads a description of it. One statement made in the entry dated October 1802, "I cannot describe what I felt," may or may not have been a conscious echo of the lines from "Tintern Abbey"—"I cannot paint / What then I was"—but their rhetorical effect is similar: they gesture at an inner intensity that must remain unspoken, and so they compel the reader to project an imagined subjective state on to the text.[26] The gesture is recognizable: it belongs to a particular historical moment in the development of prose style. Emotions so intense that they cannot be expressed are virtually *de rigueur* for the late eighteenth-century writer of sensibility. It is part of the new emphasis on writing as process and on the object of writing as the realization of "states of mind without objects," the movement which in prose fiction is closely associated with Laurence Sterne and in poetry with Collins, Burns, and the "silent poet" figures invoked by William Wordsworth.[27]

This effect, which can be found repeatedly in most nineteenth- and twentieth-century journals in one form or another, makes the journal as a textual artefact a good candidate for inclusion in Lyotard's definition of the postmodern as "that which, in the modern, puts forward the unpresentable in presentation itself" (81). (For some, it might merely confirms the suspicion that postmodernism is nothing more than romanticism's negative image.) The point I have tried to stress here is that there are historical determinants behind the romantic and modernist drive to witness to the unpresentable and that the compulsions of the 1790s are not in all respects identical with those of the 1990s.

Must this mean, though, that in the postmodern the individual loses the empowerment of the text, the possibility of using text as a means and measure of personal development, "the history of my own mind for my own improvement"? Does the postmodern put an end to the idea that producing text is a form of "labor," as is suggested in Habermas's well-known accusation against the postmodernists Derrida, Foucault, and Bataille?[28] The extreme form of the postmodern form of knowledge as outlined by Lyotard would certainly ignore or dissolve the connection between subjectivity and history. The postmodern collapses history. Like the symbolist aesthetic derived from the form of epistemological idealism that argues that everything exists only as it is perceived, postmodernism relishes outrageous or playful juxtapositions—say, a Titian, a World War II recruiting poster, and a cave painting from 40,000 BCE—because our technology makes all of them instantly available for reproduction and study. Journals can be read this way too, but they have other uses for students of nineteenth-century culture. They can demonstrate in considerable detail how personal experience exists within the matrix of actual circumstance. Since as we have seen the journal cannot be received as if it defined or contained the real self of its author, it may be the form that more than any other breaks down the "authority" accorded in modernist criticism to the permanent and transcendent self. A journal can be read as a series of testimonies to an inadequately imagined self, speaking more by negatives, by difference, than by positive definition. The very elusiveness and processual nature of the self that is witnessed to in a writer's journal may be a far better justification for an interest in journal literature than the idea that it provides privileged access to that author's subject position or to "the heart of her experience."

The philosopher Charles E. Scott has argued that discourse that abjures transcendental self as the centre of meaning also gives up the violence which accompanies the older, metaphysically grounded discourse. The poststructuralist's focus on the idea of difference, Scott suggests, "functions to break connections of identity or to offset the centers of traditional comprehension." This change can bring about "a releasing effect on thinking...one that lacks a particular kind of violence as it finds expression through its own way of offsetting itself."[29] Journal literature remains significant as a literature which itself marks "difference", which is created, in the form in which we know it, by the modern (late-eighteenth to early-twentieth century) way of conceiving subjectivity, but which exists for us as a site where subjectivity exists only from moment to moment, in evident incompleteness and temporality.[30] The journal or day-book is a textual space where the postmodern "war on totality" and the literary scholar's interest in historicizing authorship can both find hospitable ground.

Notes

1   Hugh J. Silverman, citing Husserl, William James, and Freud, says that the "modernist conception takes the subject as the center...and determinate authority for all conscious life"—*Textualities: Between Hermeneutics and Deconstruction* (New York: Routledge, 1994), 32.

2. Anne Stevenson, *Bitter Fame: A Life of Sylvia Plath* (London: Penguin, 1990), 176.

3. Richard Holmes, *Coleridge: Early Visions* (London: Hodder and Stoughton, 1989), 363. "W. N. P. Barbellion" (Bruce Frederick Cummings, 1889–1919) was the author of *Journal of a Disappointed Man*, published in 1919.

4. William L. Howarth and Robert Sattelmeyer, "General Introduction," in Henry D. Thoreau, *Journals*, gen. ed. John C. Broderick (Princeton: Princeton University Press, 1981–), 1:590.

5. Quoted in Christopher Janaway, *Self and World in Schopenhauer's Philosophy* (Oxford: Clarendon Press, 1989), 17.

6. Nietzsche's notebooks 1885–1886, quoted in Christopher Janaway, *Self and World in Schopenhauer's Philosophy* (Oxford: Clarendon Press, 1989), 17. For the need to historicize authorship, see especially Felicity A. Nussbaum, *The Autobiographical Subject: Gender and Ideology in Eighteenth-Century England* (Baltimore: The Johns Hopkins University Press, 1989), xi; David Saunders and Ian Hunter, "Lessons from the 'Literary': How to Historicise Authorship," *Critical Inquiry* 17 (1991):479–509; Nancy Armstrong and Leonard Tennenhouse, *The Imaginary*

Puritan: Literature, Intellectual Labor, and the Origins of Personal Life (Berkeley: University of California Press, 1992), 6–9 and *passim*. On the development—relatively recent in human history—of the "category of 'self,'" see Marcel Mauss, "A category of the human mind: the notion of person; the notion of self," trans. W. D. Halls, in *The Category of the Person: Anthropology, Philosophy, History*, ed. Michael Carrithers, Steven Collins, and Steven Lukes (Cambridge: Cambridge University Press, 1985), 1–25.

7. Michel Foucault, "What is an Author?," trans. Josué V. Harari, in *Textual Strategies: Perspectives in Post-Structuralist Criticism*, rpt. in *The Foucault Reader*, ed. Paul Rabinow (New York: Pantheon, 1984), 102.

8. Jean-François Lyotard, *The Postmodern Condition: A Report on Knowledge*, trans. Geoff Bennington and Brian Massumi (Manchester: Manchester University Press, 1984), 37; Thomas Hardy, "Preface" (1895), in *Jude the Obscure* (New York: Signet, 1961), v.

9. Felicity A. Nussbaum, "Toward Conceptualizing Diary," *Studies in Autobiography*, ed. James Olney (New York and Oxford: Oxford University Press, 1988), 131, 135, 131–32. Cited hereafter in the text.

10. Jane Flax, *Disputed Subjects: Essays on Psychoanalysis, Politics, and Philosophy* (New York: Routledge, 1993), 93.

11. Rachel Blau DuPlessis and Members of Workshop 9, "For the Etruscans: Sexual Difference and Artistic Production—The Debate over a Female Aesthetic," in *The Future of Difference*, ed. Hester Eisenstein and Alice Jardine (Boston: G.K. Hall and Co., 1980), 140.

12. For the distinction between the person (*personne*) and the self (*moi*), see Mauss, "A category of the human mind: the notion of person; the notion of self," 20.

13. Virginia Woolf, *The Diary of Virginia Woolf*, ed. Anne Olivier Bell, 5 vols (London: Hogarth Press, 1977–1984), 1:266. Quoted by kind permission of the Hogarth Press and of the executors of the Virginia Woolf Estate.

14. Tilottama Rajan, "Is There a Romantic Ideology? Some Thoughts on Schleiermacher's Hermeneutic and Textual Criticism," *Text* 4 (1988):65, 66, 74.

15. Lyotard, *The Postmodern Condition*, 32. One example of what such a history might look like is Gerald N. Izenberg, *Impossible Individuality: Romanticism, Revolution, and the Origins of Modern Selfhood, 1787–1802* (Princeton: Princeton University Press, 1992).

16. See Saunders and Hunter, "Lessons from the 'Literary,'" 505, 509.

17. S.T. Coleridge, Notebook 36 (British Museum Add. MS 47531), ff 5, 22. The sentence preceding the first of these extracts reads: "Strange! that so many ingenious men should <not> have detected the confusion in their minds between *the Life*, and the various agents that excite a Living Body to manifest it's Life!" Quoted by permission of Princeton University Press.

18. S.T. Coleridge, *Notebooks*, ed. Kathleen Coburn, Bollingen Series 50 (New York: Bollingen Foundation / Pantheon Books; Princeton: Princeton University Press, 1957–), 3 (1973) 3325. Hereafter cited in text. (Consistent with usual practice in citing the Bollingen edition of the *Notebooks*, references are given to volume number followed by entry number, with foliation where needed for clarity.) All quotations from the *Notebooks* are copyright 1961, 1973, 1990 by Princeton

University Press. Reprinted by permission of Princeton University Press.

19. Flax, *Disputed Subjects*, 27.

20. For a sympathetic exposition of Coleridge's concept of personhood and the ethical responsibilities of the individual see Anya Taylor, *Coleridge's Defense of the Human* (Columbus: Ohio State University Press, 1986). Kathleen Coburn's own studies of the notebooks, *The Self Conscious Imagination* (London: Oxford University Press, 1974), and *Experience Into Thought: Perspectives in the Coleridge Notebooks* (Toronto: University of Toronto Press, 1979), remain valuable, though based on a view of Coleridge's thought and personality from which I would dissent.

21. Sonia Hofkosh, "A Woman's Profession: Sexual Difference and the Romance of Authorship," *Studies in Romanticism* 32 (1993):247–48.

22. S.T. Coleridge, *Biographia Literaria*, ed. James Engell and W. Jackson Bate, *Collected Works*, Bollingen Series 75, vol. 7, 2 vols (London and Princeton: Routledge and Kegan Paul and Princeton University Press, 1983), 1:110. Copyright 1983 by Princeton University Press. Reprinted by permission of Princeton University Press.

23. S.T. Coleridge, *Confessions of an Inquiring Spirit*, ed. H. St J. Hart (London: Adam and Charles Black, 1956), 51.

24. "Introduction," in *Journals of Dorothy Wordsworth*, second edition, rev. Mary Moorman (Oxford: Oxford University Press, 1971), xiii.

25. Pamela Woof, *Dorothy Wordsworth, Writer* (Grasmere: The Wordsworth Trust, 1988), 19.

26. Dorothy Wordsworth, *Journals*, ed. Mary Moorman (London: Oxford University Press, 1971), 17, 22, 161.

27. See Northrop Frye, "Towards Defining an Age of Sensibility," *ELH* 23 (1956):149; on the silent poet figure see Jonathan Ramsey, "Wordsworth's Silent Poet," *Modern Language Quarterly* 37 (1976):260–80.

28. Jurgen Habermas, "Modernity—An Incomplete Project," *Postmodernism*, ed. Thomas Docherty (New York: Columbia University Press, 1993), 107.

29. Charles E. Scott, *The Language of Difference* (Atlantic Highlands, NJ: Humanities Press International, 1989), 156.

30. See Nussbaum, *The Autobiographical Subject*, 132: "the diary, tolerant of multiple subjectivities and discourses, is especially resistant to representing the self as a unified, rational, and intentional subject."

The De-Gendered Self in
William Blake's Poetry
by Marjean D. Purinton

Evolving from post-Enlightenment thought and Romantic revolutions, the modern self (and to some extent, the postmodern, decentered self) occupies the mythopoesis of William Blake's projects. The treatment of the gendered self in Blake's poetry is problematic. For Blake and other "modern" thinkers, "self" is a culturally and politically constructed notion.[1] Its seeming privatization is an implicit part of the social contract that determines custom, habit, and law. Its prescribed patterns of behaviors, functions, and activities appear as "naturally" gendered. Blake's poetry, however, destabilizes dichotomies and upsets unitary models of gender identity. As revisionist myth-making, Blake's poetry deconstructs simplistic self-identities and binary oppositions. His mythos challenges a monolithic understanding of gender identity based on patriarchal paradigms, negative stereotypes, and post-Enlightenment thought.[2] In the flexible models of Blakean identities, self is de-gendered and transformed in ways that expose the oppression embedded in the Western philosophical understanding of selfhood.

Blake's poetry shows us how pervasively gender divisions are symbolically manifest in the cultural binarisms of post-Enlightenment philosophy. With the political and cultural revolutions of the late eighteenth century came significant conceptual changes in the identity and function of the self.[3] While late eighteenth-century and early nineteenth-century philosophers recast the binary conceptual framework in new terms, they retained the gendered patterns that privileged "maleness" and Reason. Blake's poetry emerges from a discursive arena in which confusion about the modern self evolves, and, in many ways, Blake's poetic and prophetic treatment of the gendered self anticipates contemporary debate about gender construction.[4]

Blake operated in a misogynic culture, but his poems betray resistance to the hegemonic ideology of the early nineteenth century. For several years now, his treatment of female characters has been viewed as evidence of his misogyny.[5] Without denying the validity of these insightful interpretations and without ignoring the passages in Blake's poetry that disclose and affirm the dominant male ideology, I wish to demonstrate that within his poems' surface structures and subtexts lie the seeds of contradiction. Because Blake's poems suggest that binary classifications—including gender references and sexual distinctions—are artificial constructs, the poems themselves possess the potential for their own self-contradiction. Inconsistencies reflect rather than solve the social and political tensions of Blake's time. I argue that male-centered images suggest the possibility of interrelations governed by a de-gendered self, free from the fallen state of binarism and unencumbered by a hierarchy of being.

At the center of Blake's mythopoesis lies his rejection of fixed and permanent binary distinctions between men and women. His poetic projects deconstruct the terms of gender difference, and his vision offers an alternative to the bifurcation and stratification of gendered selfhood. His mythos destabilizes the powerful myths that reified gender constructions, and his poetry exposes the ubiquitous and powerful operations of gendered selfhood. In his poems, we see the dehumanizing and destructive results of interactions grounded upon gendered selfhood. The dangerous Female Will, Blake illustrates, is that which appropriates masculine competition, confrontation, and opposition. The Female Will idealizes maleness and enacts it—becomes what it beholds. Its power, however, is illusory.[6] In adopting a self-denying identification with its oppressor, the Female Will surrenders selfhood.

The self, defined and limited by socially and culturally constructed gender, is annihilated in Blake's epics. In his later and more complex poems, Blake disrupts the prevailing order of relationships and destabilizes the carefully controlled socio-political understandings of gender and selfhood. These poems demonstrate that the perverse struggles for domination characterize humanity fallen into the divisions of masculine and feminine categories. Repeatedly, the violation of woman in the epics signals the beginning of a revolution in gender relations. Like the political revolutions of the early nineteenth century, the "revolution in manners" (Mary Wollstonecraft, *A Vindication of the Rights of Woman*)[7] or "the gradual emancipation of women" (Mary Hays, *Appeal to the Men of Great Britain on the Behalf of Women*)[8] or a total change in "the manners of society" (Maria Edgeworth, *Letters for Literary Ladies*)[9] in Blake's poetry reflects issues of gender and selfhood created by *external* conditions. To read Blake's poetry as only *internal*, psychological strife limits the multiplicity of meanings inherit in his work.[10]

In the Shadowy Females and Enitharmon of *America: A Prophecy* and *Europe: A Prophecy*, Blake conflates political revolutions and gender conflicts.[11] Freeing the female constitutes one mediation of a whole series of contextual revolutions happening simultaneously in the two poems. Enitharmon's myth of delusion (the Eden story of original sin—humanity fallen into sexual divisions) and her edict "Thou shalt not" (see "The Garden of Love," Erdman edition 26; l. 6)[12] reaffirm a powerful and domineering sexual mentality. In *America*, the nameless daughter of Urthona silently brings the imprisoned Orc food and drink. Naked and vulnerable, she remains dumb and chaste until Orc tries to seize her, to embrace her, to dissolve the tyranny created by a doctrine of gender oppression. Together, Orc and the Shadowy Female instigate the political revolution that liberates America from its slavery to England and the social revolution that seeks to free the self from gendered behaviors.

The Shadowy Female of the Preludium of *Europe* separates from Orc. In becoming his "other," she is detached and unfulfilled. She functions as a limited dimension of Orc's fragmented self, a mere mouthpiece for his thoughts. The tyrant of *Europe* is Enitharmon, a powerful, external force. She sends her children, Rintrah and Palamabron, to the human race to tell them lies: "Womans love is Sin" (E. 62; 5:5). She orders her children to "sound" the myth of a promised external life in some "allegorical abode where existence hath never came" (E. 62; 5:7). She functions as the mouthpiece of an oppressive fiction—a myth that has been codified in tablet (gender-based laws) and institutionalized in political tyrants (George III). Her "womans triumph" (E. 64; 12:25) inverts the possibility that "every thing that lives is holy" (*America*, E. 54; 8:13).

The companion poems demonstrate that both men and women can use gender as a powerful weapon when selfhood and social interactions are based on binary oppositions. The prophecy implied by the poems is that as long as humankind perpetuates gendered identity, struggles for power and dominion will be generated in all aspects of human interaction. *America* and *Europe* stage in poetical terms the social controversies debated in the prose of the pre-revolutionary and revolutionary periods. In *Emile* (1762), Jean-Jacques Rousseau asserts that moral relations are based on sexual differences: "One ought to be active and strong, the other passive and weak. One must necessarily will and be able; it suffices that the other put up little resistance."[13] Mary Hays challenges this "natural" order as an unexamined opinion articulated in the language of prejudice rather than the language of truth. That men are superior beings, she claims, remains to be proven (96). Maria Edgeworth deems it absurd "to manage any argument so as to set the two sexes at variance by vain contention for superiority" (54). These writers approach the battle of the sexes from different perspectives, and they base their arguments on different premises, but they analyze essentially the same problem: confrontations ensuing from a social system based on the ideological doctrine of gender categories. It is this social system, so fundamental to Western thought, which Blake's poetry challenges.

The Book of Urizen relates Blake's genesis myth of gender division. The account emphasizes the multiplicity of divisions and the resulting fragmentations. As Urizen divides from the Eternals, the female form (Enitharmon) separates from Los. Selfhood, like Blake's "states signified" (see *A Vision of the Last Judgment*, E. 556), falls into division. Prior to the "fall," self was not distinguished by gendered identities, and humankind was not marked by sexual differences. The characters of Blake's mythopoesis come to accept this fallen state as an absolute and permanent system of thought. In binding characters' submission to the gendered dualism of the fallen world, the myth promulgates what ironically appears as a monism:

> One command, one joy, one desire,
> One curse, one weight, one measure
> One King, one God, one Law (E. 72; 4:38–40).

The Book of Urizen illustrates the process of being gendered, of becoming "self-closed" (E. 70; 3:3), and "a self-contemplating shadow" (E. 71; 3:21). In their struggles within and against this system, Blake's characters urge us to consider the origins and limits of gendered subjectivity.[14] They impel us to rethink the consequences of mindless obedience to a conception of self based on gender, "in chains of the mind locked up" (E. 75; 10:25).

"The Mental Traveller" explores these socially constructed operations and perceptions, those cognitive constructs that we believe to be true and so have codified into edicts and modes of behavior. Custom and habit become enslavement and oppression. In the Land of Men and Women, sexual roles are binary and oppositional. The male and the female continually torture each other, revealing "dreadful things" (E. 483; 3) to the mental traveller, and neither is affirmed by the text. The male rapes the female, "rends up his Manacles / And binds her down for his delight" (E. 484; 23–24). The female perverts maternal nurturing: "She binds iron thorns around his head / She pierces both his hands & feet / She cuts his heart out at his side" (E. 484; 13–15). Those in the Land of Men and Women cannot perceive a world in which genders and their accompanying conflicts do not exist. Entrapped by stratified and codified gender relations, they cannot imagine "a World in a Grain of Sand" ("Auguries of Innocence," E. 490; 1), a world sans binary oppositions. Here Blake demonstrates what happens to social relations when gendered selfhood prevails.

Thel demonstrates how the gendered self is repressed and denied the joys of life. Her experience reveals how the patterns of selfhood are forged out of fear. She constructs her selfhood from the sexual anxieties she projects onto nature. Socially constructed gendered behaviors hold her desires in check.[15] She retreats from the Land of Men and Women: "The Virgin started from her seat, & with a shriek. / Fled back unhindered till she came into the vales of Har" (E. 6; 6:21–22). While Thel refuses to interact in a society where masculine power and female will struggle for dominance, she has not annihilated gendered selfhood.

If Thel demonstrates unnatural and unhealthy repression of sexual desire, Oothoon's experience shows the oppression of demeaning and violent behaviors generated by gender dominance. *Visions of the Daughters of Albion* dislodges the culturally created images of "woman." She refuses to accept the sinful implications associated with her being "named" a whore by Bromion, her slave-master who has "rent her with his thunders. on his stormy bed" (E. 46; 1:16). Although she has been raped by Bromion and now carries his child, she argues that her soul is still untainted by sin. In refusing the label "whore," Oothoon denies a self defined by gender. Bromion's rape of Oothoon recapitulates on a domestic level the subjugation of women by men on a societal level, and Oothoon tries to escape the entrapping binarisms generated by gender identity. Oothoon subverts the culturally conditioned response to rape by refusing to behave in the "feminine" (submissive) manner codified by language.[16] She refuses to allow her "infinite brain" (E. 47; 2:32), her capacity for creativity and vision, to be confined by the construction of a gendered selfhood. Her technologies of the self seek to render it de-gendered.[17]

Theotormon, on the other hand, sees Oothoon's experience only in terms of bifurcations, and his system of classification renders Oothoon a "whore." Following social custom and codified law, Theotormon brands virgin "joy with the name of whore" (E. 49; 6:12). His conception of self is defined, described, and delimited by gender. Theotormon has learned to accept the constraints that systems of thought have imposed on him. He convinces himself that he is right, and his justification leads him to self-love, a denial of others, a logo-centric and ego-centric existence. Similarly, for Bromion, subjectivity emanates from clearly fixed dualities. For him, there is only "one law" (E. 48; 4:22) which relegates human relations to the hierarchical dichotomies of male and female. *Visions of the Daughters of Albion* seeks to dismantle the institutionalized logic that assigns unequal meanings to neutral facts of identity, such as gender.

The Four Zoas vividly illustrates how sexual love and jealousy are the consequences of dualistic thought. Like *The Book of Urizen*, *The Four Zoas* recapitulates the genesis of the fall, but it details in more particular forms the gender-generated conflicts which result. The emanation Enitharmon, the embodiment of emotion, femininity, and bodily senses, unleashes gender-based strife. Early in the account of the domestic strife between Los and Enitharmon of Night the First, Los abuses Enitharmon: "Then Los smote her upon the Earth twas long eer she revivd" (E. 306; 11:3). In Night the Fourth, Tharmas demonstrates his power by raping Enitharmon. His abusive action propels Los to revenge. Selfhood fashioned by the social codes and practices that dictate gender relations results in division and fragmentation. The cycle is self-perpetuating: "terrified at the Shapes / Enslavd humanity put on he became what he beheld" (E. 336; 53:23–24). Regardless of the character, assuming gendered identities and behaviors simply ensures ongoing conflicts.

All the characters of *The Four Zoas* construct subjectivity based solely on their sensory perception. In Night the Sixth, Urizen laments: "Beyond the bounds of their own self their senses cannot penetrate" (E. 347; 70:13). Selfhood is illusionary and delusionary. It is inextricably connected to the language which gives abstractions particularized meanings; these meanings become accepted as stable, ontological constructs. In Night the Eighth, we learn that False Females (e.g., Vala and Rahab) are False Forms. These forms, however, are the same as Satan. We have simply particularized the same abstraction and deluded ourselves into thinking that the different manifestations of the same concept are indeed different by assigning them different names. Like Enitharmon, we weave a delusive net of language in constructing a gendered self. Like Theotormon, we adhere to a system of thought based on one law. Night the Ninth raises the possibility of an imaginative identity in which gender distinctions are blurred, when "the Expanding Eyes of Man behold the depths of wondrous worlds" (E. 406; 138:2–5). The "end" of the epic reveals that the wars of domestic strife are temporarily subdued, but the chains of mental entrapment are refigured within the conceptual framework of philosophy. *The Four Zoas* ends as it begins—with the consequences of gendered subjectivity.[18]

Throughout Blake's poetry, then, we see repeated patterns of conflict that challenge the prevailing ideological basis of selfhood. It is important to recognize that Blake's poems are situated within a discursive arena in which issues of selfhood appear in diverse forms. Enitharmon's femininity stimulates corporeal senses and creates a fall. The battle of the sexes depicted in the various domestic scenes of the epic represent a larger, ideological doctrine of separate spheres based on man's defeat by Female Will.

Anxieties about gender-bending behaviors do not appear exclusively in Blake's poetry. Hays asserts that "women may be truly masculine in their conduct and demeanor without wounding the delicacy of men" (180). Like Los and Tharmas of *The Four Zoas*, Rousseau reflects fear of a powerful Female Will: "Finding that their pleasures depended more on the will of the fair sex than they had believed, men have captivated that will by attentions for which the fair sex has amply compensated them" (360). In *A Vision of the Last Judgment*, Blake asserts: "In Eternity Woman is the Emanation of Man she has No will of her own There is no such thing in Eternity as a Female Will" (E. 562). Only in the divine imagination can the Female Will, a product of gendered selfhood, cease to exist. Meanwhile, within the prevailing social structure, bifurcated gender roles dictate relationships. The potential embodiment of a Female Will is held in check by the double standard, and the doctrine of separate spheres prevents potential destabilization of hierarchial relations through gender bending. The double sexual standard that impedes Thel's self-realization or that destroys Oothoon's selfhood becomes in Blake's epics a basis for his exploration of an ideology giving validity and strength to such a system.

Milton suggests that selfhood defined by binarisms is false through shattering the basis on which any gender dichotomies exist. The oppositional customs inscribed as gender in *Milton* are transcribed in Eternal Imagination, where there are no sexes and there are no genders.

In *Milton*, Blake relies on the dualities created by gender to undermine the systems that perpetuate such dualities. In other words, he uses gender divisions to repudiate gender divisions. Subtly and implicitly, Blake's projections of female imagery in *Milton* undermine the way we perceive gender. Like Wollstonecraft's *Vindication of the Rights of Woman*, Blake's *Milton* suggests that we see two sexes—male and female— because we have been indoctrinated with this ideology. Wollstonecraft's argument that the distinction of sex is inculcated in us at young ages and that women are formed to gender-specific roles indicates how "self" came to be limited by gender (19). Wollstonecraft also alleges that girls and boys would play harmlessly together, "if the distinction of sex is not inculcated long before nature makes any difference" (43).

Milton impels us to ask, what if there are no sexes? What if "male" and "female" are concepts constructed by our own mental processes and imposed as an uncontested and universal view of humanity? Conceptually beyond androgyny, Blake contends that in our Eternal Imagination it is possible that self is de-gendered. We are trapped into accepting gendered roles, functions, and traits by our Vegetable States. In our Divine Selves, however, no gender distinctions exist. Because our perception is limited, we simply cannot see beyond the dualism so thoroughly embedded in our social consciousness. Blake's inversions of genders, his reversals of roles, his Emanations, Shadows, and Spectres— even his seemingly misogynic treatment of female characters—urge us to reconsider our blind acceptance of the prevailing ideological doctrine of gender.

Milton recapitulates the genesis and self-destruction wrought by gender. Leutha confesses that she enters Satan's brain nightly so that she may stupefy the masculine perceptions. As "the Author of this sin" (E. 105; 11:35), she keeps only the feminine awake. Thus, Satan is both masculine and feminine, or genderless, until Leutha creates the divisions. Such divisions become "a Hell of [their] own making" (E. 106; 12:23). Leutha exercises "a feminine delusion of false pride self-deceiv'd" (E. 105; 11:26). It is after this gender distinction has been marked that Satan "Hence rose his soft / Delusory love to Palamabron: admiration join'd with envy / Cupidity unconquerable!" (E.105; 12:6–8). Homoerotic love violates gendered behaviors dictated by the prevailing social system, and it is thus labeled perverse. The same linguistic system that brands Oothoon a whore marks as sin the desire Satan expresses for Palamabron. Homoerotic relations might mitigate, even arrest, gender conflicts, and characters re-affirm heterosexual love. Enitharmon creates a "New Space to protect Satan from punishment" (E. 107; 13:13). She fuels sexually generated conflict; her Female Will excites jealousy and confrontation. The Assembly thunders approval. With soft words, Elynittria further encourages Leutha to try to inflict her feminine wiles on Palamabron "in moments new created for delusion" (E. 107; 13:38). Sexually generated jealousy and rivalry beget continual division and strife.

This gender system is the tradition Milton inherits. His own shadow is hermaphroditic—male and female—sexless. It is, however, enclosed in a body subjected to a tradition of gender division. As with the earlier characters depicted in The Bard's Song, conflict ensues and results from Milton's efforts to fulfill the socially determined expectations of gender. Blake, no doubt, agreed with Wollstonecraft's refutation of Rousseau on the doctrine of separate spheres. Wollstonecraft challenged Rousseau's contention that the sexes unite to pursue one common object but in different manners. She repudiated Rousseau's belief that one sex should be active and strong and the other passive and weak, that one sex should exert power and will while the other should offer little resistance (*Vindication* 78–79; *Emile* 358). Milton must annihilate a selfhood that has been fashioned in the Rousseauvian mold. In giving up his Selfhood, Milton might resume his female forms, who "in blood and jealousy / Surround him dividing & uniting without end or number" (E. 110; 17:8). These female divisions write in thunder, smoke, and fire Milton's dictations—his epic that codifies the sin of sexuality.

As Milton passes to Golgonooza, the place where his self will be de-gendered, similar sexually generated conflicts occur. Enitharmon confides to her daughters her fear of Milton's coming to unloose her bond. Seeing Milton, the Shadowy Female howls her lamentations and vows: "I will put on the human Form & take the Image of God" (E. 111; 18:19). Orc implores her not to take on human form; instead, he pleads for her to take on a female form "that cannot consume in Mans consummation" (E. 111; 18:29). Because the female form evokes pity and compassion, gender becomes a covert but powerful weapon. Rejecting this gendered behavior, the Shadowy Female responds to Milton's appearance with jealousy and darkness: "Howlings fill'd all the desolate places in accusations of sin / In Female beauty shining in the unformd void, & Orc in vain / Stretch'd out his hands of fire, & wooed; they triumph in his pain" (E. 112; 18:43–45). The dualisms of gender roles create conflicted selfhood and suffering. Milton is instructed by these visions as he passes to Golgonooza.

Ololon first appears amidst Milton's confrontation with the two-fold form: hermaphroditic and double-sexed (female-male and male-female). Self-dividing, this hermaphroditic form appears "before him in their beauty & in cruelties of holiness. / Shining in darkness" (E. 113; 19:34–35). The fires of youth are bound with the Chain of Jealousy. To comply with masculine-defined feminine selves, women must forfeit the power of love. Viciously, Tirzah renders beauty and perfection mere sports among her victims. She numbers her experiments on men:

> She ties the knot of nervous fibres into a white brain!
> She ties the knot of bloody veins into a red hot heart!
> Within her bosom Albion lies embalmd, never to wake.
> Hand is become a rock; Sinai & Horeb is Hyle & Coben;
> Scofield is bound in iron armour before Reuben's Gate!
> She ties the knot of milky seed into two lovely Heavens,
> Two yet but one, each in the other sweet reflected! (E. 113; 19:55–60, 20:1).

As objects of male desire, women like Tirzah work their artful wiles against male power that is legitimated by the prevailing social system.

Feminine charms, like those practiced by Tirzah, are variously discussed in the philosophical discourse of the period. In response to Rousseau's assertion that woman is made specially to please man and to be subjugated by man (358), Wollstonecraft counters that woman "was created to be the toy of man, his rattle, and it must jingle in his ears whenever, dismissing reason, he chooses to be amused" (34). She insists that "men endeavour to sink us still lower, merely to render us alluring objects for a moment" (8). Rousseau argues that women's only weapons are her art and her beauty (371), that to be a woman means to be coquettish (365), and that it is by dispensing coquetry artfully that she makes the strongest chains for her slaves. Defensively, Hays responds: "Women are taught and expected to exercise artful snares" (223). Woman, she claims, must have some schemes of her own employment or "accept that she is a mere nothing and her merit next to nothing" (57).

Hays's most vehement defense of women's artful snares could be applied to Tirzah's experiments on men: "If women do avail themselves of the only weapons they are permitted to wield, can they be blamed? No…since they are compelled to it by the injustice and impolicy of men. Petty treacheries, mean subterfuge, whining and flattery, feigned submission, all the dirty little attendants which compose the endless train of low cunning cannot be severely censured when practiced by women" (91). Similarly, Wollstonecraft justifies women's deceitful behaviors: "Women...sometimes boast of their weakness, cunningly obtaining power by playing on the weakness of men" (40). In the land of men and women which Wollstonecraft, Hays, Rousseau, and Blake experience, these gender games occur routinely; they are not merely fanciful machinations of Blake's epic world. Inextricably caught in the trap and conflicts of this gender duality, men and women entreat Milton to come to the Three Heavens to be bound: "And let us bind thee in the bands of War & be thou King" (E. 114; 20:5). They yearn to bind Milton conceptually to the delusion, the fallen vision, of sexual dichotomies.

Fearful that Milton might perceive the results of gendered selfhood, the Daughters of Los scurry to weave a new Religion from a new Jealousy. Wailing prophetically and acting deceitfully, they weave their theological net: "Miltons Religion is the cause: there is no end to destruction!" (E. 117; 22:39). The Miltonic, or Urizenic, sexually-based dualities could be undermined if Milton perceives their delusive nature. Rahab creates Voltaire, and Tirzah creates Rousseau to perpetuate "War & Glory to perpetuate the Laws of Sin" (E. 117; 22:45). These laws of sin emanate from the dichotomy of gender roles. Universal acceptance of the male/female dualism makes it is possible to pervert biblical myth (as Hyle and Coben had done to the Mosaic laws of Sinai), to reduce Jerusalem to a Harlot, and to raise up for reverence the Virgin Harlot, Mother of War. While the women seem to be given pejorative treatment in these parallel confrontations, *Milton* reminds us that the men codify and perpetuate the destructive myth of genders.

It is significant that Ololon descends in a place called Beulah in Book II of *Milton*, "a place where Contrarieties are equally True" (E. 129; 30:1), a place of "the Eternal Great Humanity" (E. 129; 30:15). What is depicted in Book II stands in contrast to the chaotic, deceitful, gender-generated conflicts of Book I. The Seven Angels of Presence tell Milton that Forms exist forever. Imagination is not a state; it is a Human Existence itself, and it is not defined by sex or gender. Science explicitly exists in Time and Space. Since the biological divisions of sex implicitly occupy time and space, they cannot exist in the Eternal Imagination. Similarly, gendered dualisms exist in finite historical and spatial contexts; as culturally determined modes of identity, they are irrelevant in Infinity. In the existence of Divine Imagination, there is neither a female-male separation, nor a division between divine and human. Elsewhere, mental and corporeal strife continues because divisions exist. In Beulah, Ololon and Milton will be transformed for Divine Eternity. Milton and his Sixfold Female will be reunited just as Jerusalem—now a wandering harlot in the streets—will be reunited with God. To this end, Milton must annihilate his Selfhood and his sexuality. Miltonic ideas or concepts themselves "may be slain in offerings for sin" (E. 135; 35:6).

Considerable critical controversy exists about the nature of Ololon and what she represents. She is neither simply an aggressive, independent female nor a mere passive, dependent feminine creature.[19] Ololon is the most complex and problematic female in the Blake canon prior to *Jerusalem* because she confounds, reverses, and contradicts traditional gender associations. Her metalanguage thus serves as a discourse about the nature of femininity. In drawing attention to the concept of femininity and its sexually-bound language, Ololon brings the entire gender dichotomy into question.

None of Blake's earlier females project such complexity. They embody femaleness, but they do not challenge the very concept—or language—that defines, characterizes, and restricts them. Gendered dualisms ultimately impose limitations and confinement, and the language ascribed to femininity reinforces those limitations. In dismissing the condescending feminine phrases men use to soften females' slavish dependence, Wollstonecraft declares in the *Vindication*: "The first object of laudable ambition is to obtain a character as a human being, regardless of the distinction of sex" (9–10). Interestingly, all distinctions of selfhood in Rousseau's *Emile* rest upon sex-linked language (see 358, for example). Conversely, Hays, like Wollstonecraft, questions the "fanciful system of arbitrary authority" based on "the language of prejudice" which men have so assiduously erected in their own favor (52; 91). Declaring the word "masculine" a "bugbear" (11), Wollstonecraft illustrates how gender and gender-bound language impose restrictions on humanity. Blake likewise suggests this notion in insisting that both Ololon and Milton are Imagination when they annihilate the limitations that gender roles inscribe. Ololon must be freed from femininity, and Milton must be freed from patriarchy.

Looking down into the Heavens of Ulro, Ololon is fearful. The Daughters of Beulah marvel how "the Wars of Man" (E. 134; 34:50) are made to appear "in the External Sphere of Visionary Life" (E. 135; 34:51). They marvel that "those Visions of Human Life & Shadow of

Wisdom & Knowledge / Are here frozen to unexpansive deadly destroying terrors" (E. 135; 34:55, 35:1). In Ulro, visions, wisdom, and knowledge are fixed forms. As Wollstonecraft observes, fixed forms, like gender dichotomies, are so readily inculcated in us that we often do not recognize them. Under the laws of fixed forms (Mosaic/Urizenic/Miltonic), the "Brotherhood is changed into a Curse & a Flattery" (E. 135; 35:4), and the self defined by gendered dualities becomes a "corroding Hell" (E. 135; 35:3).

Ololon seeks to change these conditions. Simultaneously with Milton, she descends to Ulro to transcend gender conflicts. Ololon is herself transformed into a liberating process as she transforms the entrapments that emanate from the prevailing ideological doctrine of gender roles, activities, and identities. As she steps into the Polypus within the Mundane Shell, Ololon descends as a twelve-year-old virgin. This is the age traditionally associated with sexual activity, an age at which it is biologically possible to conceive and bear children—the sexually procreative functions of the female. She bears all the "baggage" of femaleness just as Milton's descending shadow bears all the "baggage" of patriarchy. Milton descends "to put off Self" (E. 139; 38:49), to redeem Ololon (as Ololon reciprocates by simultaneously redeeming Milton), and to teach humankind that the laws of gender roles are false.

For Ololon to "put off Self," to shed virginity (the trappings and baggage of femaleness), to annihilate the female hidden in a male, to destroy false femininity, means that her union does not affirm a male-female division. Like Milton, she frees herself from the chains of sexually defined codes. The Laws of Eternity demand that "each shall mutually / Annihilate himself for others good" (E. 139; 38:35–36). Moral virtue is exposed as "a Female hidden in a Male, Religion hidden in War /...[a] cruel two-fold Monster shining bright" (E. 141–42; 40:20–21). Ololon dissolves the delusion that holds humankind to gender-determined selfhood.

Ololon's liberating process invites us to suspend our blind acceptance of dichotomies and hierarchies that limit self. Sexually derived powers and gender-based roles are rendered unnecessary if we can see beyond their divisive influence. Like Milton and Ololon, we must "cleanse the Face of [our] Spirit by Self-examination / To bathe in the Waters of Life; to wash off the Not Human" (E. 142; 40:37–41:1).

If the Blakean myth seeks unity and reintegration, if there is One Universal and Divine Family in his mythopoesis, and if all of his thematic presentations are mediations of the same conflict, then it seems reasonable that Blake's myth would seek to dissolve gender distinctions. Identity is generally determined in Western culture by a sex-oriented paradigm. Identity rendered by classification requires division—frequently sexual division. *Milton* implies that we have anthropomorphized each other (the divine human) just as we have anthropomorphized deities. Our mental processes have constructed "male" and "female" concepts. We have then invented sexist languages to complement and codify our dichotomies. Finally, we have become entrapped by our own gender-generated systems. *Milton* emphasizes the ubiquity of the destructive myth of genders and the fallen vision of the male/female dichotomy. *Milton* suggests a radical new way of conceiving identity. *Milton* suggests that the power of the constructed self is neither feminine nor masculine, and the epic casts in poetical terms ideas shared by philosophical writers. Wollstonecraft, for example, writes that "the sexual distinction which men have so warmly insisted upon is arbitrary" (193). In *Appeal*, Hays twice asserts that "the mind is of no sex" (104; 187), and she encourages us to reconsider the "pretentions of the sexes" as a method of identification (291). Even the moderate reformer Edgeworth insists that "woman, as well as man, may be called a bundle of habits" (62).

Of course, we can never achieve the ideal of a genderless existence, a genderless self—even in our imaginations.[20] If sexually determined behaviors are the bases for all power struggles, we may not wish to annihilate them totally or permanently. Positive competition can be productive and yield beneficial results. At the end of *Milton*, the speaker's soul returns to its mortal state, and the Shadow of Delight trembles by the speaker's side. All, it seems, returns to normal. The possibility of genderless selfhood does not seem to be within our grasps. The epic does "tease us out of thought," and it requires us to sustain "a willing suspension of disbelief." Nonetheless, *Milton* urges us to consider, even if momentarily, the gendered self in new ways that are bound to liberate our culturally bound perspectives. The discovery of how pervasive and powerful gendered dualisms really are may be the most that *Milton* should accomplish.[21]

If *Milton* implies that the gendered self is a concept that we have created and then become trapped by, *Jerusalem* shows us the redemption of sexual bifurcations. In Chapters 3 and 4, we perceive selfhood as a unified whole, not torn by divisions and gender-generated conflicts. With

Los, we learn that the Urizenic way of thinking—our perceptions about gendered selfhood—can be corrected. Correction is initiated with imagination, however, and not with reason. Los admonishes the Divine Family against war-like behavior and the pride of gendered selfhood. In the state of gendered selfhood, Los reminds them, they are nothing; they are diseased by rational philosophical thought.

In Chapter 1 of *Jerusalem*, we encounter the now familiar domestic strifes that emanate from sexual divisions. These family struggles are soon blown into full-scale war with a number of parallel conflicts raging. "Laws of Moral Virtue" (E. 147; 4:31) rule these relationships, and Humanity (what annihilated selfhood had achieved in *Milton*) is a dying concept, almost swept over by the victory of "war & princedom" (E. 147; 4:32). Punishment reigns over forgiveness, and wrath rules pity. Cambel and Gwendolen busily weave the webs of war and religion (powerful institutions of patriarchy). The wheels of science "with cogs tyrannic / Moving by compulsion each other" (E. 159; 15:18–19) grind away. A pretence of love veils its destruction—"false / And Generating Love" (E. 161; 17:25–26). Los, on the other hand, resolves to build Golgonooza, to "Create a System, or be enslav'd by another Mans" (E. 153; 10:20). In this world of gendered dualities, "All Love is lost! terror succeeds & Hatred instead of Love / And stern demands of Right & Duty instead of Liberty" (E. 167; 22:10–11). Divine Vision (Jerusalem) is hidden and veiled. It is Divine Vision that can see beyond sexual dichotomies, Female Will, and gender-based war, if she can be liberated. Like Ololon, Jerusalem is willing to annihilate her self to remove the "Veil of Moral Virtue, woven for Cruel Laws" (E. 168; 23:22).

The prevailing ideological doctrine of gendered behaviors underlies all conflicts in Chapter 2 of *Jerusalem*. Albion assumes the role of judge and punisher; Eden becomes envied horror and jealousy. Los laments female power over men: "What may Man be? who can tell! but what may Woman be? / To have power over Man from Cradle to corruptible Grave. / There is a Throne in every Man, it is the Throne of God / This Woman has claimd as her own & Man is no more!" (E. 176; 30:25–28). Los reasons that the God-given privilege of man is being unfairly challenged. Gendered selfhood breeds distrust and competition. These sexual divisions clearly exist as unharmonious relationships rather than as complementary pairs. But is not sexuality merely a distinction of sensory perception? Los rationalizes: "If Perceptive Organs vary: Objects of Perception seem to vary" (E. 177; 30:55). His eyes "became what they beheld" (E. 177; 30:54). His vision is shaped by a philosophy that privileges one sex over the other. About the creation of a Female Will, Los remarks to Albion: "Consider Sexual Organization & hide thee in the dust" (E. 177; 30:58). Through Los's eyes, we perceive that sex dichotomies exist because we are conditioned to see them: "What seems to Be: Is" (E. 179; 32:51).

Los comes to recognize the error of his vision. In selfhood, the Divine family remains diseased. Their selfhood must be annihilated and thus redeemed: "That Man may be purified by the death of thy delusions" (E. 195; 45:66). But Los's furnaces are in ruin, and the Divine Family is not yet ready to annihilate selfhood. As terrible separations continually occur, they seek refuge from the wrath of Albion's iron law. In response to patriarchal tyranny, the Daughters of Albion assert female power over man in Chapter 3. Los despairs at man's fall to woman and moans that women who delight in such power "tremble at the light therefore: hiding fearful / The Divine Vision with Curtain & Veil and fleshly Tabernacle" (E. 206; 56:39–40). Their femaleness is their power base, and they do not want the delusion corrected. Los wails: "O Albion why didst thou a Female Will Create" (E. 206; 56:43). It should be obvious by now that no character creates a Female Will; it is a condition that is a result of sexual divisions. It is a condition that seeks to counterbalance the oppressive, tyrannical patriarchy. It is "created" by our own perceptions and acceptances of gender-generated concepts.

This assertion of destructive female power differs from the linguistic construction of self that Oothoon tries to advance in *Visions of the Daughters of Albion*. In Chapter 3 of *Jerusalem*, feminine power is merely an appropriation of the tyranny inflicted by the dominant male gender as its own. As long as characters are "locked in" to the doctrine of gender dualism, the exchange of power can pass between male and female, but the combative, destructive relationship survives. At the end of Chapter 3, Los begins to question the ideology upon which gender divisions exist: "What is a Wife & what is a Harlot? What is a Church & What / Is a Theatre? are they Two & not One? can they Exist Separate? / Are not Religion & Politics the Same Thing?" (E. 207; 57:8–10). Los could have just as easily have asked: Are not male and female one? Los's interrogatives conceptually echo those of Oothoon when, in *Visions*, she questions the label that signifies her as whore.

Just as both Milton and Ooloon must annihilate selfhood in *Milton* to discover their de-gendered selves, so must Los and the Daughters of

Albion learn to see the delusion of the myth of genders. Coming before Los as one, the Daughters cry: "The Human is but a Worm, & Thou O Male: Thou art / Thyself Female, a Male: a breeder of Seed: a Son & Husband: & Lo. / The Human Divine is Womans Shadow" (E. 215; 64:12–14). Pejorative language traditionally leveled at women is here turned around and leveled at men. The Daughters remind Los that he is, after all, "Woman-born / And Woman-nourishd & Woman-educated & Woman-scorn'd" (E. 215; 64:16–17). The sexually charged language further alienates males and females. The Daughters have merely taken on the "masculine" impulse to separate, to divide, to dominate. These gender inversions, taken to extreme, illustrate the artificiality of gendered dualisms. The gendered dualisms in which the Daughters are conceptually entrapped reflect and reproduce patriarchal relations.

The Daughters of Albion then unite in Rahab and Tirzah and form a Double Female. They "Wove a Male, they divided / Into a Female to the Woven Male" (E. 220; 67:9–10). Having woven this male, they circumscribe the brain. The male becomes reason, doubt, and despair. In essence, they recreate the myth of genders and its bondage. The myth is likened to disease: "Then all the Males combined into One Male & every one / Became a ravening eating Cancer growing in the Female" (E. 223; 69:1–2). The Daughters draw the free loves of Jerusalem into "infernal bondage" (E. 223; 69:9), and "they refuse liberty to the male" (E. 223; 69:14). Under this system, jealousy becomes murderous, and religion is chastity, "forming a Commerce to sell Loves / With Moral Law" (E. 223; 69:34–35). The Daughters can, it seems, pervert sexual activity under the guise of moral law as artfully as Albion. Repeatedly in *Jerusalem*, we are reminded that all dualisms have their origins in the basic male/female dichotomy and that dualisms necessarily involve hierarchies.

The system appropriated by the Daughters forces the male to be "severe & cruel filled with stern revenge" (E. 223; 69:36). In their system, "Mutual Hate returns & mutual Deceit & mutual Fear" (E. 223; 69:37). Feminine power is thus a "Brooding Abstract Philosophy to destroy Imagination, the Divine / Humanity" (E. 224; 70:19–20). *Jerusalem* demonstrates in recapitulated frames of male/female conflict that substituting feminine power for masculine power does not redeem humanity; it destroys the Divine Imagination. Chapter 3 of *Jerusalem* shows us how this erroneous system evolves and then becomes thoroughly ingrained in our cultural consciousness. The self is so thoroughly grounded in gender that we do not recognize it. Chapter 3 also reveals that the substitution of feminine hegemony for masculine hegemony is not a viable alternative to the confrontations emanating from gender dualisms.

In Chapter 4 of *Jerusalem*, battles for dominance precede the annihilation and redemption of selfhood. Gwendolen and Cambel continue to weave falsehood, jealousy, and envy by perpetuating the myth of gender division. Their allegory maintains that in "Beulah the Feminine / Emanations Create Space. the Masculine Create Time, & plant / The Seeds of beauty in the Space" (E. 243; 85:7–9). When Los attempts to instruct Enitharmon in the doctrine of gender division, she rebels. Los's Spectre delights in the ensuing domestic strife—the masculine and feminine separations. He laughs: "The Man who respects Woman shall be despised by Woman" (E. 247; 88:37). He recapitulates the genesis of the Female Will, and his story fuels the cycle of hate and power: "Continually building, continually destroying in Family feuds / While you are under the dominion of a jealous Female / Unpermanent for ever because love & jealousy" (E. 247; 88:40–42). This mythical allegory promises that as long as there exist the divisions of male and female, love and wrath will likewise exist. Although Los strikes the Spectre with his hammer, the delusions continue. The Double Female appears in the Tabernacle: "Religion Hid in War, a Dragon red & hidden Harlot / Each within other" (E. 249; 89:52–53). The double female becomes "One with the Antichrist & are absorbed in him" (E. 249; 89:62). Repeated within this theological context, the cycle of gender division begins anew: "The Feminine separates from the Masculine & both from Man, / Ceasing to be His Emanations, Life to Themselves assuming!" (E. 249; 90:1–2). The female no longer wants to be an extension of the male, a part of his being; she wants to be independent, a self-entity, and she wants to exercise a power that is not male-defined but female-defined. This division means that "no more the Masculine mingles / With the Feminine, but the Sublime is shut out from the Pathos / In howling torment, to build stone walls of separation, compelling / The Pathos to weave curtains of hiding secresy from the torment" (E. 249; 90:10–13). As we have seen in *The Four Zoas* and in *Milton*, replacing the male hegemony with a female hegemony is not a cure; it succeeds only in reversing the role of those who inflict the curse. Genders continue to define and delimit self. The Divine Imagination remains veiled.

Los finally perceives the folly of the gender doctrine. He realizes the cycle of hatred and destruction will continue unless it is broken at its ideological foundation. He cries: "Sexes must vanish & cease / To be" (E. 252; 92:13–14). Unity, not division, is their salvation. Annihilating selfhood means annihilating gender, and all the delusions and dualities it creates. Unity existed before the fallen vision of gender dichotomies. Los now recalls the times of old before "Two Wills they had; Two Intellects" (E. 245; 86:61). Jerusalem repeats Los's insight: "O Vala! Humanity is far above / Sexual organization" (E. 236; 79:73–74). Jerusalem demonstrates that they can achieve the unity with which they were once blessed. This unity, however, is a unity of multiplicities, not a unity of dualities, for the possibilities of selfhood are infinite. Los deconstructs the allegory that had held them in bondage: "When the Individual appropriates Universality / He divides into Male & Female: & when the Male & Female, / Appropriates Individuality, they become an Eternal Death" (E. 250; 90:52–54). They have, Los now realizes, been "Hermaphroditic worshippers of a God of cruelty & law" (E. 250; 90:55). They have been victims of their own system of gender dualism.

Milton implies the fallen vision of sexual dichotomies that *Jerusalem* explicitly illustrates and corrects. Just as Reasoning Power with its "Laws & Moralities" (E. 229; 74:12) destroys the Imagination and lead the "Divine Body, by Martyrdoms & Wars" (E. 229; 74:13), so the concept of dual genders generates destructive powers and entraps the Divine Imagination. To redeem ourselves from this system, we must, like Ololon, Milton, Los, and the Daughters of Albion, put off Selfhood, or gender, and work with—not against—Humanity as a genderless Divine being. Of course, a de-gendered selfhood obviates gender-generated conflicts and language. Like *Milton, Jerusalem* presents the process of gender separation and proposes dissolution of the gendered self. Unlike Blake's previous poems, however, *Jerusalem* concludes with the hope of a de-gendered self.[22] The epic demonstrates that the human imagination is capable of both; we have to see with our imaginations beyond culturally created descriptive and doctrinal blinders.

At the level of literary ideology, Blake's poetry inscribes gender issues which preoccupy the philosophical discourse of the late eighteenth century and early nineteenth century and which anticipate the interdisciplinary topoi of contemporary criticism. Blake has been dutifully recognized as a revolutionary thinker—one who was a product of his time but refused to be bound by it. Some degree of reform was encouraged by most of Blake's contemporaries. Although Rousseau's fictitious tutor warns Emile that "the revolution most to be feared belongs to the age over which [they] are now keeping watch" (432), Rousseau acknowledges that maladroit French institutions have made women dissembling (430). Equity between the sexes, Hays claims, involves many public and political, private and domestic concerns; "in its progress new points of view must open" (100). Only Blake's poetry considers a radical, imaginative direction. He refuses to privilege gender, whether masculine or feminine. He resists some kind of symbiotic unity of sexes or androgyny. Instead, he exposes the entire social system from which gender-based arguments emanate as fictitious and false.[23]

While Blake could not foresee the complexities and technologies of the construction of selfhood at the turn of the twentieth century, his mythopoesis does anticipate the conceptual paradigms and interpretative frameworks of our efforts to negotiate and neutralize confrontations generated by gendered roles and behaviors. Because Blake's poems challenge the dualistic mode of thought advanced by Enlightenment thinkers, his poems enable us to see fluid relationships among identity, gender, and ideology. His characters as "states signified" blur gender distinctions that come to be defined and codified during the nineteenth century. His poetry destabilizes the controlled socio-political understandings of gender and selfhood. In the divisions and conflicts of his poems, Blake draws attention to what it means to be gendered. In disrupting the prevailing order of gender relationships, Blake's poetry impels us to recognize the possibilities of a self not defined and delimited by gender. A prophetic poet, Blake points the way toward our creation of the modern and the postmodern self.

Notes

1. As gender is a discursive practice, so "self," claims Roland Barthes, is "an activity of production," *Image—Music—Text*, trans. Stephen Heath (New York: Hill & Wang, 177), 157. Teresa de Lauretis, *Technologies of Gender: Essays on Theory, Film, and Fiction* (Bloomington: Indiana Univ. Press) and Michel Foucault, "Technologies of the Self," in *Technologies of the Self*, ed. Martin H. Luther, Huck Gutman, and Patrick H. Hutton (Amherst: Univ. of Massachusetts Press, 1988) articulate in theoretical terms what Blake depicts in poetical forms: a gendered self is the product and the process of a number of social technologies.

2. For recent discussions about the masculine paradigm in Western thought, see for example, Jean Grimshaw, *Philosophy and Feminist Thinking* (Minneapolis: Univ. of Minnesota Press, 1986), and Moira Gatens, *Feminism and Philosophy: Perspectives on Difference and Equality* (Bloomington: Indiana Univ. Press, 1991).

3. I am indebted to anthropological work which has explored the issues of gender and subjectivity. It is not crucial, argues Nancy Chodorow, for us to maintain a stable sexual identity; see "Being and Doing: A Cross-Cultural Examination of the Socialization of Males and Females," in *Women in Sexist Society: Studies in Power and Powerlessness*, ed. Vivian Gornick and Barbara K. Moran (New York: Basic Books, 1971), 193.

4. I am referring to the discursive polemics generated by cultural and gender studies that, like Blake's mythopoesis, seek to unsettle our understanding of gender in binary terms. For example, in *"Am I That Name?" Feminism and the Category of "Women" in History* (Minneapolis: Univ. of Minnesota Press, 1988), Denise Riley demonstrates the unstable nature of "women," a category that is historically constructed. In *Gender Trouble: Feminism and the Subversion of Identity* (New York: Routledge, 1990), Judith Butler argues that the construct called "sex" is as culturally constructed as gender, a shifting and contextual phenomenon. Gender is performative, constituting the identity it is purported to be. Gender is doing rather than being, a fluid activity. Butler contends that because the category of "sex" is itself a gendered category, there is no distinction between sex and gender.

5. Blake's portrayal and treatment of female characters has been variously debated during the last two decades. In his psychological study *Symbol and Truth in Blake's Myth* (Princeton: Princeton Univ. Press, 1980), Leopold Damrosch, Jr., maintains that Blake's female emanations operate as "emotional storm center[s]" (181) and that they are treated by Blake in three distinct ways (181–90). In his Marxist study *The Social Vision of William Blake* (Princeton: Princeton Univ. Press, 1985), Michael Ferber excuses Blake as a child of his time making use of traditional misogynic symbolism, and he encourages feminists to forgive the disturbing connotations of female imagery in Blake's poetry (89–115). And, in his posthumously published book *Witness Against the Beast: William Blake and the Moral Law* (New York: The New Press, 1993), E.P. Thompson clearly acknowledges that Blake employed anti-feminine imagery (81).

6. In *Gender and the Politics of History* (New York: Columbia Univ. Press, 1988), Joan Wallach Scott argues that gender identity is constructed through language and that gender is the primary field within which power is articulated. For her discussion of gender as an analytic category, see 28–50.

7. Mary Wollstonecraft, *A Vindication of the Rights of Woman*, ed. Carol H. Poston, 2nd ed. (1792; New York: Norton, 1988), 45. Page numbers of subsequent quotations from this volume will be cited parenthetically in the text.

8. Mary Hays, *Appeal to the Men of Great Britain on the Behalf of Women* (1798; New York: Garland, 1974), 277. Hereafter, the page numbers of passages quoted from this volume will be cited parenthetically in the text.

9. Maria Edgeworth, *Letters for Literary Ladies* (1795; New York: Garland, 1974), 52. Hereafter, the page numbers of passages quoted from this volume will be cited parenthetically in the text.

10. Elizabeth Langland has encouraged us (much as Blake does) to question the ways meaning has been foreclosed within a critical tradition and to remain receptive to alternative possible readings that expose patriarchal (i.e., gender) bias. See "Blake's Feminist Revision of Literary Tradition in 'The SICK ROSE'" in *Critical Paths:*

Blake and the Argument of Method, ed. Dan Miller, Mark Bracher, and Donald Ault (Durham, NC: Duke Univ. Press, 1987), 231–43.

11. Following David V. Erdman's *Blake: Prophet Against Empire: A Poet's Interpretation of the History of His Own Times*, rev. ed. (Princeton: Princeton Univ. Press, 1969), a number of critics have explored political issues inscribed in Blake's poetry. Jon Mee argues, for example, that Blake represents sexual liberation as part of the political liberation associated with the revolutions in America and Europe. See *Dangerous Enthusiasm: William Blake and the Culture of Radicalism in the 1790's* (Oxford: Clarendon, 1992), 129–145.

12. All quotations from Blake will be cited from *The Complete Poetry and Prose of William Blake*, ed. David V. Erdman (New York: Doubleday, 1982), noted parenthetically as E.

13. Jean-Jacques Rousseau, *Emile or On Education*, trans. Allan Bloom (1762; New York: Basic Books, 1979), 358. Hereafter, the page numbers of passages quoted from this volume will be cited parenthetically in the text.

14. Paul A. Cantor points out that the sexual attraction of Los and Enitharmon provides the first movement of unity in *The Book of Urizen*. The sexual union of male and female produces, however, merely another male *or* female, not the androgynous being that the myth would seem to dictate. See *Creature and Creator: Myth-making and English Romanticism* (Cambridge: Cambridge Univ. Press, 1984), 52. I argue that in a fallen world—in a world of gendered selfhood—the cycle of sexual regeneration will continue.

15. Stephen C. Behrendt argues that Blake neither condemns nor criticizes Thel; rather, he portrays in her "unnatural" learned resistance to her "natural" sexual impulses. See *Reading William Blake* (New York: St. Martin's Press, 1992), 74–84.

16. Patricia Yaeger notes in *Honey-Mad Women: Emancipatory Strategies in Women's Writing* (New York: Columbia UP, 1988) that Theotormon and Bromion refuse (by their silence) to recognize Oothoon's power of self-definition. To be controlled by a woman's body of speech is frightening for Theotormon and Bromion, for it portends the loss of masculine boundaries (159).

17. Oothoon as a revolutionary agent is problematic. According to Thomas A. Vogler, *Visions* emphasizes the futility rather than the power of Oothoon's utterance of political and sexual liberation. See "'in vain the Eloquent tongue': An Un-reading of *VISIONS of the Daughters of Albion*," in *Critical Paths: Blake and the Argument of Method*, ed. Dan Miller, Mark Bracher, and Donald Ault (Durham, NC: Duke Univ. Press, 1987), 279.

18. James King points out in *William Blake: His Life* (New York: St. Martin's, 1991) that the discord between men and women in *The Four Zoas* is not resolved, an indication that Blake was not sure how to bridge the gulf separating the sexes; see 124–28. While I agree with King that "the separation into male and female remains for Blake *the* metaphor for the fragmented nature of life" (128), I argue that rather than bridge the gap dividing the sexes, Blake simply eliminates the social constructions which rendered the division.

19. A number of important studies focusing on the problematic female in Blake's poetry have encouraged a reassessment of Ololon. See Susan Fox, "The Female as Metaphor in William Blake's Poetry," *Critical Inquiry* 30:3 (1977): 507–19; Anne

K. Mellor, "Blake's Portrayal of Women," *Blake/An Illustrated Quarterly* 16:3 (1982–83): 148–55.

20. In "The Road of Excess: My William Blake," Alicia Ostriker admits that while she cannot "imagine the world non-dualistically," she is working on it (78). Susan Morgan has argued in connection with nineteenth-century fiction that since gender is the product of the human imagination, it can be re-imagined, *Sisters in Time: Imagining Gender in Nineteenth-Century British Fiction* (New York: Oxford Univ. Press, 1989), 13.

21. In "Women's Time," trans. by Alice Jardine and Harry Blake, *Signs* 7:1 (1981): 13–35, Julia Kristeva asserts that the "de-dramatization" of the battle of the sexes lies not in reconciliation but in a recognition of each person's multiple identifications.

22. About the fallen state of gender redeemed into de-gendered selfhood in *Jerusalem*, see Thomas R. Frosch, *The Awakening of Albion: The Renovation of the Body in the Poetry of William Blake* (Ithaca: Cornell UP, 1974), 159–77.

23. Eleanor Wilner notes that visionary imagination is rarely embraced during its lifetime. The crisis that produced Blake's vision was not yet society's; he became aware of contradictions in a system long before those contradictions, through their historical consequences, were to become apparent to society. See *Gathering the Winds: Visionary Imagination and Radical Transformation of Self and Society* (Baltimore: Johns Hopkins Univ. Press, 1975), 47–8.

Modern Identity in a Postmodern World

The Postmodern Self: "Decentered," "Shattered," "Autonomous," or What? A Study of Theoretical Texts by Deleuze and Guattari, Glass, Kohut, and Meyers
by Carole J. Lambert

> The oddity of postmodern thought is that it has clung to a liberal image of negative freedom even while deconstructing the self who could embody that freedom.[1]

The theoretical concept of the "decentered" self, as posited by Gilles Deleuze and Félix Guattari in *Anti-Oedipus, Capitalism and Schizophrenia*, represents one aspect of postmodern thought. Countering this model of the "desiring machine" is the research of James M. Glass in *Private Terror/Public Life, Psychosis and the Politics of Community* and *Shattered Selves, Multiple Personality in a Postmodern World*. Working with psychiatrists, psychotherapists, and survivors of psychological trauma, he demonstrates the real suffering of persons clinically diagnosed as "decentered" selves—those experiencing schizophrenia and multiple personality disorder. Glass advocates the necessity of a centered self that can make responsible choices about the discourses surrounding it. His position is supported by Heinz Kohut's theory of the self in *The Restoration of the Self* and Diana Meyers's advocacy of autonomy in *Self, Society, and Personal Choice*. Deleuze and Guattari, Glass, Kohut, and Meyers all have the same goal: personal, individual freedom of the self. The problem is how to arrive at this liberation—through wandering away from community (Deleuze and Guattari), through a Rousseauian integration into community (Glass), through psychotherapy (Kohut), or through the practice of "autonomy competency" (Meyers). This essay will explore the strengths and weaknesses of each theoretician's position and will emphasize the need for interdisciplinary dialogue about diverse approaches to the self.

Theories of the self need to be analyzed juxtaposed to each other and across the disciplines because adherence to any one perspective on the self can result in a dangerous tunnel vision that ignores the approach's weaknesses and overemphasizes its strengths. "The oddity of postmodern thought" which John McGowan has highlighted—"it has clung to a liberal image of negative freedom even while deconstructing the self who could embody that freedom"—exemplifies such tunnel vision. The outcome of my examination of only four perspectives illustrative of the diverse voices now speaking about the self favors a centered self, in touch with both its own authentic desires, if such authenticity is possible, and the social constructions of reality in which it lives and about which it thinks. The decentered self is an interesting theoretical construct but does not seem to be viable for persons required to live in community with others; truly decentered selves, those fractured by mental illness, lose their personal, autonomous freedom which thus defeats the goal posited for such a self.

Deleuze and Guattari's *Anti-Oedipus, Capitalism and Schizophrenia*

Gilles Deleuze, educated in philosophy, and Félix Guattari, a practicing psychoanalyst,[2] propose a release of desire from the unconscious, a freeing of the "schizzes." They express anger and frustration because of the power psychiatrists and psychoanalysts exert over their patients through the use of the Freudian paradigm. Deleuze and Guattari want persons to become in touch with their real desires, not always to be pleading "daddy-mommy-me."[3] Using technological vocabulary, they describe their approach:

> How can we sum up this entire vital progression? Let us trace it along a first path (the shortest route): the points of disjunction on the body without organs form circles that converge on the desiring-machines; then the subject—produced as a residuum alongside the machine, as an appendix, or as a spare part adjacent to the machine—passes through all the degrees of the circle, and passes from one circle to another. This subject itself is not at the center which is occupied by the machine, but on the periphery, with no fixed identity, forever decentered, *defined* by the states through which it passes (20).

The center is the "desiring machine" not the core of identity. The ego has abandoned the center and is dispersed to the margins, to the "circles that converge on the desiring-machines." There is dynamic movement as the subject "passes from one circle to another." Because of this mobility, there can be no fixed identity for the subject; it becomes defined by the circles it traverses.

The "desiring machine" is the unconscious set free from cultural conditioning. Deleuze and Guattari explain the difference between their "schizoanalysis" and psychoanalysis: "Schizoanalysis attains a nonfigurative and nonsymbolic unconscious, a pure abstract figural dimension ('abstract' in the sense of abstract painting), flows-schizzes of real-desire, apprehended below the minimum conditions of identity" (351). The ideal for this decentered subject is "*orphans* (no daddy-mommy-me), *atheists* (no beliefs), and *nomads* (no habits, no territories)" (xxi). Paradoxically, this revolutionary figure strongly resembles the hero of modernism—he who is liberated from all ties to women, family, religion, nation, and culture, Stephen Dedalus par excellence. Yet Deleuze and Guattari would eschew the modern hero in favor of the postmodern "desiring machine." The somber nostalgia that the modern hero experienced for all that he had left behind is replaced by technological "play"—in both the sense of the immediacy of children's play and the play of smoothly running machines.

Deleuze and Guattari's paradigm is intended to precipitate the healing of those driven mad by capitalism. Their "schizoanalytic approach" will forge a new subjectivity—"anti-Oedipus" (xxii–xxiii). Anti-Oedipus is not the same as Stephen Dedalus because he is perpetually in motion with no synthesizing psychological stability. Deleuze and Guattari explain: "I am God I am not God, I am God I am man: it is not a matter of synthesis that would go beyond the negative disjunctions of the derived reality, in an original reality of Man-God, but rather of inclusive disjunction that carries out the synthesis itself in drifting from one term to another and following the distance between terms. Nothing is primal" (77).

In keeping with postmodern suspicion of origins and a stable truth, they want to destroy original signifiers—the signifieds of God and Freudianism—so that their decentered subject can flow around its psychological circumference. "Schizoanalysis proposes to reach those regions of the orphan unconscious—indeed 'beyond the law'—where the problems of Oedipus can no longer even be raised" (81–82).

Capitalism "sets in motion schizo-flows that animate 'our' arts and 'our' sciences, just as they congeal into the production of 'our own' sick, the schizophrenics" (245). Capitalism would seem to be a positive force if it "sets in motion schizo-flows" since Deleuze and Guattari want a freeing of the "schizzes." However, capitalism does this only to provide a limit to the flow; schizophrenia represents the farthest limit of capitalism, yet capitalism survives only by inhibiting the free flow of desire: "Capitalism therefore liberates the flows of desire, but under the social conditions that define its limit and the possibility of its own dissolution, so that it is constantly opposing with all its exasperated strength the movement that drives it toward this limit. At capitalism's limit the deterritorialized socius gives way to the body without organs, and the decoded flows throw themselves into desiring-production" (139–140).

Capitalism "axiomatizes with one hand what it decodes with the other" (246). Anti-Oedipus or "the desiring machine" exceeds the boundaries of capitalism and must be repressed, restrained, and confined.

Schizoanalysis begins then with "discovering in a subject the nature, the formation, or the functioning of *his* desiring-machines, independently of any interpretations" (322). For the "desiring-machine" to be liberated, capitalism must change so that it will stop preventing the "schizo-flows." Deleuze and Guattari outline a radical program that could bring about their utopia:

> A true politics of psychiatry, or antipsychiatry, would consist therefore in the following praxis: (1) undoing all the reterritorializations that transform madness into mental illness; (2) liberating the schizoid movement of deterritorialization in all flows, in such a way that this characteristic can no longer qualify a particular residue as a flow of madness, but affects just as well the flows of labor and desire, of production, knowledge, and creation in their most profound tendency. Here, madness would no longer exist as madness not because it would have been transformed into "mental illness," but on the contrary because it would receive the support of all the other flows, including science and art—once it is said that madness is called madness and appears as such only because it is deprived of this support, and finds itself reduced to testifying all alone for deterritorialization as a universal process. It is only its unwarranted privilege, a privilege beyond its capacities, that renders it mad. In this perspective Foucault announced an age when madness would disappear, not because it would be lodged within the controlled space of mental illness ("great tepid aquariums"), but on the contrary because the exterior limit designated by madness would be overcome by means of other flows escaping control on all sides, and carrying us along (321).

Thus, all aspects of culture need to be liberated so that there is no limit to the "flow of madness;" the "flows of labor and desire, of production, knowledge, and creation in their most profound tendency" would create an environment where all desires would be acceptable. The "reterritorializations" of capitalism and classical psychiatry would no longer exist; the flow of "schizzes" would not be reversed. The "social machine" (255) must give way to the "desiring machine."

Lacking in *Anti-Oedipus* are specific case histories or even literary examples of schizophrenics who have been liberated by the freeing of their "schizzes." Deleuze and Guattari struggle with the same question that tormented Rousseau: how can the desiring individual live out his or her desires in community with other desiring individuals also living out their desires? Their utopian vision would allow persons in all fields to fulfill their wants. The vision may seem to be postmodern, but the craving behind it can be traced to Enlightenment origins. If Deleuze and Guattari sketched out their vision in more detail, they would end up with a community of desiring schizophrenics no doubt finding difficulty living in proximity to each other. Rousseau at least filled in the details of his utopia in *On Social Contract*, and Glass shows actual contemporary communities of decentered selves.

Glass's *Private Terror/Public Life, Psychosis and the Politics of Community* and *Shattered Selves, Multiple Personality in a Postmodern World*

James M. Glass is aware of the Rousseauian dilemma about desire, but he advocates the limitation of desire for the sake of community: "Further, the utterance of the mad (or, better, the psychically homeless) may be considered Rousseauian in the sense that it is the language of the heart (the self unmediated by social forms), a linguistic place that constitutes a view or commentary on the structures of civil society and its values. For the seriously mentally ill to attain, much less establish, a faith in community is a transformation as compelling as for Rousseau's natural man to leave nature for the moral benefits and interdependencies of political association."[4] Glass's "psychically homeless," "the self unmediated by social forms," sounds like Deleuze and Guattari's "desiring machine," but it is not the same, for Glass's "mad" function out of a "linguistic place," not the "nonfigurative and nonsymbolic unconscious...below the minimum conditions of identity."[5] A "linguistic place" is highly symbolic, capable of "commentary on the structures of civil society and its values." Yet Deleuze and Guattari's "desiring machine" also is capable of commentary, in their case negative commentary on the capitalism which drives its subjects to madness. Their commentary would have to be derived from the "decentered self" located in the "circles" surrounding the "nonfigurative and nonsymbolic unconscious."

Glass rejects the idea of capitalistic society undergoing transformation into a utopian state where all will have their wishes met. As a professor of political science and a researcher at the Sheppard and Enoch Pratt Hospital in Towson, Maryland (*Private Terror*, xi), his stance is grounded on his experience of working with the mentally ill, those suffering in real life "decentered selves" because of schizophrenia and multiple personality disorder.

These persons live in worlds of their own creation, but the capitalistic society or real world they inhabit does not cooperate with their visions of reality. Critical of Deleuze and Guattari's theory, Glass affirms that "to couch the argument only in terms of ideology is to obscure and minimize the very real suffering of persons with mental illness" (*Private Terror*, 214). The "decentered self" in reality is frightening, not freeing. The delusion or psychotic state is not a pleasant utopia of unleashed desires but one where the normal symbols of fantasy and dream become, from the perspective of the deluded, concrete realities (*Private Terror*, 15). "In dissolving boundaries, psychosis (in Lacan's terms) made the Imaginary into the Real. It abolished fixed, external points of reference and led to a mammoth confusion over the relation between identity and reality" (*Private Terror*, 34). Thus, a non-psychotic's dream images become, for the psychotic, real settings peopled by real creatures from which he or she cannot escape.

Glass argues that delusions serve to preserve the wounded self's integrity from total shattering. His "wounded self," shaken in its core identity, could be equated with Deleuze and Guattari's mobile self traversing its "circles," no longer occupying its center, the center being the place of the "nonfigurative and nonsymbolic unconscious." Glass describes the results of the wounded self's delusions: "Delusion's elaborate inner scenarios destroyed the human foundations of action: its seeming perfection protected the self from acknowledging deep-seated feelings of worthlessness and badness" (*Private Terror*, 52). Deleuze and Guattari could respond that those "feelings of worthlessness and badness" need to be "scoured": "Destroy, destroy. The task of schizoanalysis goes by way of destruction—a whole scouring of the unconscious, a complete curettage. Destroy Oedipus, the illusion of the ego, the puppet of the superego, guilt, the law, castration" (311). Such severe action, however it could be accomplished, would doubtlessly remove the schizophrenic's feelings of "worthlessness and badness," but one wonders if any feelings at all would remain.

Deleuze and Guattari's strong stance makes one question what indeed is reality and who gets to define it. Glass affirms that "delusion is an attack on ideals, cultures, histories, and, most important, on consensually validated patterns of meaning" (*Private Terror*, 16). The French theoreticians would probably agree with Glass, but would further assert that such attacks need to be made on a society dominated by capitalism. They propose that the creators of reality are mad, and that the mad are actually sane. Glass describes the schizophrenic state: "both cognition and emotional structure have disintegrated, the structures of civil society have been assimilated into a delusional logic or system" (*Private Terror*, 57). Anti-Oedipus would need to undergo this disintegration but would remain unsupported in his or her delusions as long as society remained unchanged. That is why Deleuze and Guattari must advocate a breakdown in society. They critique all systems that proclaim an original truth—Freudianism, capitalism, religion—which thus empowers these systems to structure reality. Given that society, at least in the near future, will not change in order to accommodate the delusions of the schizophrenic, the current end result of schizophrenia is extreme isolation from others. "Delusions lack any empathic capacity; their function lies in fragmenting, isolating, destroying, and dominating" (*Private Terror*, 122).

Both Deleuze and Guattari's thesis and Glass's research focus on the problem of identity. Theories of so-called normal psychological growth, such as Eric Erikson's, describe the development of identity in the context of one's family, country, age group, race, gender, social class, and other givens. The invasion of delusion reshapes the contexts that have been called realities. "Delusional time and space replace the self's rootedness and identity in interpersonal and social situations; the result is a loss of the self's public being, a reversion to private knowledge systems, and most important, a complete loss of the sense of community" (*Private Terror*, 212). Deleuze and Guattari's orphans, atheists, and nomads would seem to have to suffer from their alienation from community, not rejoice in their total liberation. If all members of a community became like them, there would be no community, only wanderers, unless some new type of community for wanderers could be imagined.

Glass's mentally ill also long for psychic liberation: "Further, to be free psychically becomes from the patient's perspective a vital, social good, since the psychically displaced find themselves afflicted and dominated by knowledge that maintains the self in varying degrees of unfreedom, knowledge that imprisons and victimizes through the imposition of pain" (*Private Terror*, 4). This knowledge is not forced upon the patient by others but rather resides in the troubled mind, out of the sufferer's conscious control. Glass describes such a tormented self:

> Neither fully delusional nor integrated in community, the self moves back and forth; it feels lost, out of control, ineffectual, and terribly confused. Lacking the certainty of any firm belief structures but not so psychotic that consciousness has been completely absorbed by delusion, the self searches for moorings and familiarity. Delusion fails to provide any comprehensive or detailed epistemological direction. While inwardly the self experiences despair and hopelessness, its outward appearance may seem organized or together. It is a state of mind and being characteristic of borderline psychological states (*Private Terror*, 127).

This "borderline" self is on the verge of retreating fully into its private self away from public interaction that would serve to help it maintain contact with external reality.

Glass acknowledges the importance of "poetry and metaphor ask[ing] disturbing questions of reason" (*Private Terror*, 20). He continues, "The poet argues that passion—or, in Lacan's word, desire—is stronger than artifice or reason;" the French theoreticians' focus on desire is almost poetic. However, the outcome of this emphasis negates reason as a factor necessary for balancing desire. Glass states, "Deleuze and Guattari's use of the schizophrenic's experiences as a kind of revolutionary model misses entirely the terrible psychological costs of a fragmented existence: a severing of the self's connection to any known and recognizable consensual reality and existence in delusional space in which otherness appears in the nihilistic wanderings of delusional action."[6] Without the counterweight of reason, their desire driven utopia becomes dystopia.

A decentered self, the desiring machine, has no stable personal narrative. It is exposed to multiple narratives in its surrounding world. It is the nexus of varied, continual, floating discourses, yet it is not controlled by any one paradigmatic discourse, including its own life narrative. Abstractly, such a self can be imagined. In reality, the human being formed by these floating discourses becomes an identityless response to all that surrounds him or her.

Identityless responses are extremely vulnerable to manipulation by external others. The loudest or most predominant discourse can end up controlling the decentered self. Developmental psychologists such as Erikson generally posit adolescence and young adulthood as the time for the crucial stage of growth that results in the breaking away from surrounding important others, usually the parents, in order to establish adult identity. The decentered self risks existing as a pre-adolescent, subjected to others' discourses for a lifetime, unable to make sophisticated decisions or perform complex, creative acts since this self's faculties would be controlled by others' external discourses tracing through it.

A real decentered self would talk in fragments and perform incomplete activities. The controlling center that provides rationality in language and judgment in action would be missing. Glass summarizes, "If anything, the postmodern self is a naive, malleable self, incapable of reflecting anything other than social/ideological/cultural impositions, a self constituted only by practices and power" (*Shattered Selves*, 25). The desiring machine is virtually helpless if those in charge of the surrounding discourses are unable or unwilling to fulfill its desires.

Glass believes that for someone suffering from multiple personality disorder, desire itself can only be recovered through a consolidation of the compartmentalized personalities, that is, those selves which each proclaim his or her own narrative (*Shattered Selves*, 72). Thus in multiple personality disorder, one experiences a moving from one discourse to another, each calling itself a true self, and desire, which requires some kind of personal unification, is impossible, for within this fragmented self are selves, each with his or her own desires, and sometimes with a desire that conflicts with that of another self.

Glass continues, "The postmodern critic or philosopher, in focusing primarily on texts and not survivors or victims, creates a highly intellectualized self, a textualized self, a self made up of letters and words, not feelings and psychological fractures" (*Shattered Selves*, 26). The freedom sought by Deleuze and Guattari, the choice to reject psychoanalytic theory and social conventions, can best be attained by an integrated self in touch with its own history and fully responsible for its choices, not by a self momentarily dictated by this or that discourse. A key issue then is who controls the self? A strong self with a history that can clearly be narrated, has, after all, been created by the discourses surrounding her or him. Michel Foucault "argues that the self is not an objective reality to be described by our theories but a subjective notion that is actually constituted by them. The self is an abstract construction, one continually being redesigned in an ongoing discourse generated by the imperatives of the policing process."[7] Society generates theories of the self which become powerful. Yet, how can the self defend itself from the power of these theories unless it has the maturity and self-development to sort these theories out? The overall goal of postmodernism is to deconstruct the "metanarratives" which have controlled knowledge in the past. A Freudian narrative is targeted by Deleuze and Guattari, but their theory of the desiring machine evolves out of their education, particularly their formation in Freudianism. They themselves are centered selves rationally positing the freedom of the decentered self. A truly decentered self would not be able to think and speak with their sophistication. Glass summarizes his stance toward the postmodern decentered self: "One can live with a healthy postmodern skepticism toward truth, absolutes, causality, and rationality yet at the same time acknowledge and recognize how critical a core sense of self is to the project of life itself" (*Shattered Selves*, 13).

Kohut's *The Restoration of the Self*

In *The Restoration of the Self*, Heinz Kohut, a Viennese-trained psychoanalyst and neurologist who practiced and taught at the University of Chicago, posits a theory of the self for the twentieth century which he believes is more fundamental and relevant to this age than the Freudian paradigm used to treat structural neuroses and other similarly constructed psychological phenomena.[8] He believes that "from the beginning, the drive experience is subordinated to the child's experience of the relation between the self and the self-objects" (80). He maintains that one is born with a basically healthy self and that the Oedipus complex is an outgrowth of damage to this self. Mental illness is the result of a lack of accepting, loving mirroring from one parent and an impossibility of idealizing throughout the stages of growth the other parent. He states, "Defects in the self occur mainly as the result of empathy failures from the side of the self-objects—due to narcissistic disturbances of the self-object" (87).

If there is damage in one area, it may be compensated for by success in another. For example, a patient who had an emotionally unresponsive mother but who was able to share in the idealized power and success of the father will be healthier than a client who was frustrated in both realms. He advocates that unhealthy aggression is the result of a child's normal assertiveness not being welcomed by the parents as appropriate to early stages of growth (116–117). Parents who do not find joy in their children's progress through the various steps of maturity also do harm to their children. "But clinical experience tells us that in the great majority of cases it is the specific pathogenic personality of the parent(s) and specific pathogenic features of the atmosphere in which the child grows up that account for the maldevelopments, fixations, and unsolvable inner conflicts characterizing the adult personality" (187).

His therapy requires a "working through" of the stages of growth where the child's reactions were inappropriately received by parental figures. This working through occurs with the therapist in the transference relationship. Kohut emphasizes the need for empathy, which he defines as "vicarious introspection," in the therapist's reactions to the patient; lack of genuine empathy and care will only cause a repetition of the same originally frustrating situation (90–91). Healthy response to the client's anger or other needs can bring about healing. He describes the steps to be followed in this working through process:

> To put the description of these microstructural changes in the classical transference neuroses into a nutshell: (1) interpretations remove defenses; (2) archaic wishes intrude into the ego; (3) under the repeated impact of the archaic strivings, new structures are formed in the ego which are able to modulate and transform the archaic strivings (discharge delay, neutralization, aim inhibition, substitute gratification, absorption through fantasy formation, etc.). The analysand, in order to keep open the access of the archaic strivings to his ego, despite his anxiety (in the classical transference neuroses; castration anxiety in the face of incestuous libidinal and aggressive strivings), uses the analyst as the self-object—even in the analysis of structural neuroses!—, i.e., as a precursory substitute for the not-yet-existing psychological structures....In brief: through the process of transmuting internalization, new psychological structure is built (32).

Most of Kohut's case studies portray persons suffering from narcissistic personality disorders and experiencing disturbed self-acceptance and fragmentation of the self (94) as manifested in their low self-esteem, disorientation in their surroundings, excessive rage, hypersensitivity to slights, hypochondria, depression, lack of initiative or purpose in life, perversion, delinquency, addictions, or sometimes a feeling of not being connected to their bodies (193). The end result he seeks in his therapy is, indeed, the "restoration of the self" that has been fragmented to some degree because of childhood traumas of abandonment, emotional coldness, or neurosis and even latent psychotic behavior in the parents.

He defines the healthy "nuclear self": "This structure is the basis for our sense of being an independent center of initiative and perception, integrated with our most central ambitions and ideals and with our experience that our body and mind form a unity in space and a continuum in time" (177). To maintain a healthy nuclear self, the adult continues to need both a mirroring of the self in his or her love objects as well as objects or persons to idealize (188). Kohut's "nuclear self" is opposite to Deleuze and Guattari's "decentered self." The healing or restoration of the client's self through interaction with a therapist represents the power relationship that the French theoreticians despise. The focus on the narcissistic wounding of the patient by parents lacking in caring empathy repeats the "daddy-mommy-me" paradigm, although it is without the Freudian Oedipal emphasis, which Deleuze and Guattari scorn in their promotion of orphans, atheists, and nomads. They assert that their paradigm fits the postmodern era; Kohut feels that his description of the self, particularly in its critique of classical Freudian psychoanalysis, is appropriate for the second half of the twentieth century.

Kohut argues that his theory of the self is fitting for the modern and postmodern ages in the Western world since "significant changes in the human condition have been taking place since the decisive decade from 1890 to 1900 when the basic formulations that determined the direction in which analysis developed were laid down" (285). In Freud's era, children were overstimulated by being too much the focus of family members and servants, by being kept within the confines of the home and the family's expectations:

> Until comparatively recent times the dominant threat to the individual was unsolvable inner conflict. And the correlated dominant interpersonal constellations to which the child of Western civilizations was exposed were the emotional overcloseness between parents and children and intense emotional relationships between the parents—perhaps to be looked upon as the unwholesome obverse of such corresponding wholesome social factors as firmness of the family unity, a social life concentrated on the home and its immediate vicinity, and a clear-cut definition of the roles of father and mother (269).

Now children are understimulated—left alone with minimal emotional support by working parents with few figures to idealize. They do not experience the parental selves at their best in the work situation but, rather, relate to parents during their leisure, often when they are fatigued (269–270). Kohut explains:

> The environment which used to be experienced as threateningly close, is now experienced more and more as threateningly distant; where children were formerly *over*stimulated by the emotional (including the erotic) life of their parents, they are now often *under*stimulated; where formerly the child's eroticism aimed at pleasure gain and led to internal conflict because of parental prohibitions and the rivalries of the oedipal constellation, many children now seek the effect of erotic stimulation in order to relieve loneliness, in order to fill an emotional void (271).

Parents who cannot provide the empathy needed and the sharing of idealized power promote fragmentation of the self in their children. Thus changing social structures provide changing psychological problems for which new paradigms, like his, are necessary.

Similar to Glass, who admires the poet's attack on reason, Kohut also believes that twentieth century fragmentation is accurately and prophetically depicted by artists:

> The musician of disordered sound, the poet of decomposed language, the painter and sculptor of the fragmented visual and tactile world: they all portray the breakup of the self and, through the reassemblage and rearrangement of the fragments, try to create new structures that possess wholeness, perfection, new meaning. The message of the greatest of them—Picasso's perhaps, or Ezra Pound's—may be expressed with such visionary originality, through the employment of such unconventional means, that it is still not easily accessible (286–287).

He also admires the impressive works of Franz Kafka, Eugene O'Neill, Henry Moore, and Igor Stravinsky (287–288).

Like Deleuze and Guattari, Kohut also questions the validity of the Freudian paradigm for all cases of mental illness, but his theory of the self provides an alternative that serves to unify the self rather than fragment it. He affirms, "Within the framework of the psychology of the self, we define mental health not only as freedom from the neurotic symptoms and inhibitions that interfere with the functions of a 'mental apparatus' involved in loving and working, but also as the capacity of a firm self to avail itself of the talents and skills at an individual's disposal, enabling him to love and work successfully" (264).

Meyers's *Self, Society, and Personal Choice*

Diana T. Meyers, an American professor of philosophy, is also sensitive to the lack of freedom resulting from mental illness. She defines "personally autonomous agents" as those who do "what *they* really want to do within the sphere of moral permissibility." These persons "control their own lives" and are not victimized by the following threats to personal autonomy: "social pressure, externally applied coercion, internalized cultural imperatives, and individual pathology." Like Deleuze and Guattari, Meyers wants her autonomous individual "to live in harmony with one's true—one's authentic—self"[9] and "to reclaim the distinction between real and apparent desires" (26). Like Kohut, she recognizes the inevitable acculturation or socialization that occurs in childhood. However, she refuses to analyze autonomy "as a state of having overcome socialization through self-consciousness" because this leads to "an epistemological regress" (30). Self-consciousness does not always result in autonomy.

Meyers advocates self-knowledge, as do all of the theoreticians studied so far, but she emphasizes that this self-knowledge must be linked to action. She defines action oriented self-knowledge as "*autonomy competency*": "autobiographical retrospection, detection, and reconciliation of conflicts within the self, and identification with preferred components of the self" (53). The function of "autonomy competency" is "to secure an integrated personality" which will be able to maintain control over one's life while acting spontaneously (59–60). The integrated personality is "complex and evolving, yet unified" (70). The unification occurs in the process of "self-discovery and self-definition" (80). As one gives oneself direction and then discovers oneself on the journey, then one's definition of oneself must be revised (96). In short, "autonomous people consult their selves, discover their abilities, inclinations, and values, and organize their desires into life plans" (99).

Meyers's work is more of a descriptive paradigm of how the autonomous self should act than a recipe for how one arrives at this autonomous self, the central concern of the first three theoreticians. She is discontented with those who focus fundamentally on "how people can elude socialization, that is, how the authentic self can transcend the impact of social causes" (40). Her emphasis will be on "how a person can live in harmony with his or her self" (40). The authentic self which acts spontaneously and avoids cultural conditioning resembles Deleuze and Guattari's decentered self. The autonomous self which identifies "with preferred components of the self" (53) echoes Kohut's therapy as he tries to help his client build on the character strengths which have evolved because of at least one parent's empathetic understanding. Glass's deep concern for the victims of incest who often develop multiple personality disorder is heard in Meyers's own plea against injustice resulting from lack of autonomy: "The most poignant evil of socialization that produces minimally autonomous individuals, then, is that it helps to secure its victims' collaboration with the injustices they may suffer" (253). Drawing extensively from Simone de Beauvoir's *The Second Sex*, Meyers is aware that culture encourages men to act more autonomously than women (136); hence, women are at the greater risk of being victimized by men because of their lack of autonomy.

Similar to Deleuze and Guattari, Meyers advocates social changes that will enhance autonomy, particularly for women. Traditional feminine socialization coerces girls "into a dependent mindset which curtails their control over their lives" (207). Socialization must stop emphasizing role preparations—"it will be necessary to dismantle those social and economic institutions that depend on docile acquiescence in preordained roles. Rather, socialization practices aimed at awakening and cultivating autonomy competency must be coupled with a social and economic climate that supports the exercise of this competency" (188). Meyers would have parents and teachers encourage children to pay attention to their real desires and then help them find means to act on their insights (193). This would help a child gain confidence in his or her own authentic choices and find creative means to fulfill legitimate desires.

This type of pedagogy is quite different from that shown in Rousseau's *Emile* where the preceptor manipulates the child into learning by discovery. In *Emile*, the desire comes from the preceptor, not the child, although the goal is for Emile to become an autonomous adult. Meyers summarizes:

> Now, keeping in mind that the objective of Emile's education is to make him an autonomous man—a man capable of supporting himself and of thinking for himself—it is paradoxical that Emile always draws a preordained conclusion. From his religious convictions to his choice of a wife, Emile follows the course his mentor sets out for him....Rousseau seems to think that by concealing his own authority and power over his pupil while nurturing the boy's rationality, Emile will become so unaccustomed to acquiescing to other people and so accustomed to deciding for himself that he will be autonomous. The trouble with this scheme is that it leaves out the true self (194–195).

The true self must learn to think, feel, and choose for itself in order to arrive at authenticity. Rousseau's isolation of Emile from communal interactions with others denies the child the contact with society necessary for autonomous choices and for increased self-understanding and social awareness. The child is exposed to only one discourse, not several from which he can choose and through which he can discern his own real desires. His self-concept is at the mercy of only one shaper rather than a community of diverse approaches to life.

Although both Meyers and the French theoreticians of the "decentered self" would like revisions in the social order so that role expectations are reduced (Meyers) or capitalism is eradicated (Deleuze and Guattari), overall, Meyers would have to disagree with the Anti-Oedipus paradigm because it, too, like the Rousseauian individualism advocated in *Emile*, lacks the integration of the autonomous individual into communal settings. In short, autonomous individuals need the foil of roles and conventions surrounding them in order to discover their true, perhaps non-traditional, desires and goals. Emile's isolation exposes him only to the discourse of his teacher, and he responds obediently but ignorantly because he has no knowledge of the other discourses from which he is kept isolated.

Although Meyers does not comment directly on the work of Deleuze and Guattari, Kohut, and Glass, her "personally autonomous agents" embody the healthy freedom they admire. Her "agents" can choose authentically to be alone or in relationship with others because they are in touch with their real desires and are not victimized by society or internal psychological pathology. "Self-directing people are not simply driven to behave one way or another. They act in accordance with their own reasons. Fractured personalities are incapable of autonomy to the extent that they are incapable of sustaining reasons, and they are incapable of sustaining reasons to the extent that they are fractured" (69). The "decentered self" may be a "fractured personality;" certainly the mentally ill whom Glass mentions fit this category.

Behind the "reasons" that motivate "self-directing people" are "characterological strands" which "unite the disparate elements of the true self" (70). She defines these dominant qualities:

> These strands can be stylistic qualities (vivacity or melancholy), virtues (patience), vices (arrogance), or foibles (excitability); they can be ways of processing experiences (careful sifting of accumulated evidence or quick intuition); they can be ardently held principles ("the environment must be saved

from the ravages of toxic waste"); they can be commitments to a role (community leader), to a career (film director), or to other people (one's children). In an integrated personality, the same characterological strands are not in evidence at all times—that is the difference between an integrated and an obsessive personality (70).

Yet, Meyers's "true self," her definitions of autonomous persons and descriptions of persons in literature and real life who live autonomously, ignores the very real power of unconscious pathological desires which, as Glass shows, can so overtake a person that he or she is victimized by these internal forces. The "characterological strands" could well include more negative than positive qualities like most of those mentioned above. An unspoken given in her argument is that she is beginning with basically healthy persons.

Her choice to focus on the theoretically defined autonomous individual is made in a vacuum; few people could just decide to live according to her definitions without the support of caring others—a therapist, a community, or a friend. She asserts, "Nevertheless, since such emotional sustenance is not always forthcoming—others may have all sorts of reasons for not wanting one's authentic self to be expressed—autonomous people need to be capable of standing by their own judgments despite the opposition or faint encouragement of others" (84). Her ideal is very attractive—persons living with no regrets (55)—but the means of achieving and sustaining the ideal are lacking. Unlike Kohut, who argues that a healthy adult needs persons to love and to idealize and those who mirror his or her self, Meyers's adult needs to be capable of acting on personal desire without support. Outside encouragement is less necessary than the steady exercise of autonomy competency.

Conclusion

This study has presented only four of many views about the self. It is a topic that can be analyzed historically from a philosophical point of view, as Charles Taylor in his *Sources of the Self, The Making of Modern Identity* has done so well, or synchronistically, by evaluating recent theories of the last twenty-five years. Louis A. Sass, in "The Self and Its Vicissitudes in the Psychoanalytic Avant-Garde," for example, provides an excellent comparative analysis of the approaches of one of my theoreticians and three others: Roy Schaefer, an advocate of the autonomous self; Heinz Kohut, whom Sass designates as the "champion of the expressivist self,"[10] James Hillman, a proponent of a Jungian archetypal approach to the self; and Jacques Lacan, representative of the postmodern theorists who permit "self and world [to] simply disappear into the middle term, the language-like structures that replace these supposedly outmoded polarities."[11] I chose to analyze the works of theoreticians selected from not only the field of psychology (Guattari and Kohut), but also from the domains of philosophy (Deleuze and Meyers) and political science (Glass). The study of the self is obviously interesting to many across several disciplines. Those who write theoretically about the self often use examples from both literary texts which graphically portray fictive selves and case studies.

Deleuze and Guattari, Glass, Kohut, and Meyers all see the self as basically sound but distorted by outside forces—capitalism, powerful others, lack of empathetic "self-objects," and socially imposed roles, respectively. Rousseau has been invoked by Glass and Meyers as a forefather in studies of the self. Glass focuses on the natural man's surrender to the social contract, and Meyers deplores the manipulative education inflicted on Emile. All four theoreticians accent desire for freedom. Deleuze and Guattari want freedom from the Oedipus paradigm and capitalism; Glass advocates freedom for the mentally ill through the responsibilities of working in community; Kohut tries to liberate his narcissistically wounded patients through the transference experience of therapy, and Meyers proposes "autonomy competency" as a way for persons to live freely regardless of past traumas. This desire for freedom in all of them can also be found in Rousseau and hence stems from Enlightenment origins.

Charles Taylor, believing that "our visions of the good are tied up with our understandings of the self,"[12] shows in *Sources of the Self* the philosophical and cultural origins of the self. There is a shift from the Platonic reason as good to the Augustinian loving God as good to the Cartesian inward moral choice as good to the Lockean objectifying different domains as good to the Rousseauian self as source of unity and wholeness as good. Romanticism and modernism emphasized the desire for this unified self in a threatening and later fragmented world.

The modern self is both conscious of being unique and is also aware of the conflicts around and within itself. Social alienation results in reflective introversion and the effort to take care of oneself on one's own and to establish one's values according to personal, internal authority, not external frames of reference.

The postmodern decentered self does not oppose but rather evolves from the modern self. It represents the introverted modern self without a center. It is exposed to external discourses which traverse it, but it is fixated on none. As A. T. Nuyen notes, the decentered self "is no longer at the center of some grand unified story that contains the totality of knowledge, such as the Hegelian story."[13] The postmodern self desires freedom from metanarratives such as marxism or Freudianism. Our study has shown this to be, in Taylor's terms, the "good" of our era, but it is doubtful if this liberation can be achieved without agency which requires a core sense of self.

Looking at the self from four points of view accentuates the dilemma of bondage to something—others, personal pathology, social conventions—and provides supplementary, if not complementary, perspectives on the same central problem. Each theory tells a part of the story of the postmodern self's dilemma. With the exception of Deleuze and Guattari, each theoretician tries to support his or her viewpoint with specific examples from art or life.

It has been said that male postmodernists are able to risk theorizing about the "decentered self" because they have reigned so long as "centered selves." Women as objects of the male gaze have been denied subjectivity. It is thus understandable that women now do not want to lose their center of control over themselves and, to whatever extent possible, over their lives, because they have had so little power in the past. Reginia Gagnier describes "feminist postmodernism":

> The poet Audre Lorde was one of the first to articulate what has since come to be called "feminist postmodernism," the theory of the diverse components of complex modern identities. In male theory, postmodernism can mean the disempowerment and dispersal of the self, the threatening "death of the author" in the face of institutional powers obliterating the individual; but feminist postmodernism posits a still strong, if fractured and contingent, subjectivity. In "Age, Race, Class, and Sex: Women Redefining Difference," Lorde described herself as "a forty-nine-year old Black lesbian feminist socialist mother of two, including one boy, and a member of an inter-racial couple." In feminist postmodernism, no part of such a complex identity can be sacrificed to any other: one will not be feminist at the cost of being racist, nor a socialist at the cost of being antifeminist.[14]

If feminists fear becoming "decentered selves," then this postmodern approach will not survive because, theoretically, whoever chooses to remain "centered" will have power over those who become "decentered" since their discourse, like that of Emile's mentor, will be the loudest, longest, and most prevalent. The empowering of some at the cost of others negates the goal of all: personal freedom.

An examination of the strengths of each theoretician's approach may advance the current understanding of the "self." Deleuze and Guattari's emphasis on a mobile, fluid self motivated by pure, authentic desire, uncontaminated by social pressures, is attractive. In spite of the opaqueness of their technological vocabulary, one admires the freedom of anti-Oedipus, "the desiring machine," from manipulation by capitalists and psychiatrists. Although their focus is on decenteredness, the overall impression their text provides is a call to autonomy—freedom from "daddy-mommy-me" and the falsity of capitalist society.

Glass counters their view of the self with the necessary balancing factor of real life experience. Those who try to live entirely according to their desires, at times pathological, encounter solid obstacles to their wishes in the form of communal norms about reality. One who for too long speaks incoherently and acts out of keeping with societal norms will be marginalized and perhaps eventually incarcerated. Living as a decentered self results in enormous personal pain and potential loss of basic freedoms provided by a society. Glass's focus on the delusions by which decentered selves live without the equilibrium of reason shows two important aspects about self-understanding: even a decentered self will create a narrative, a personal discourse to justify its existence, or, in the case of multiple personality disorder, several unified narratives, each presented by several selves in one body; further, those who share consensually validated patterns of meaning have power over the decentered selves.

I chose Deleuze and Guattari as representatives of the postmodern view of the self, and I wanted to directly juxtapose Glass's vehement objections to their approach. I then turned to Kohut, in psychoanalytical fields, except for strict, orthodox Freudians, a highly respected advocate of the centered self. Interestingly, Kohut's definition of the healthy self would probably be acceptable to Deleuze, Guattari, and Glass: "This structure is the basis for our sense of being an independent center of initiative and perception, integrated with our most central ambitions and ideals and with our experience that our body and mind form a unity in space and a continuum in time" (177). Deleuze and Guattari definitely want their anti-Oedipus to be "an independent center of initiative and perception," operating freely from the center which is uninhibited desire, perhaps to be equated with Kohut's "central ambitions and ideals."

Deleuze and Guattari's technological vocabulary makes the self sound more like a disembodied machine than a human being, but this is because they must try to negate the usual soul or self/body dichotomy that has prevailed in Western history. Their decentered self realistically can be expressed only in action via a body and can only operate within the normal human limitations of space and time. However, if they insist on equating anti-Oedipus with an authentic schizophrenic, then they renounce the possibility of a self living in normal time and space, capable of waging war against capitalism. As Fredric Jameson, another outspoken opponent of capitalism, remarks:

> It is because language has a past and a future, because the sentence moves in time, that we can have what seems to us a concrete or lived experience of time. But since the schizophrenic does not know language articulation in that way, he or she does not have our experience of temporary continuity either, but is condemned to live a perpetual present with which the various moments of his or her past have little connection and for which there is no conceivable future on the horizon. In other words, schizophrenic experience is an experience of isolated, disconnected, discontinuous material signifiers which fail to link up into a coherent sequence.[15]

Whether or not Deleuze and Guattari could agree with part or all of Kohut's definition of the self, they would strongly object to the process of psychotherapy, with an emphasis on transference through the artificial self-object or parental substitute, the therapist, which Kohut takes for granted. Glass, an advocate of the mental health professions, would have no difficulty accepting Kohut's definition, but would combine or sometimes even replace one-on-one therapy with communal projects and work in either the broad society outside of the hospital or a special society created by mental health practitioners. Again, the focus of Deleuze, Guattari, Glass, and Kohut is personal freedom from internal pathology and external, abusive social pressures. The differences among them are what constitutes abusive social pressures—capitalism, repressive environments such as concentration camps, mentally ill parents—and how one arrives at freedom—renouncing psychiatrists and society, community work, or psychotherapy.

I included Diana Meyers in my essay because she represents the feminist concern noted above which eschews decenteredness and advocates autonomy even at the expense of loneliness. Her "autonomy competency" paradigm suggests a way to negotiate living in society while having many of one's personal desires met, without delusion and without therapy. She affirms Deleuze and Guattari's emphasis on the flowing, evolving desirer, but she refuses to dissolve personal identity. Her theory is action oriented rather than therapy grounded. Ideally, a person who has adopted autonomy skills can function according to his or her volition within society.

There are also weaknesses in each paradigm. Meyers could be accused of reverting to essentialism when she speaks of one's "true self" composed of "characterological strands." Since such a charge does not appear in her text, she makes no defense of her unpostmodern sense of a "true self." She also ignores the power of the unconscious to motivate desires that may or may not be in keeping with the "true self." Glass's deluded try to live competently and autonomously in their delusional worlds. Her ideal, authentic, autonomous self is admirable, as in many ways is Deleuze and Guattari's decentered self, but both selves are not grounded in reality. Autonomous selves and decentered selves will falter when their desires are prevented from being fulfilled by powerful others.

Glass's and Kohut's approaches balance the excessive abstractness of the theories of Deleuze, Guattari, and Meyers, but weaknesses can be found in them as well. Glass deemphasizes the very real possibility that the deluded may have even deeper insights into the foibles and injustices of society than the average person and should be taken seriously, even if their visions of reality do not adhere to current norms. He admires the visionary power of the artist but is comfortable with this power only because it is balanced by reason, the quality lacking in the deluded. Kohut also affirms the power of the mental health professions over the patient in his facile acceptance that "doctor knows best." Unlike Meyers, who strongly critiques the social roles foisted on boys and girls since birth and calls for a new understanding of what is male and female, Kohut regrets that mothers and fathers do not follow their stereotypical roles and in so doing damage their children. Kohut frequently criticizes parents without following through on his thinking as to how social structures could have frustrated the growth and development of these parents so that eventually their pathology is inflicted on their children.

This essay has revealed the theme common to all four theoreticians—the desire for personal freedom—and points the way to additional commentary on the self which will enhance the strengths and correct the weaknesses shown in the texts of Deleuze and Guattari, Glass, Kohut, and Meyers. My attempt to allow each critic to converse with the others is paradigmatic of what needs to continue in future studies of the self. All of the disciplines have an important voice in describing how decentered, centered, or communal the postmodern self may be and how its desire for freedom may best be expressed.

Notes

1. John McGowan, *Postmodernism and Its Critics* (Ithaca: Cornell University Press, 1991), 211.
2. Brian Massumi, *A User's Guide to Capitalism and Schizophrenia* (Cambridge: The MIT Press, 1992), 2.
3. Gilles Deleuze and Félix Guattari, *Anti-Oedipus, Capitalism and Schizophrenia*, trans. Robert Hurley, Mark Seem, and Helen R. Lane (Minneapolis: University of Minnesota Press, 1990), xxi. All quotations from *Anti-Oedipus* are from this translation. Subsequent page numbers are noted parenthetically in the text.
4. James M. Glass, *Private Terror/Public Life, Psychosis and the Politics of Community* (Ithaca: Cornell University Press, 1989), 233. Subsequent page references to this book are cited parenthetically.
5. Deleuze and Guattari, 351.
6. James M. Glass, *Shattered Selves, Multiple Personality in a Postmodern World* (Ithaca: Cornell University Press, 1993), 59. Subsequent page references to this book are cited parenthetically.
7. Patrick H. Hutton, "Foucault, Freud, and the Technologies of the Self," in *Technologies of the Self*, ed. Luther H. Martin (Amherst: University of Massachusetts Press, 1988), 135.
8. Heinz Kohut. *The Restoration of the Self* (Madison, Connecticut: International Universities Press, 1986), 68. Subsequent page references to this book are cited parenthetically.
9. Diana T. Meyers, *Self, Society, and Personal Choice* (New York: Columbia University Press, 1989), 19. Subsequent page references to this book are cited parenthetically.
10. Louis A. Sass, "The Self and Its Vicissitudes in the Psychoanalytic Avant-Garde," in *Constructions of the Self*, ed. George Levine (New Brunswick: Rutgers Univ. Press, 1992), 32.
11. Sass, 49.
12. Charles Taylor, *Sources of the Self, The Making of the Modern Identity* (Cambridge: Harvard University, 1989), 105.
13. A. T. Nuyen, "Postmodern Theology and Postmodern Philosophy," *Philosophy of Religion*, 30 (1991): 66.
14. Reginia Gagnier, "Feminist Autobiography in the 1980s," *Feminist Studies* 17.1 (Spring 1991): 140.
15. Frederic Jameson, "Postmodernism and Consumer Society," *The Anti-Aesthetic, Essays on Postmodern Culture*, ed. Hall Foster (Port Townsend: Washington: Bay Press, 1983), 119.

Discourse, Home, and Travel: The Place of the Self in Modern Travel Writing
by Sally M. Silk

My grandfather used to say: "Life is astoundingly short. To me, looking back over it, life seems so foreshortened that I scarcely understand, for instance, how a young man can decide to ride over to the next village without being afraid that—not to mention accidents—even the span of a normal happy life may fall far short of the time needed for such a journey."   Franz Kafka, *The Next Village*

For parts of the time the conversation centred on the story *The Next Village*. Brecht says it is a counterpart to the story of Achilles and the tortoise. One never gets to the next village if one breaks the journey down into its smallest parts, not counting the incidental occurrences. Then a whole life is too short for the journey. But the fallacy lies in the word 'one'. For if the journey is broken down into its parts, then the traveller is too. And if the unity of life is destroyed, then so is its shortness. Let life be as short as it may. That does not matter, for the one who arrives in the next village is not the one who set out on the journey, but another.
Walter Benjamin, Understanding Brecht

Introduction

Although current theoretical work on the modern self cannot resolve the question "What is the self?" once and for all, some of the confusion around the issue can come into clear focus if one examines the self with regard to language and the dialectic that ensues between the opposing tropes of home and travel. In particular, modern travel literature has witnessed definitive changes in the constitution of the self that perhaps no other genre can claim so boldly. I shall first discuss the relationship of language to the constitution of the self by invoking the tropes of home and travel. I will emphasize the relativist nature between these two, demonstrating that their seeming opposition is in fact an intimate relationship where the supposed dividing line between them is forever blurred.

Having established that the notions of home and travel are mutually interdependent, I will next argue that modern travel writing foregrounds the dispersed voice of the modern self to such a degree that it makes visible an activity I call discursive homelessness. This is a condition of language in which the self is understood as a transitive activity because it keeps moving from one voice to another, provoking transitions as it eludes centering.

This condition, in which the presence and absence of home coincide in language, occurs in Céline's *Voyage au bout de la nuit*, a text in which the narrator narrates various episodes from his travels as a younger man. As a final means to identifying what discursive homelessness is and how it operates, I shall offer an analysis of certain key passages from this novel. I will demonstrate that the idea of discursive homelessness allows us to read Céline's text, not only as a study in abjection and the subversion of language for which it is well known, but as a study of Bardamu's obsession with carving out narrative space for himself. His anxious relationship to language when describing his travels can be explained by the precarious positioning of the self vis-à-vis the tropes of home and travel.

The Traveler vs. the Storyteller

Quoted at the beginning of this essay, Benjamin's reading of Kafka's story illuminates the problematic of the self in travel writing that I shall investigate here. Benjamin believes that Brecht, in imagining that it is difficult to complete a journey given the shortness of life, has misread the text. While Brecht locates the problem in the journey, Benjamin locates it in the traveler. Brecht's focus on the journey remains thematic, in contrast to Benjamin who sees the problem on a more formal level: that of the traveling subject. For Benjamin, the traveler cannot remain identical to himself as long as he travels.

Benjamin's discussion of the traveler brings him to a second point, seemingly unrelated to the first. What he subsequently finds of interest in Kafka's story is not that life is too short, but rather that its "true measure is memory."[1] He distinguishes his reading from Brecht's when he explains that the elderly narrator of this story, like "all those for whom life has become transformed into writing, (...) can only read the writing backwards. That is the only way in which [writers] encounter themselves."[2] Travelers, in other words, can entertain no hope of finding themselves. Only narrators, in the act of writing, "encounter themselves."

Brecht's supposed misreading of Kafka is important for Benjamin because it introduces the opposing figures of a narrator and a traveler. Benjamin frames his discussion of *The Next Village* around the *possibility* of finding oneself, of knowing oneself, and, finally, of being able to hold onto oneself: a narrator might achieve these goals; a traveler certainly cannot. What is it about the grandfather telling the story that holds out such promise for Benjamin?

Benjamin privileges the act of telling as an event in which the self can be found.[3] Although his attitude towards finding the self through writing reflects an approach to texts that appears dated today, his focus on the status of the writing self senses the crisis in subjectivity that will preoccupy poststructuralists decades after his death. Poststructuralist theory has demonstrated that the very act of writing problematizes rather than resolves the encounter with the self.

Benjamin's reading of Kafka's tale foreshadows the poststructuralist dilemma of the relationship of the self to writing and recognizes the complexity of this narrative situation. In the novel to be examined here, *Voyage au bout de la nuit*, I take this complicated situation one step further: the traveler and the narrator are the same. In what terms can we come to understand the self who is both narrator *and* traveler/protagonist in his own narrative fiction?

Language: Tropes of Travel

I have chosen to locate this complicated dynamic within the very particular genre of travel literature. Reading, writing, and signification themselves can all be considered different forms of travel. It is not difficult to imagine the reading process itself as an exercise in travel. Our eyes literally move across words, lines, and pages when we read, evoking an act of displacement, one that can be likened to travel in the most basic physical sense. Michel Butor's claim that the general reading public today engages in the activity of reading primarily when they are trying to get from one place to another makes this all the more resonant as a trope.[4] In particular, he sees the subway, train, and airplane as major sites of reading in contemporary society. Thus reading both resembles and is contiguous to an act of travel. Metaphorically and metonymically, the process of reading is bound to travel.

Secondly, writing, too, commands a powerful relationship to travel. In its most basic form, the movement necessary to the physical act of writing, as with reading, shares with travel the process of movement through space. On the other hand, writing presented as an experience, as in the simple statement "I like her writing," offers a cognitive displacement, a mental elsewhere in which one resides as long as the experience is sustained. As a concept writing can be regarded as another formal reality, albeit an ambiguous one, as demonstrated in Barthes's early work.[5] Although writing for Barthes is considered both an act and a moment, it also brings to mind the idea of travel: precisely because it functions as another formal reality writing evokes a very specific space through which a text must pass. From a different perspective, Derrida's view of writing, that it is a decentered and deferring process, also suggests a connection between writing and travel.

Thirdly, poststructuralist linguistics sees the signifying act as one of continual displacement, and, as such, signification itself can be understood as an exercise in travel. Meaning threatens to escape control because the dynamics between signifier and signified are understood as unstable, if not antagonistic. The Derridean concept of *différance* shows that meaning is produced and driven by movement, thus creating a direct relationship between travel in particular and the production of signs in general.

All texts, therefore, have something to do with travel. The operation of displacement inherent in reading, writing, and signification makes travel not simply a trope, but a basic part of the way texts operate. Indeed, to say that "all narratives are travel narratives"[6] suggests that every narrative, at the level of the text rather than that of the story, shares essential properties with travel. What, then, are the implications of this claim for literature whose central thematics is travel?

An obvious answer is that the activity of continual displacement is even more pronounced in narratives about travel. Yet, this is a gross overstatement, one that conflates topos with textuality so that the two are seen as virtually complementary when, in fact, they are often at odds. In the modern text to be analyzed here, the voice in the narration from beginning to end is actually disembodied from the story it is telling.

In order to make apparent the profound nature of this disjunction between what is told and the act of telling it, in *Voyage au bout de la nuit* I focus on the relationship between voice and the textual subject. My interest here is the enunciative situation, the utterance, the being of the communicative act itself. This approach permits a paradoxical situation to come to light: how a dispersed voice can be heard.

Discursive Homelessness/Home and Language

I have chosen to give the name discursive homelessness to the process by which the narrative voice seeks representation of its own fragmentation. It is important to point out that I am not describing the disintegration of narrative voice (although this may at times occur) for this would suggest that the voice in the text was once whole. On the contrary, the term discursive homelessness is particularly appropriate because it designates a condition of discourse wherein voice never settles into the text, but remains free-floating and distinctly separate from the story through which it is heard. Tension ensues between story and narration, creating conditions for a new reading of Céline's text.

Homelessness is a highly charged term in late twentieth-century America, and for that reason I do not use the term lightly. Actual homelessness, as a grave social ill, represents a totally different kind of crisis from that examined here. It does reflect, however, an extreme putting into question of the notion of home that also lies at the root of this study of language in travel writing. I shall demonstrate here that the term resonates in discourse. Our relationship to language is profoundly complicated because language engenders a particular kind of critical difficulty. For to participate in language is to renounce the very idea of home. What is there about home that makes it such an impalpable concept?

Scholars avidly seek its definition because the primordial meaning of the term is so difficult to grasp. Even in mythology, a field in which one can systematically learn the origins of people and events, the difficulty of isolating the meaning of home is apparent. Ancient myths about home become interesting not so much for the stories they tell, but for their attempts to get at the essence of the trope. For example, the ultimately divine presence of Hestia, goddess of the hearth, made it difficult for the Greeks to represent her through statues and paintings, as well as through stories.[7] When such representation did occur, curiously, it was in the context of her relationship to Hermes, the messenger-god venerated for his ability to move, effect transitions, travel. What is surprising, however, is that Hestia, although she was neither his lover nor family relation, should be depicted side by side with him; connected to Hermes not by blood or desire, Hestia relates to him through a "functional affinity"[8] that can be read as their shared power in the domination of space. The two are mutually interdependent, demonstrating that the supposed constancy of home is, in fact, utterly relational. Hestia's reign may be the space of home, while Hermes' is all that is circumscribed outside of it, but just where one stops and the other begins is impossible to say. If Hestia is both a principle of permanence and movement,[9] then properties assigned to the idea of home—origins, centeredness, stability—become severely problematized.

The meaning of Hestia persists as a metaphysical issue, one that is related to this study of discourse in travel literature. In light of Hestia's virtual unrepresentability, "should we be surprised that she is, in some way, Being, irreducible to any perceptible being? If there is no way to determine her shape, is she not, then, what evokes being as being for us?"[10] This dilemma in representation raises the essential question "What is the relationship between home and *language*?" As language seeks to represent the thing itself, it cannot be what it says. And because language can only represent and never be, "it is only the forgetting of being which causes representation to take place."[11] To avail oneself of language, therefore, is to submit to incompleteness. Language requires a concept of home because it represents its own inability simply to be; representation can only take place where being is not. Language's sole capacity to represent consistently reminds us that it is not home.

Yet, it is important to point out that language does not derive from a concept of home abandoned. That is, home cannot be posited as a point of origin that language had to leave behind in order to operate. Language is already not home, although it nevertheless always needs the idea of home because the power of language resides in its unique ability to evoke that which it will never be. Language defines itself against home in a way that demonstrates its dependence on it.

Home is an ultimately inexpressible idea. To talk about discursive homelessness should not suggest, therefore, that one can also elaborate what is meant by discursive home*ful*ness. Some may venture to say that texts from an earlier tradition exhibit the latter, but as long as there is language, there can be no such entity as a discursive home. This is not to say that discursive homelessness in earlier texts functions the same way as in modern ones. Indeed, this is not the case. Earlier texts about travel posit home as something discourse can work towards, even though it can never actually operate there. The illusion of a discursive home is a strong one, and it determines the degree of authenticity to which a text aspires.

Faith in epistemology guides texts to greater or lesser degrees. In early modern travel literature, even though one can find evidence that the voyage threatened the notion of self, ontology nevertheless played a fundamental role in the quest for self-knowledge. Seventeenth-century travel writing, for example, although it does problematize features of narrative, is marked by a certain naïveté and belief that truth can be located in what one observes.[12] P. Paul le Jeune, for example, in his *Relation de ce qui s'est passé en la Nouvelle France en l'année 1633*

(...) of 1634, quoted an old Latin proverb that says that "one eyewitness is worth more than ten ears."[13] Seeing entitled the traveler to speak authoritatively and, more importantly, unquestioningly, of his experience.

In the eighteenth century, although the travel writings of Rousseau particularly attest to the fact that travel complicates the very idea of the self,[14] they still rely on the idea of a virtual home that can serve as some kind of transcendental vantage point from which the self may be brought into question. Rousseau, for instance, shifted the metaphysical question of "Who am I?" to "Where am I?,"[15] thus foregrounding the importance of place for ontology. Although he undoubtedly did not expect that the realization of self-knowledge should depend on home, he nevertheless brought the issue of home, or more precisely, the absence of it, into the scope of his ability even to consider such metaphysical questions. In *Emile* he writes that "In breaking the knots that attached me to my country, I extended it to include the whole earth."[16] The power of home to center the self is invoked as a concept that especially allows him to apprehend the self when it is away from home.

By contrast, in the example of twentieth-century French travel writing that I analyze here the potential to formulate the most basic ontological question becomes very difficult. In *Voyage au bout de la nuit* discourse resists ontology so that the traveling subject is in a position to ask neither "Who am I?" nor "Where am I?" Indeed, the voice in the text is too dispersed to be able to take up such grounding questions. The inability of the narrative voice to cohere is the defining characteristic of discursive homelessness. The term is more than just a metaphor for a fragmented voice in travel writing; it denotes a crisis in textuality. My reading of Céline's novel shall expose discursively how the traveling subject is subverted in writing.

Discursive homelessness may not be particular to travel writing since it can be regarded as a condition of language in general. Yet, I consider it a theory of travel. For if the textual subject has no natural and essential self, travel, on the other hand, *is* "man's natural place."[17] Because it always represents movement towards somewhere travel provides us with a motif of continual displacement that is one of narrative's constitutive features.[18] The impossible representability of home apart from travel is indicative of this state of perpetual motion and suggests that discourse can never find its way home. Because the traveler "displaces himself at the *limits of representation*,"[19] he does not concern himself with representing, but focuses instead on the process of displacement essential to any act of representation. From a discursive perspective, this state makes travel literature into an extreme genre: all discursive activity therein operates 1) through displacement and 2) in some kind of markedly marginal space.

Poststructuralist theory, motivated by a dialectic between structure and agency, has shown subjectivity to be a site of conflict. In modern travel writing subjectivity is doubly aggravated because the textual subject can only write from a position of displacement that is located in the margins. This liminal environment is what makes possible the reading conducted here. The course of discursive homelessness requires a certain exacerbated state in the narration in order to be followed. Without it the process of fragmentation remains buried in the text.

Voyage au bout de la nuit: **The Functioning of a Homeless Discourse**

When Bardamu claims that "everything is bound to end up in the street,"[20] he suggests there is no such state as privacy. The issue of privacy leads us to a question that warrants examination here: considering that Bardamu is an extremely solitary and isolated figure, is the *text* itself willing to accept dialogical properties that necessarily guarantee the absence of privacy from discourse? This question needs to be explored in order to learn how discursive homelessness produces a narrative without a center.

In *Voyage au bout de la nuit* discourse is completely ravished by the process of telling. To locate where this occurs, the dynamics of various enunciative situations need to be examined, ones that will reveal, among other things, great differences between Bardamu the protagonist and Bardamu the narrator; the hero's relationship to language needs to be distinguished from the narrator's in order to show how decentering operates in the text.

Bringing the Battlefield to Paris: Why Bardamu Can't Handle His Own Stories

Bardamu the narrator describes how, as a younger man institutionalized in a psychiatric hospital for cowardice on the battlefield, he fabricated tales of his own bravery in a faraway land for the bourgeois visitors paying social calls to the hospital. A local actress finds his stories fascinating and asks his permission to relate them to a poet friend of hers, so that he may put them into verse for her to recite one evening at the

Comédie Française. He attends the performance and works himself into a frenzy upon hearing the soaring rhymes and pathos of the poet's version of his own lies. The evening becomes an ultimate failure when neither the audience nor the actress nor the poet choose to acknowledge him when the curtain falls. The poet, who incarnates the otherness of his discourse, becomes a powerful rival via the actress. Bardamu, now a pitiful sight, leaves the theater, dejected and anxious to take refuge in the safety of the hospital where it all began.

Suffering thus from having his storytelling prowess appropriated by others for their own ends, Bardamu is unwilling to admit mediation in language. Although the scene occurs early in the story, Bardamu continues to deny this essential dimension of communication throughout the novel. The episode suggests the effect on discourse resulting from the Nietzschian contract between telling and deception,[21] a situation that leads to the exploitation of Bardamu the protagonist's stories and accounts for Bardamu the narrator's mistrust of language. He explains:

> We're never suspicious enough of words, they look like nothing much, not at all dangerous, just little puffs of air, little sounds the mouth makes, neither hot nor cold and easily absorbed, once they reach the ear, by the vast gray boredom of the brain. We're not suspicious enough of words, and calamity strikes.[22]

Nevertheless, having realized the errors of his younger "self's" naïve attitude towards language, Bardamu the narrator is still caught: words being the only possible medium at his disposal for relating his various travels, *Voyage au bout de la nuit* can be read as a study in discourse gone awry because of a vain search for the point at which a home can be located in language, where discourse does not have to be shared with another.

The suspicion with which Bardamu the narrator views language conditions discursive activity throughout the novel all the way down to its jesting but desperate "Help! Help!"[23] The wide range of the narrating self in this text, with the young storyteller poised at one end and the accomplished narrator of *Voyage au bout de la nuit* at the other, cannot accept the issue of language as social material, as something that does not stay in one place long enough to be owned.

The Move to Africa: Bardamu's Fear of Losing a Western Interlocutor

If Bardamu's storytelling self is mediated through numerous others so that they may exercise discursive control from which he cannot escape in Paris, in Africa the problematics of control are only one part of his dilemma. The case of his old acquaintance Robinson highlights the mediating power of the alter ego whose character represents a voice that Bardamu is continually in search of. When he does find this voice, Bardamu appropriates it but discovers that it does not work for him as it does for Robinson. From Bardamu's position, Robinson's voice rings wrong and gets him into trouble, for his pursuit of the alter ego results in the death of the latter and the homeless state of the former. Bardamu's inability to subdue his alter ego means that Robinson, "the only one on his island, the only one in his night...the personification of a shipwrecked consciousness,"[24] secures discursive decentering in the novel.

Bardamu's stay in Africa, besides resulting in a confrontation with the alter ego, also addresses an imperialist discourse that the text both explores and resists. Because it does not help Bardamu master the natives, he abandons the all-powerful discursive position occupied by his French predecessors in the jungle. Such a definitive move, however, involves reconsidering the representation of the black as absence and negation in western discourse. Henry Louis Gates points out that blackness as a trope "has no essence; rather it is signified into being by a signifier."[25] If the sign of blackness is pure invention devoid of an essence, a rhetorical construct to the core, then Bardamu's reconsideration of this sign necessarily means not only playing with the trope, but resisting it as well (this can be seen as early as the initial scene in which traditional western discourse is destabilized as Bardamu watches the "corocoro" white man take advantage of the black family selling rubber). This is not to say that Bardamu rejects the validity of the trope, but simply that discursive activity in those scenes demonstrates a certain defiance of it.

What occurs in discourse in *Voyage au bout de la nuit* is something similar to that which is represented by the Signifying Monkey, "he who dwells at the margins of discourse, ever punning, ever troping, ever embodying the ambiguities of language."[26] In addition, discursive decentering here reveals that the text does not blindly accept the trope of blackness since in capsizing the authority of western discourse Bardamu necessarily shakes the foundations of its preconceptions. Fragmentation of the subject thus takes on dramatic proportions because, like Ishmael Reed's poem of a *parody* of the trope of blackness in which the parodic elements demonstrate a refusal "to be duped by figuration,"[27] Bardamu's narrative also refuses deception. For, no longer unsuspecting enough to submit naïvely to another's exploitation of self through narrative, Bardamu as narrator turns the reader into his confidant in contrast to the distinct absence of this dimension in his story.

The confidential mode is a response to the discursive problems he experienced as Bardamu the protagonist; confiding to the reader, even pathetically, eliminates the risks involved in the theatrical style he used in Paris and looked for in Africa. The confidential style draws the reader into the enunciative situation, thus guaranteeing the narrator he will be listened to. His bare honesty makes the reader both pity and admire him, and consequently assures him that the reader is completely uninterested in exploiting his narrative for the reader's own ends. Bardamu's desperate appeal to the reader represents an attempt to keep discourse from slipping away, into the mouth of another. It reveals Bardamu trying to bring discourse home once and for all.

America: Bardamu's Frantic Search For Any Listener At All

In America, the protagonist's dilemma is ontological because of the failure of the phatic. Unable to establish any contact whatsoever with both the waitress in a New York dive and the passersby in the street below his hotel window, Bardamu is entangled in an enunciative situation whose rules he would like to ignore. He fumbles every chance of catching the waitress's attention and ends up causing a dramatic scene that has him thrown out of the place by a huge bouncer of indescribable proportions. Similarly, back in his cheap hotel, lamenting his failure to capture the young woman's heart, he literally screams out the window so that those below should take notice of him. Both efforts at attracting attention fail miserably.

In this episode, an ontological crisis has replaced the discursive one experienced in France and Africa because of the protagonist's unwillingness to accept the rules of any discursive process, that is, that language is an act of shared expression between individuals rather than an isolated act of individual expression.[28] He fights the assumptions inherent in the relationship between addresser and addressee where on both sides, the illusion of a complete communication code takes a positive aspect: a meaningful communication is impossible without the presupposition, by both communicating parties, of a complete and non-ambiguous system of communicational devices. This is an illusion, but a necessary and shared one. We may consider it to be a nuclear instance of the ideological mediation of social integration.[29]

The marginal social status of Bardamu the protagonist can be explained by his resistance to the "illusion." Inept at understanding the implications of discursive homelessness, he relentlessly tries to make contact with an other who ignores him. Bardamu the narrator, on the other hand, has achieved an excellent understanding of the conditions of homelessness to which his younger "self" was subjected. The older and, perhaps, wiser narrator has learned to keep narrative exploitation at bay through a style of abjection that reduces the threat of the power of the other because the latter would not deem an abject voice worthy to compete with. The confessional mode that inheres in this style means not only that he is assured an addressee, but also that he has a very particular addressee in mind when he writes, one that does not stand poised ready to abuse his narrative. Thus the narrator's form of homelessness in discourse differs from the protagonist's because the former must adopt a particular voice in order to feel secure about being heard while the latter falls into discursive traps wherever he goes.

In either case, however, both Bardamus, although from different motives, anxiously attempt to procure for their disparate selves a discursive home. They are either always scrambling to escape discursive control (Bardamu the protagonist), or shrewdly attempting to master a confidentially abject style (Bardamu the narrator) as a guarantee of a phatic that will not aggressively turn on him (as in Paris), elude him (as in Africa), or ignore him (as in America).

Conclusion

In Paris the storyteller *par excellence* throws himself into discourse where he is sapped of ownership of his words; in Africa he completely gives himself over to others so that he must literally be carried out of the jungle by natives who sell him for a profit to a Spanish ship captain; and in America he searches for contact but bungles it so completely that he is forced to scream out of a window with no hope of a response.

If neatly escaping from one place to the next is what Bardamu the protagonist does best in the *story*,[30] perhaps it is in response to his failure in *discourse* to execute a decisive escape from an impossible situation. His failure to procure the addressee of his wishes elicits a reaction on the part of Bardamu the narrator, who compensates for this unfulfilled desire by a narrative obsessed with the position of an addressee that cannot disappoint or surprise him. The voice of the narrator becomes dependent on the reader because it is constituted solely according to the reader's position in the enunciative situation.

For Bardamu the narrator, the hard truth, although he will not accept it, is that a voice cannot actually own what it says. The energy of the text is evidence of this rejection as he actively seeks to compensate for this "sad" fact in the freedom inherent in the confessional mode. Abjectly confiding in the reader compensates for the abuse he took as protagonist because it allows him to spill all. The narrator's wild use of language draws the reader's attention to this energy so that he makes himself highly visible.[31] Indeed, the more visible he is in the text, the greater the indication that he is fighting a lack of discursive autonomy in the act of narrating. He frantically searches for a place where he can be at home in discourse, where the threat of the other can be held back.

Bardamu as narrator and Bardamu as protagonist would not have found much consolation in the idea that if we cannot own what we say, "we may at least *rent* meaning."[32] Both Bardamus, although they represent the problem in different ways, manage poorly the mediating position in which travel places them, suffering in language the consequences of an unwillingness to "rent meaning" when it is in fact the only way to go. In this text, traveling means that discourse suffers mediation at the expense of the self: home is not a place towards which the self can move nor is it a place from which it ever set out. It becomes impossible to distinguish clearly between home and travel in language because desire for the former is awakened only by the discursively mediating force of the latter.

The problematic idea of home has enabled this study of homelessness in discourse. Home both excludes the outside and protects the inside; it occupies two spaces rather than the nucleus of a single thing. Textually, the narrative voice permits these two spaces to come into view simultaneously. Voice is compelling because it is where the configuration of self becomes visible as it speaks through others in writing. Like the figure of the grandfather in Kafka's tale, for whom life is meaningful only because he can "read the writing backwards," the notion of home is only significant "retroactively,"[33] when one inhabits some other space, occupying an elsewhere that is ultimately the salient feature of travel. A definitively homeless voice characterizes discursive activity in *Voyage au bout de la nuit* because the text invites us to experience language from a variety of necessarily conflicting directions.

Notes

1. Walter Benjamin, *Understanding Brecht* (London: Verso, 1983), 112.
2. Benjamin, 112.
3. Benjamin distinguishes between two kinds of telling: the traditional storyteller conveys information and the modern novelist asks about the meaning of life. "The Storyteller," *Illuminations*, Hannah Arendt, ed. (New York: Schocken Books, 1969), 83–109.
4. Michel Butor, "Le voyage et l'écriture," *Répertoire IV* (Paris: Minuit, 1974), 12.
5. Roland Barthes, *Le degré zéro de l'écriture* (Paris: Seuil, 1953), 14.
6. Michel de Certeau, *Arts de faire* (Paris: 10/18, 1980), 206.
7. Jean-Pierre Vernant, *Mythe et pensée chez les grecs* (Paris: Editions de la Découverte, 1985), 155–7 and *passim* (rpt. [Paris: Maspero, 1965]).
8. Vernant, 156.
9. Vernant, 201.
10. Jean-Joseph Goux, "Vesta, or the Place of Being," *Representations* I.1 (1983): 101. Goux goes on to establish that both Plato and Heidegger, even through different linguistic derivations, "arrive at the same divinity, signifying or evoking 'the beingness of being:' she who is named Hestia or Vesta" (102).
11. Goux, 103.
12. Normand Doiron, "De l'épreuve de l'espace au lieu du texte: le récit de voyage comme genre," *Biblio 17, Voyages: Récits et imaginaires*, ed. Bernard Beugnot 11 (1984): 19.
13. Quoted in Doiron, 20. Interestingly enough, the same proverb was found in the 1638 French translation of a German text, *Brief discours de la manière de voyager*, trans. Maistre Yves Dugué, 9 (Doiron, 20).
14. Georges Van Den Abbeele, *Travel as Metaphor: From Montaigne to Rousseau* (Minneapolis: Univ. of Minnesota Press, 1992), 85–130. Van Den Abbeele's lucid readings of travel literature by Montaigne, Descartes, Montesquieu, and Rousseau are, to my mind, the most engaging analysis to date of early modern travel writing. His theory of an economy of travel is founded on fundamental issues in metaphysics.
15. Van Den Abbeele, 105.
16. Quoted in Van Den Abbeele, 105.
17. Bernard Beugnot, "Préface," *Biblio 17, Voyages: récits et imaginaires* 11 (1984): xv.
18. The idea of displacement as essential to the narrative process has been discussed in a variety of critical works. From a literary perspective see, for example, Peter Brooks's work on the relationship of desire to the idea of plot as a dynamic figure of displacement in *Reading for the Plot* (New York: Vintage, 1985). Displacement is also fundamental to psychoanalytic practice as evidenced from the very beginning in the Freudian notion of *Nachträglichkeit*, where temporality prevents the self-containment of an event so that action is always necessarily deferred (Jean Laplanche and J.-B. Pontalis, *The Language of Psychoanalysis*, trans. Donald Nicholson-Smith [New York: Norton, 1973], p. 111). Lacan's concept of the simultaneous anticipation and insistence of the signifying chain demonstrates that

meaning can only occur through displacement (Jacques Lacan, "L'instance de la lettre dans l'inconscient ou la raison depuis Freud," *Écrits* [Paris: Seuil, 1966], 502).

19. Doiron, 23; his emphasis.

20. Louis-Ferdinand Céline, *Journey to the End of the Night*, trans. Ralph Manheim (New York: New Directions, 1983), 308.

21. In *The Will To Power* Nietzsche explains that telling by its very nature is deceptive. Friedrich Nietzsche, *The Will To Power*, trans. Walter Kaufmann and R.J. Hollingdale (New York: Vintage Books, 1968), sec. 492 and 512, pp. 272 and 277 respectively.

22. Céline, 419–20.

23. Céline, 180.

24. Philip Stephen Day, *Le miroir allégorique de Louis-Ferdinand Céline* (Paris: Klincksieck, 1974), 87.

25. Henry Louis Gates, Jr., *Figures in Black* (New York: Oxford, 1987), 274.

26. Gates, 236.

27. Gates, 276. The poem, entitled "Dualism: in ralph ellison's invisible man," demonstrates "Reed's signifying relation to Ellison." See Ishmael Reed, *Conjure: Selected Poems, 1963–1970* (Amherst: University of Massachusetts Press, 1972), 50. Quoted in Gates, 275.

28. Although it is not my intention to bring Céline's political beliefs into the scope of this study, I cannot help but observe a certain affinity between Bardamu's resistance to positing some discursive power in an other and Céline's own fascist ideology. The latter represents an attempt to produce another, as submissive, who will accept the subject's self-presentation as "in control." This totalitarian refusal to cede power cannot be divorced from the unexpected discursive trouble Bardamu experiences as a storyteller in Paris and an entrepreneur in Africa.

29. Rastko Mocnik, "Toward a Materialist Concept of Literature," *Cultural Critique*, 4 (1986), 176.

30. Cf. When he flees Africa, he writes, "That was the time to get away" (105), and, similarly, when he leaves Molly in Detroit, he sadly writes: "I was very fond of her, but I was even fonder of my vice, my mania for running away from everywhere in search of God knows what" (197). Whenever Bardamu leaves somewhere for good, whether it be a hospital or a town, the departure is always portrayed in terms of suddenly breaking loose from that place.

31. For an interesting exploration of the relationship between grammatical structures in Céline and the notion of visibility, see Annie Montaut, "La poésie de la grammaire chez Céline: mise en substance de la forme et objectivation de l'intelligibilité," *Poétique*, 50 (avril 1982). Montaut claims that if Céline subverts language, "it is not by infraction, but by excessive visibility" (228).

32. Michael Holquist, "The Politics of Representation," *Allegory and Representation: Selected Papers from the English Institute, 1979–1980*, ed. Stephen J. Greenblatt (Baltimore: Johns Hopkins Univ. Press, 1981), 164.

33. Van Den Abbeele, xviii.

Lest We Not Forget: Memory in Semprun's *The Long Voyage*
by Howard Giskin

In the winter of 1943, Jorge Semprun, an active member of the French resistance, was captured in occupied France and sent to Buchenwald, where he spent two years as a political prisoner. His five-day train voyage to the concentration camp and subsequent imprisonment inspired a thinly veiled autobiographical account in which memory forms the central axis of the narrative. The story is told through Gérard's recollections, which alternate between the train, camp, and scenes after his liberation. Semprun's aim in remembering is twofold: to heal himself of a split in his consciousness by making sense of these traumatic events, and to tell the world about Nazi inhumanity. He wishes to guard against the dangerous psychic consequences (depression, schizophrenia, or neurosis) of the death camp experience by recalling and integrating what has happened, which is a fundamentally modernist approach to the project of psychic centering. To do this, he must examine the nature of the repression that he suffers at the hands of the Nazis. While aware that the modernist self is capable of injustice, Semprun does not embrace the postmodern conception of the decentered self, because he believes that this kind of decenteredness enables, rather than prevents, Nazi atrocities.[1] His final and no less important goal, however, is to ensure continued awareness of the atrocities committed in Buchenwald which have caused so much suffering and decenteredness in its victims.

As Patricia A. Gartland points out, Semprun's novel attempts to reconcile the relentless presence of the camp experience in individual memory.[2] In an effort to recall the events of the war and put them into personal perspective, Gérard has to integrate alien and disturbing memories. C. G. Jung argues that assimilation of unconscious or repressed psychic contents guards against a dangerous isolation which everyone feels when confronted with incomprehensible and irrational aspects of personality. Such isolation, according to Jung, often signals the beginning of a psychosis or severe neurosis.[3] Gérard must assimilate devastating memories of his deportation in order to avoid possible derangement because of a dangerous psychic splitting off of these very memories. While it is true, as Sally M. Silk suggests, that Semprun's shift (in Part II) from first person to third person signals a separation in the narrational self, it is by no means true, as she argues, that this split is absolute.[4] The very act of telling his story is crucial in reconciling Gerard's alienation from self, for, as holocaust researcher Anton Gill has argued, survivors must ventilate their feelings or a sense of isolation gets the upper hand.[5]

Deportation constitutes a reality so difficult to fathom that the task of communicating it to others can seem insurmountable to the survivor. "One had to be there," argues Elie Wiesel, "in order to understand that there are some kinds of loneliness that can never be overcome. Only those who lived through the Event know what it was; the others will never know."[6] Gérard, like Wiesel, understands that what has happened to him and others has little precedent in history.[7] Few who survived deportation escaped the psychological aftereffects of confinement in Nazi prison camps.

These effects have been studied by a number of psychiatrists since the end of the war. Gill carefully details the mental disturbances survivors are subject to, which include a general inability to adapt to the normal stresses and demands of society, as well as a host of particular symptoms. He argues that frequently the experiences survivors suffered were of such traumatic intensity that it was simply impossible for a normal person to accept them. Survivors, therefore, often tried to negate their memories of death camp atrocities, giving themselves the impression that they were not true.[8]

Yet, the results of denial are equally unpalatable, resulting in a host of neuroses or even a complete mental breakdown.[9] Gérard's project to recall what he has seen and suffered has therapeutic value, since it is aimed at helping him survive the disintegration at the center of the Nazi project, the destruction and shattering of the body and mind in an attempt to reduce persons to a state where "the body is about to break into little pieces" (122). Gérard knows intuitively that to survive and integrate this experience is its ultimate negation.

Not surprisingly, Semprun devotes considerable space in *The Long Voyage* to Gérard's examination of the nature of the Nazi mentality. By plumbing the Nazi psyche, Gérard hopes to understand what he has stood for and against; his recollections lead us through a series of experiences during which he tries to fathom the mind-set that has given rise to such catastrophic events, while he simultaneously defines and heals himself. The majority of these memories center on acts of inhumanity committed by German civilians, soldiers, and functionaries. Perhaps most inexplicable to Gérard is the behavior of the common folk, since they are not directly involved in the guarding, transport, or killing of prisoners, yet they are extraordinarily hostile as a rule. On one occasion a young boy, encouraged by his parents, heaves a large stone as hard as he can against the boxcar opening that Gérard stands beside. Gérard ducks down quickly, and the stone ricochets off the barbed wire, just missing someone inside (36).

This gratuitous violence perplexes Gérard, though evidently, he concludes, society is partially to blame. Nazi inhumanity and indifference to suffering, Semprun here suggests, have their foundation in the social production of moral indifference in a system where actions have no intrinsic moral value. The curiously pointless actions of the youth are merely required behavior, necessitated by his role as a good citizen in Germany at that time. Since he does exactly what is expected of him, he is by most definitions normal.

Numerous recent attempts, in fact, to interpret the holocaust as an outrage committed by born criminals, sadists, and madmen have repeatedly failed.[10] That most of the perpetrators of genocide were "normal" individuals (something Gérard realizes), who would likely pass conventional psychiatric tests, is deeply disturbing to him. The most difficult problem to be solved by the Nazis was how to overcome the natural pity normal men and women feel when in the presence of physical suffering.

How, in other words, Gérard wonders, were ordinary Germans transformed into mass murderers? According to Herbert C. Kelman, moral inhibitions against violent atrocities are lowered only when three conditions are met, singly or together: violence must be authorized by superiors, the actions are routinized, and the victims are dehumanized through ideological indoctrinations.[11] Gérard examines all three of these conditions in his narrative, paying particular attention to the SS.

The German SS is perhaps the most striking example of the success of the authorization, routinization, and dehumanization of violence. Amazingly, according to recent psychological data, no more than ten percent of the SS could be considered abnormal by conventional clinical criteria.[12] SS leaders actually expressed concern for the mental sanity of their subordinates; they counted on organizational routine and discipline, not individual zeal.[13]

Yet, Gérard senses that something has gone terribly wrong with humanity. Scenes involving S.S. atrocities draw the most poignant commentary, since they are undeniably at the center of the Nazi project of genocide. Semprun portrays S.S. behavior as bordering on the absurd, for their actions are so consistently and deliberately without humanity that one finds it difficult to accept them as real and not the invention of some perverted literary mind. The S.S.'s love of order and symmetry is responsible for ludicrous, yet horrific, situations. Officers of the camp become annoyed when they have to extinguish crematorium fires during allied air raids (35). On another occasion thirty thousand prisoners' heels "click to an impeccable attention...[while] thirty thousand prisoners' berets were seized by thirty thousand hands and slapped against thirty thousand right legs, in a perfect chorus-like movement" (52).

The S.S. carries out its murderous duty with a precision and efficiency which apparently precludes even the slightest twinge of conscience; it is all done in a way in which the most insignificant of details are taken care of and usually so as to leave the victim in doubt about his fate until the moment of execution. Soviet officers are taken individually into what they believe is a shower stall, given a bar of soap and a bath towel,

> but the water didn't flow. Through a loophole concealed in the corner, an S.S. would send a bullet into the Soviet officer's head. The S.S. was in an adjoining room, he calmly aimed at the Soviet officer's head, and he sent a bullet into his head. They removed the corpse, they gathered up the soap and the bath towel, and they turned on the shower to erase any trace of blood. When you have understood the simulacrum of the shower and the piece of soap, you will have understood the S.S. mentality (71).

In a discussion of findings by psychologist Stanley Milgram, Zygmunt Bauman notes how the most striking of Milgram's conclusions is the inverse ratio of readiness to cruelty and proximity to its victims. It is always easier, Bauman argues, to inflict pain on a person we see at a distance, and still easier in the case of a person we can only hear.[14] A key S.S. strategy was to distance themselves from their victims, both psychologically and physically, as in assassination through a small hole in the wall, for, in avoiding bodily contact, the perpetrator is allowed the comfort of denying the causal link between his actions and his victim's suffering.

Gérard finds this calculated distancing of killer and victim appalling;

the mentality of the S.S., he reasons, cannot be reasoned with and altered. It must be simply eradicated, because "with an S.S. man, dialogue becomes possible only after he is dead" (78). Yet he adds, as if to stress that the issue is not merely one of personal aberration, the essential problem is to change the historical structure which allows the existence of the S.S.[15] But once the S.S. man is there, there is no choice but to liquidate him whenever the opportunity arises in the course of battle (78). It is more difficult to talk with a German soldier than to read Hegel, Gérard admits, especially to talk with him about truly essential matters, about "life and death, about the reasons for living and dying" (43). Writes David H. Hirsch, "what the German soldier has done defies both basic ideas of human decency and justice, as well as logic. Hegel, though difficult, can still be understood if one makes the effort."[16] Throughout *The Long Voyage* Semprun investigates this problematic mentality.

The dilemma of German reaction to the holocaust, still relevant, has demanded the attention of many, including Primo Levi, Elie Wiesel, and Bruno Bettelheim. In an essay entitled "The Dispute among German Historians," Levi discusses the disturbing phenomenon of revisionist historians who downplay the significance of the holocaust as a unique event in world history. Worse still are some who categorically deny that a systematic annihilation of Jews and others took place. Levi argues that polemic in Germany between those who tend to banalize the Nazi slaughter (Nolte, Hillgruber) and those who insist on its uniqueness (Habermas and many others) cannot leave us indifferent. The former argue that there have been slaughters in all centuries, especially during modern times. During the Second World War, they argue, Germans did nothing but adapt themselves to a horrendous but already established procedure.[17]

Yet, even Gérard pities Germans who have been caught in the inexorable cogs of the Nazi war machine, for he knows that the affable German soldier from Auxerre who has befriended him, "for years now...hasn't understood why he is what he is" (46). His life has been made uninhabitable, and he has not the slightest awareness of the social forces which have molded him. Atrocities nevertheless have occurred. Who is responsible, Gérard wonders, for trainloads of Polish Jews shipped to death camps in the dead of winter, padlocked nearly two-hundred in each boxcar, arriving frozen solid after eight days without food or water (97), or Jewish children murdered by S.S. clubs and dogs

(164–66)? The answer, for Gérard, is that a kind of collective insanity has descended upon Europe, an ideology whose credo is the submersion of individuality and the death of critical self-consciousness. Curiously, Gérard's effort to remember what he has experienced hinges upon coming to some tentative understanding of the mentality he struggles against.

James Glass's argument for the necessity of a unitary, self-conscious self sheds light on the effects of depersonalization on the Nazis' victims. Glass deals specifically with the question of postmodernism's unrealistic (in his opinion) conception of the capabilities of a decentered self. Glass points out that, based upon his observations in clinical settings, the true psychological significance of an unstable sense of identity for those suffering from schizophrenia and other diseases involving a radical decentering of consciousness, is not a liberation from subjugating power, but rather "feelings of abandonment, terror, and implosion," in other words, a sense of absolute enslavement to external forces.[18]

Contrary to postmodern concerns with decentered texts, Semprun focuses on the decentering of actual selves and the resulting pain they feel as they disintegrate and die. For, as Glass argues, human beings are not texts, and since persons are capable of suffering, while texts are not, humans must be treated differently than words on a page.[19]

The enigma of Nazi behavior, Gérard realizes, resides in progressive dehumanization and depersonalization of the "enemy." Camps were geared to reducing men and women to a sub-human, animalistic existence with but one aim, to survive at any cost, ultimately converting those who survived into emotional basket cases or psychic replicas of their persecutors.[20] Glass refers to the daughter of a camp survivor who was treated so badly by her father that she ended up institutionalized until she was able to integrate what had been done to her. Her psychic state eerily conforms to the idealized decentered self of postmodernists, yet rather than feel a sense of freedom, she lived in constant paralyzing dread of psychological disintegration, which often resulted in suicide attempts.[21]

The borderline psyche's energy is wholly occupied with merely holding itself together and is therefore incapable of any but the most rudimentary tasks involving creativity, organization, or control. It is weak, ineffectual, unappealing, subject to exploitation by others, and unlikely to pose a threat to dominant power interests, a result which undoubtedly conformed to the German vision of German superiority over the other peoples of Europe.[22]

Gérard is engaged in a dual project, one of both understanding and healing. To complete the circle of healing, he must not only remember and comprehend, but also tell his story. Psychologically, however, there is very little reason to desire to preserve the memory of a nightmare. As Freud has argued, repression consists of striving against acceptance (in Gérard's case remembering) of a painful piece of reality.[23] Emblematic of forgetting are two encounters Gérard has, one with a Jewish woman he has earlier helped to find a house she was looking for in Paris, and another with a young German woman after the war. Recalling the incident with the frightened Jewish woman, he wonders "whether she took the voyage that we're taking," or perhaps, if she has taken the voyage, "she hasn't taken it the same way we are. Because there is still another way of traveling for the Jews" (93). After his release he recognizes her and tries to strike up a conversation, though she repeatedly refuses to acknowledge that she knows him, as if *that* past is too painful to recall. Gérard, in contrast, perseveres; "I lean over" Gérard remarks,

> toward her and take her right arm, her wrist, and my fingers lightly graze her white, delicate skin and the blue number from Oswiecim [Auschwitz] tattooed on her white, delicate, already withered skin. "I was wondering," I tell her, "I was wondering whether you had finally made this voyage." Then she withdraws her arm, which she hugs to her breast, and she retreats as far as possible into the lounge chair. "Who are you?" she says. Her voice is choked...Silently she begins to cry. "But who are you?" she begs..."I don't know you," she says...She's still crying silently. "I don't know who you are," she says. "Leave me alone" (95).

Gérard concludes, "if you've forgotten, it's true that I didn't see you. It's true that we don't know each other" (96), ironically foreshadowing another conversation which is to make clear the peril of failing to remember.

Gérard's episode with the young and beautiful Sigrid, who appears either unaware or uninterested in the recent past of her country, serves to emphasize the powerful forces working to consign wartime atrocities to mere footnote status in history. Yet, Gérard knows that if these events are not actively recalled to memory they will become unreal and insignificant; of course, then they are likely to recur. Remembering, we are reminded, involves seeing the truth, even in its repulsive and shattering aspect: the stench of the ill and the infirm, the dying, crematoriums, lampshades made out of human skin, complete with blue tattoos (140).

After the war Germans are taken to bear witness to the camps' atrocities firsthand. The men and women from Weimar, "in their new spring finery," are taken by the Americans to see these things: "with their professor- and grocer-like glasses, [they] will start to cry, start to scream that they didn't know, that they aren't responsible" (140). Knowing and preserving the truth, however gruesome, Gérard realizes, is the first step to coming to terms with it. While it is natural to wish to repress a shameful past, this cannot be allowed to happen. Whether justly or not, Sigrid bears the brunt of Gérard's anger, for she too wishes to treat the Nazi years as if they have nothing to do with her, as if Germany's past has no relation to the present. Though she personally cannot have been responsible for atrocities, her willful ignorance of the horrors committed still seems, in Gérard's eyes, unpardonable. After she repeatedly denies that her father was in the Gestapo, or in the Waffen-S.S., Gérard derisively comments, "'And he was never a Nazi, of course,'" to which she replies, "'I don't know.'" Gérard sardonically adds, "'That's true,…you don't know anything. Nobody knows anything any more. There was never any Gestapo, never any Waffen-S.S., never any Totenkopf. I must have been dreaming'" (143).

In an essay entitled "Children of the Holocaust," Bruno Bettelheim, himself a camp survivor, writes of the need for survivors to speak of the things they have experienced, so as to free themselves and their descendants of the burden of their memories.[24] "If these ancient wounds are not dealt with," he writes, "they will continue to fester from generation to generation," a malady which applies to victim, persecutor, and indeed western society itself, as Levi, Lyotard and others have argued.[25] Bettelheim tells of a woman whose parents were both survivors of extermination camps; their inability to speak about it severely damaged her life, even though she grew up in the United States, far from war and physical suffering. Though never separated from her parents, nor exposed to excessive hardship, she suffered from their unspoken pain, carrying within her "an iron box which she buried deep," and which made life so very painful for her.[26]

Semprun, like Bettelheim, argues for the necessity of remembering, for that which is denied and cannot be named, is that which oppresses. Things thus repressed, he knows, have an existence of their own which destroys life. Yet, the desire to forget is powerful for victim and persecutor alike, for the holocaust persistently resists rational explanation and thus contains within itself something of the eerie, the kind of thing we do not like to face unless forced. "After we have gone through the facts," writes Andreas Huyssen, "we will still be haunted by that core of absolute humiliation, degradation, and horror suffered by the victims."[27] Intuitively, however, Semprun realizes that only memory itself can call the dead to testify to their fate and help prevent similar atrocities in the future.

"'Tonight, wake not those who are sleeping'" (143). With these words, Gérard signals the immense difficulty of rousing to awareness those who wish to consign their own history to oblivion. Still, he is not without sympathy for the terrible weight of collective memory which must be carried yoke-like by new generations. He realizes that Sigrid "must have left her country, her family, no doubt because of the burden of this past of which she wants no part, not the slightest part, this past she is trying to erase, through an infinite succession of meaningless gestures" (145), a past which *she* may choose to deny, but which Gérard cannot; remembering is as essential to his discovery of himself, his purpose and meaning, as forgetting seems necessary to others. Memory, for Gérard, is an indissoluble link with humanity's enduring dignity and spirit; remembering the atrocities, the dead, the misery, is an act of defiance and negation of inhumanity. Memory, furthermore, wakes him from the stupor of oblivion he has fallen into, signaling the work of recalling and telling to be done (147).

Sigrid, who struggles to dissolve a past which cannot be erased, personifies the "burning tension" between the weight of this past and the refusal to remember this past (148). Intrusion of this painful past, however, so deeply buried in Gérard's memory, wakes him from the dream (forgetting) he has fallen into, making it possible for him to write his book, whose purpose is to "evolve some semblance of order for myself out of my past" (126). Memory transports him to a past which impinges on the "empty, hazy happiness" (126) of a present threatening to obscure the events of his voyage. Luminescent memories rise from the willful oblivion of the voyage with the "polished perfection of diamonds that nothing can impair" (126).

On one occasion, during dinner with friends, the taste and texture of Russian black bread catapult him back to prison camp when "we used to eat our ration of bread, when, with Indian-like stealth, we used to stretch it out, so that the tiny squares of wet, sandy bread which we had cut off our daily ration would last as long as possible" (126). Sitting motionless, his arm raised with a buttered slice of good black bread in his hand, and his heart pounding like a jackhammer, he cannot tell his host that he is "in the throes of dying, dying of hunger, far from them, far from the wood fire and the words we were saying" (126).

Telling, however, becomes part of the voyage for Gérard, surely crucial for his personal evolution; only the transformation of a jumbled mass of disjointed memories into a coherent and communicable account can ascribe meaning to his pain. His suffering transformed into art has a deep regenerative and healing power capable of benefiting not only himself but also the community at large.[28] Through telling via writing, his story leaves the purely personal realm and enters the public arena, where some good may come of what he has suffered. Gérard's journey follows the ancient tradition of the trip to the Underworld, for ultimately he must return to the realm of the living to tell his tale. Just as Odysseus, after meeting the dead, must return to his men, so too must Gérard finally unburden himself in the light of day.[29] What he has suffered has little meaning, Gérard understands, until it is expressed and shared.[30] His vow "never again to talk about this voyage" (105) is destined to be broken, for, he adds, "I knew, though, that this would not be possible" (105). It is not possible simply because there is too much that needs to be known and cannot be forgotten, and too many ghosts which will find peace only when they have been given voice.

Speaking out, Gérard comes to understand, is a sacramental act, a sacred duty to those who were silenced by a tyranny they scarcely understood. It is an act of solidarity with the Jewish children from Poland who were slaughtered by the S.S. on a cold winter day, children who, sixteen years later, would be adults, had they lived. Locked within Gérard's mind is the vision of that terrible day. The time, he realizes, has come to break the silence, to let the voices of the dead ring out. "And maybe," we read,

> I shall be able to tell about the death of the Jewish children, describe the death in all its details, solely in the hope—perhaps exaggerated, perhaps unrealizable— that these children may hear it…to tell of their death on this broad avenue of the camp in the middle of the final winter of the war, that story which has never been told, which has lain buried in my memory like some mortal treasure, preying on it with a sterile suffering…from now on I can remember everything…I feel compelled to tell it. I have to speak out in the name of things that have happened (163).

Attempts to derive conclusive meaning from the holocaust have been notoriously unsuccessful. The enormity of the devastation was in some ways similar to earlier historic events such as the destruction of Armenians at the hand of the Turks around the turn of the century or more recently the mass genocide of more than a million in Cambodia by the Khymer Rouge. In an insightful and far-reaching talk given at the 1978 symposium, "Western Society After the Holocaust," Leszek Kolakowski reflected on the lessons to be learned in the light of Nazism's destruction. The Third Reich, he remarked, was a perfect example of the ideological state ruled by one *Weltanschauung*, in which those in a position of higher authority guaranteed the truth. What they wanted to destroy was the belief, long rooted in western culture, that universal criteria for truth are the property of all mankind, not merely of one privileged group. Nazi ideology, he argued, was based on the belief that "some segments of mankind—the supreme race and its leaders— have a deeper insight which no arguments based on ordinary logical criteria could invalidate."[31]

Particularly disturbing is the seemingly inexplicable fact that the same society which had produced Himmler and Eichmann had nurtured Mann and Einstein.[32] Semprun provides a provisional response to the problem of systemized repression in his persistent focus on ideology and depersonalization, two factors particularly salient in totalitarian regimes and which have an especially ruinous effect on the human spirit. Activation of memory and reconciliation of the psychic split created by Gérard's war trauma in effect provide an antidote to the threat of totalitarianism. Semprun's rehumanization of Gérard (and others through his account) constitutes a process which, if successful, can reduce the chances of history repeating itself. While totalitarianism is, Kolokowski suggests, a possible (though not desirable) solution for a society in deep crisis, it is the worst possible solution not only because of the horror it brings about, but also because of the damage it does to society as a whole.[33]

The reestablishment of an autonomous self tied to humanity through a common sympathetic bond is the final goal of Semprun's narrative. Like Habermas, who, in response to the horrors of the holocaust, began to wonder about the ghastliness of a collectively realized inhumanity, Semprun too recognizes the dark side of modernity. He too ponders the rupture in the Enlightenment tradition in which the ideals of reason, freedom and justice had been so prominent, yet, like Habermas, he searches for a way to reclaim values which make a tolerant and cooperative democratic community of selves possible. Such a community would be based on mutual understanding and consensual action, rather than efficiency and success.[34]

Semprun aims at neutralizing the effects of postmodern ideologies which encourage the depersonalization, fragmentation, and dehumanization characteristic of the Nazis. The way to do this, Semprun suggests, begins with an honest, deep, and painful examination of oneself, precisely the kind of moral reflection Nazism prohibited. Semprun would agree with Glass that a "Rousseauian integration" is needed where empathy becomes "the foundation for understanding,"[35] and where self emerges from the "narcissistic preoccupation"[36] characteristic of both totalitarian regimes and the individuals subjugated by them. Semprun hopes that, by knowing ourselves, we can, to use Glass's words, discover "empathy…as the foundation of the core self," and as the emotion "that lies at the center of human responsiveness [which] pushes the self toward recognition of the other."[37]

This kind of reflection is most likely to affect both the collective behavior and the memory of civilization, because, as beings capable of empathy, we are unlikely to forget the inhumanity of others and less likely to repeat their acts. The solution to the enigma of genocide is thus both simple and difficult. One must know oneself with bare, brutal honesty; one must look truth in the face, however ugly, and one must be willing to tell others what one has seen. Preserving the memory of those who perished, Semprun realizes, requires constant struggle against an insidious oblivion which threatens to deprive the present of a much needed, and unquestionably sobering, voice.

In *The Long Voyage*, Jorge Semprun creates a moving fictional account of a man whose decision to join the French underground leads to his capture and transport to a German death camp. The voyage, as he calls this experience, becomes an event which not only changes the course of his life, but also imbues him with a profound sense of the human race's capabilities for both good and evil. His need to recall his ordeal and finally to tell his story is part of a necessary project of individuation and self-definition which comes out of the deep human misery he has witnessed; by telling his story, he is able to transform a private and subjective experience, thus moving his suffering out of the merely personal realm while allowing for a healing of the deep psychic wounds he has received. His sharing of his ordeal, an act of communion with the dead, concretizes events which time and willful oblivion threaten to obliterate, and allows the possibility for others to grow in awareness and find healing.

Notes

1. This is a very complex subject and cannot be fully covered in this paper. While the causes of the holocaust are many and are still the subject of passionate and sometimes rather obscure debate, it is clear that Semprun locates the source of Nazi atrocities in precisely the kind of decenteredness that postmodern theorists postulate as the predominant mode of consciousness today, at least in the postindustrial world. That is, a decentered awareness incapable of the kind of self-reflection which would recognize the inherent worth of others who are perceived as different or alien. The greatest enemy of the kind of tolerance Semprun wishes to argue for is not, as some would argue, a modernist self capable of systematic introspection, but a postmodern decentered self which has no humanistic point of reference anchored to others in a shared global community. In a tragically ironic sense, release from traditional Enlightenment values of community and self have become, rather than a liberation, an opportunity for oppressive ideologies to proliferate. As Jane Flax argues in *Thinking Fragments: Psychoanalysis, Feminism, and Postmodernism in the Contemporary West* (Berkeley: Univ. of California Press, 1990), it is possible that we are now in an age when "governments...claim to be the ultimate bastion and guarantor of freedom, progress, and human emancipation" (8), thus mocking the very values they seek to uphold.
2. Patricia A. Gartland, "Three Holocaust Writers: Speaking the Unspeakable," *Critique: Studies in Contemporary Fiction* 25.1 (Fall 1983), 51.
3. C. G. Jung, *Symbols of Transformation*, trans. R. F. C. Hull (Princeton: Princeton Univ. Press, 1976), 442.
4. Sally M. Silk, "The Dialogical Traveler: A Reading of Semprun's *Le grand voyage*," *Studies in 20th Century Literature* 14.2 (Summer 1990) 233. While Silk argues that at the end of his voyage Gérard has arrived at a point "which apparently marks for him a division of self that can no longer be joined" (233–4), I take the position in this essay that this split, though deep, can be healed to some degree by the act of writing, that is, by Gérard telling his story. The "complete rejection of the self for the other" (234) Silk argues for, would result in insanity for Gérard. In a more recent article, "Writing the Holocaust/Writing Travel: The Space of Representation in Jorge Semprun's *Le grand voyage*," *Clio: A Journal of Literature, History, and the Philosophy of History* 22.1 (Fall 1992), Silk similarly concludes that Gérard "narrates his journey through a voice that completely leaves behind a conception of self as an autonomous entity" (65), a position with which I also disagree.
5. Anton Gill, *The Journey Back from Hell: An Oral History: Conversations with Concentration Camp Survivors* (New York: William Morrow, 1988), 87.
6. Elie Wiesel, "Pilgrimage to the Kingdom of Night" in *From the Kingdom of*

Memory (New York: Summit, 1990), 108.

7. Jorge Semprun, *The Long Voyage*, trans. Richard Seaver (New York: Schocken, 1964), 40. Subsequent references will be cited in the text.

8. Gill, 94.

9. Gill, 91. See also Erich Neumann's discussion of the danger to psychic health of repression or denial of unconscious material ("Creative Man and Transformation" in *Art and the Creative Unconscious: Four Essays*, trans. Ralph Mannheim [Princeton: Princeton Univ. Press, 1972], 161).

10. Zygmunt Bauman, *Modernity and the Holocaust* (New York: Cornell Univ. Press, 1989), 19.

11. See Herbert C. Kelman, "Violence Without Moral Restraint: Reflections on the Dehumanization of Victims and Victimizers," *Journal of Social Issues* 29.4 (1973), 29–61.

12. George M. Kren and Leon Rappaport, *The Holocaust and the Crisis of Human Behavior* (New York: Holmes & Meier, 1980), 70. Quoted in Bauman, 19.

13. Bauman, 20.

14. Bauman, 155.

15. Kathleen A. Johnson's "Narrative Revolutions/Narrative Resolutions: Jorge Semprun's *Le Grand Voyage*," *Romanic Review* 80.2 (March 1989), contains a discussion of the dialectic of history as it relates to narrative voice in *The Long Voyage*.

16. David H. Hirsch, *The Deconstruction of Literature: Criticism after Auschwitz* (Hanover, New Hampshire: Brown Univ. Press, 1991), 131. Semprun, Hirsch also argues, is one of the few who has left a record of his attempt to reconcile German high culture with the reality of the death camps.

17. Primo Levi, "The Dispute Among German Historians" in *The Mirror Maker*, trans. Raymond Rosenthal (New York: Schocken, 1989), 163.

18. James M. Glass, *Shattered Selves: Multiple Personality in a Postmodern World* (Ithaca: Cornell Univ. Press, 1993), 13.

19. Glass, *Shattered*, 14.

20. Jack Bemporad, "The Concept of Man After Auschwitz" in *Out of the Whirlwind* (New York: Schocken, 1976). "Those who did survive," writes Bemporad, "often adopted Nazi attitudes, identifying themselves with their persecutors, judging themselves by Nazi standards" (479).

21. James M. Glass, *Private Terror/Public Life: Psychosis and the Politics of Community* (Ithaca: Cornell Univ. Press, 1989), 72–85.

22. Joseph H. Berke, *The Tyranny of Malice: Exploring the Dark Side of Character and Culture* (New York: Summit, 1988), 262.

23. Sigmund Freud, *The History of the Psychoanalytic Movement* in *The Basic Writings of Sigmund Freud*, trans., ed. A. A. Brill (New York: Modern Library, 1938), 939. As a chilling parallel to the type of individual repression Semprun describes, Hirsch characterizes the "French poststructuralist-deconstructionist-postmodernist phenomenon" as part and parcel of a massive repression which has taken place in the wake of the holocaust. He accuses, among others, Lacan, Barthes, Foucault, and de Man of ignoring (consciously or unconsciously) central issues relating to the holocaust in order to hide their tacit, or possibly in the case of de Man and others,

active complicity in the shameful events of the war (Hirsch, *Deconstruction of Literature, passim*).

24. Bruno Bettelheim, "Children of the Holocaust," in *Freud's Vienna and Other Essays* (New York: Knopf, 1990), 217–218.

25. Andreas Huyssen, "Monument and Memory in a Postmodern Age," *The Yale Journal of Criticism* 6:2 (1993), 251.

26. Bettelheim, 218.

27. Huyssen, 25.

28. Neumann, 187.

29. Homer, *Odyssey*, trans. Robert Fitzgerald (New York: Anchor, 1963). See Book Eleven.

30. Thoughts and experiences, Erich Neumann writes, are weak and insubstantial until they enter the physical world ("Creative Man and the Great Experience" in *The Place of Creation: Six Essays*, trans. Eugene Rolfe [Princeton: Princeton Univ. Press, 1989], 177).

31. Leszek Kolakowski, "Genocide and Ideology" in *Western Society After the Holocaust*, ed. Lyman H. Legters (Boulder: Westview, 1983), 19.

32. Ibid., 19.

33. Ibid., 22.

34. Richard J. Bernstein, *The New Constellation: The Ethical-Political Horizons of Modernity/Postmodernity* (Cambridge: MIT, 1992), 202–204.

35. James M. Glass, *Delusion: Internal Dimensions of Political Life* (Chicago: Univ. of Chicago Press, 1985), 231.

36. Ibid., 238.

37. Ibid., 239.

Piracquo's Missing Finger, Or, The Utility of the Liberal Arts
by Dan Latimer

> Every time the meaning of a discussion depends on the fundamental value of the word useful—in other words, every time the essential question touching on the life of human societies is raised, no matter who intervenes and what opinions are represented—it is possible to affirm that the debate is necessarily warped and the fundamental question is eluded....There is nothing that permits one to define what is useful to man.
>
> Georges Bataille, *Visions of Excess*[1]

> Dragons of the prime,
> That tare each other in their slime,
> Were mellow music match'd with him.
>
> Tennyson, *In Memoriam A. H. H.* (Section 56)

I.

"Utility is the great idol of the age," wrote Schiller in 1795.[2] He was in the process of finding some justification for an aesthetic education, the syllabus for which we would today call the liberal arts. "In [utility's] clumsy scales the spiritual service of Art has no weight." Schiller complains of his century's "noisy mart," from which art, discouraged and disheartened, flees (26). He speaks of art's contracting frontiers, of ever larger chunks of pastoral territory gobbled up by the Visigothic developers of science. He wonders whether he shouldn't apologize for "looking around for a code of laws for the aesthetic world" (25) when there was much more serious lawlessness abroad, when the burning question of the moment was clearly not aesthetic at all but rather political. Shouldn't we be trying to comprehend the nature of true political freedom, which if it existed would be a work of art worthy of the name? His interests are, he fears, "unseasonable," at the very least.

If they were unseasonable then, they are even more so now. Not only do very few citizens "fail to recognize the direct relevance of art to their lives," according to *American Canvas*, the latest report from the National Endowment for the Arts;[3] we live in an age in which 15,000,000 contracts are awarded by the Pentagon each year, when $.70 of every dollar spent by the government for research and development is for military research and development, when half of the military's basic research is done by the universities, and when a third of the country's scientists and engineers are directly employed by the defense industry.[4] In such a context liberal arts deans continue to represent the indispensability of their disciplines. It may be a measure of their desperation that they are sometimes driven to invoke the touchstone of Albert Speer, technician of the Third Reich, organizer of its heavy industry and of spectacular sound and light shows in Nürnberg. Speer, the deans assure us, was eager to play the role he played in the history of Europe precisely because he lacked the soul, the character, with which a couple of quarters of world literature at an American university would have equipped him.

The same salvational assumption is constantly being made by others, well-meaning and intelligent educators, who care deeply that Fredric Jameson's description of the "postmodern" character may be correct: that there is a widespread loss of coordinates of any kind, let alone the moral ones; that schizophrenia (a breakdown between signifiers) has become our dominant cultural style; that we have lost the past and any vital connection to nature; that life lacks coherent sequence; that our children live, as do we, if we are sufficiently hip, in a series of isolated orgasmic instants of intensity; that to be a postmodern citizen in the U.S. today is, in short, to be a tripped-out denizen of the simulacrum.[5] Into the teeth of this national crisis, Allan Bloom wanted to steer "the good old Great Books…, the only serious solution."[6] E. D. Hirsch (*Cultural Literacy; The Dictionary of Cultural Literacy*) and William Bennett (*The De-Valuing of America; The Index of Leading Cultural Indicators*) also continue to think the liberal arts will provide a way out of the postmodern dilemma, the curse of personality by pastiche, to allude to Jameson again. The theory is that the cultural evacuation of character leaves one vulnerable to colonization by Satanic influence, that—to return to the theories of the liberal arts dean above—such was precisely the problem of Albert Speer.

It must be said, alas, that he who finds this argument convincing has not gotten very far into *Inside the Third Reich*, nor very deeply into human nature. Not only was Speer not a soulless technician, ignorant of art and fine sentiments, he was himself always an artist. A description of his first elaborate, allegorical artwork, produced at the precocious age of twelve years, can be read on the fourth page of his memoir. As a boy he took inspirational walks in the Odenwald near Heidelberg. He dreamed in the Schlosspark with its view of that city's ancient roofs and crooked old streets.

He collected landscape paintings of the Heidelberg Romantics. He regularly saw Stefan George, the great Symbolist poet. He was passionately fond of music, "ravished by Rimsky-Korsakov," he says. "German Class assignments called solely for essays on literary subjects."[7] His own *Abitur* essay was judged the best in his class.

Suffice it to say that we are not dealing here with a man who has devoted his life to chicken bronchitis or to developing ball joints for arthritic Siberian huskies. We are dealing with a man whose primary source of inspiration was, as is ours, Classical Greece. Speer's own predilection was for the purer Doric style. He felt he detected signs of contamination in the Ionic, due to the inordinate wealth drawn by the colonies from Asia Minor.[8] But let's not pick on the Third Reich, rather an easy target, anyway, as any number of recent mini-series and "blockbuster" films have shown. Other countries and other eras are filled with wonderful examples of cultured monstrosity. Nadezhda Mandelstam, wife of the poet Osip, hence someone who should know, has provided us with instruction in the "dereliction and depravity" of men of culture and talent during the 1930s in Russia.[9] Many who were murdered during the Moscow Trials Era (Babel, Pilnyak, Vesyoly) or committed suicide (Mayakovsky, Tsvetaeva, Yesenin) or merely died in labor camps (Mandelstam) had their colleagues to thank (Fadeyev, Sholokhov, Olesha, Gorky, Aleksey Tolstoy), who, choosing to stay alive themselves, were moved to denunciation, recrimination, and cooperation to please their "Kremlin mountaineer," the very coinage, incidentally, which earned Mandelstam the malevolent attention of Stalin.[10]

One particularly exciting example of commitment by a massively cultured, highly educated, very brilliant old Stalinist is Georg Lukács, who in 1919, just before the advent of the short-lived Hungarian Soviet Republic, was at some pains to sort out questions of revolutionary morality for the ultra-leftist reign of terror he and others on the "second Central Committee" were planning for the country—a Red Terror which was itself to be followed, as always, it seems, by an even bloodier "White Terror."[11] According to Lukács's argument, *not* to act implies complicity in all the crimes of capitalism. To act is to accept personally all the deaths of the Terror. Thus commitment is both acceptable and unconscionable. The following formulation is from "Taktik und Ethik":

Nur die mörderische Tat des Menschen, der unerschütterlich und alle Zweifel ausschliessend weiss, dass der Mord unter keinen Umständen zu billigen ist, kann—tragisch—moralischer Natur sein.
Only the murderous act of the man who, shutting out all doubts, knows unshakably

that murder is under no circumstances to be countenanced, can be—tragically—of a moral nature.[12]

Here intellectual aporia leads to precipitous commitment. And we had thought it led to paralysis! Another member of the ultra-left Lukács group, Jozsef Revai, an "aesthete," in the description of a historian of the period, set pen to paper and composed a poem for his time. Its (sweepingly Oedipal) title: "My Mother, My Father, My First Teacher: You Should Die Like a Dog."[13]

It is easy to think from the distance of safety that one would have reacted differently under similar circumstances. One thinks surely that one would have made more sense than these gentlemen appear at first glance to make. The point, however, is at this stage that there are enough examples of diabolism, bloodlust, and madness among people who deal in the "liberal" arts to cause us to reconsider the terms in which we are recommending them to the young. Indeed, we educators may want to recommend them in precisely these terms, as the *Bildung* of terror. But if we do want to say that artists distill the purest essence of evil, can we then continue to go on saying that the liberal arts are the ground, the foundation, of the "love of our neighbor, the impulses toward…help, and beneficence, the desire for removing human error, clearing human confusion, and diminishing human misery, the noble aspiration to leave the world…happier than we found it"?[14] Should we go on saying that "to cultivate the liberal arts, to pursue culture is to pursue human perfection"?[15] Should we not burst out laughing when, as we consider the savagery with which we treat each other during periods of tenure and promotion, let alone during periods of social upheaval, we sanctimoniously call this perfection "sweetness and light"?

Where "bitter envying and strife" are, there culture is not, says Arnold, who wanted to believe that bitter envy and strife were exclusively products of Philistine commercial activity, products of a culture that exalts the practical, the very thing that Schiller calls "utility" in his *Aesthetic Letters*.[16] "He who works for sweetness and light, works to make reason and the will of God prevail," says Arnold in *Culture and Anarchy*.[17] Reason and the will of God: two elements which Tertullian was not sure belong together.[18] And to us, as well, the reconciliation of these two elements with each other, much less with the university, seems rather a tall order. Sometimes we imply that our colleagues in mechanical engineering or poultry science are not pursuing the same lofty ends as we.

He who works for machinery, he who works for hatred, works only for confusion.

Culture looks beyond machinery, culture hates hatred; culture has one great passion, the passion for sweetness and light....It is not satisfied until we all come to perfect man; it knows that the sweetness and light of a few must be imperfect until the raw and unkindled masses of humanity are touched with sweetness and light.[19]

Let us resist for a moment the temptation to discuss Arnold's account of the masses here as "raw and unkindled." We find this attitude very much present in otherwise rousing assaults on Wilcoxism (Philistine practicality of the upscale sort), in English novels like Forster's *Howards End* (1910), where the very idea of the urban proletariat's attempts to improve itself makes Forster swoon with laughter. And indeed we find something very similar in Schiller. Let us return to this great German's attempts to discover a justification for aesthetic education in his time.

II.

It was Schiller's impression that the natural character of man was selfish and violent and tended more toward the destruction than toward the preservation of society.[20] Society itself, far from improving on the human character, if anything made it more depraved by making it more sophisticated and refined without eradicating its selfishness. The "sensuous instinct" seems to be the source of all the trouble. It is by nature appetitive and relentless, always on the prowl. No sooner does it desire something than it seeks to gratify the desire. In its most intimate interests it often finds itself in conflict with the moral law, to which reason's interests are closely related. "But the sensuous instinct does not recognize the moral law..."[21] It wants, incorrigibly, to "enjoy" its object as soon as possible.[22] The man who is driven predominantly by this rapacious id-like "tempest" with its "brutified explosions" of affect, the man who is without the capacity to postpone enjoyment, ignore, or sublimate it, Schiller calls "the coarse soul," a raw unkindled Caliban.[23] Everything exists only to the extent that it "secures existence for him." The coarse soul sees in Nature's profusion "nothing but his prey" (*Aesthetic Education*, 114). His relation to the sensible is by "immediate contact." Since he is driven by "savage greed" (114), he imagines that every other human creature is as well, that there is "no other aim but his own advantage" (117).

Schiller writes that the aesthetic mode is the only solution to this appetitive bestiality: "There is no other way to make the sensuous man rational than by first making him aesthetic" (108). When a man becomes aesthetic, or sees aesthetically, nature becomes objectified, becomes an item of contemplation and no longer an object of desire. "Contemplation thrusts its object into the distance,...thus securing it from passion" (120). When this happens, "instantaneous calm descends upon the senses." Time stands still. The chaotic darkness of the inner man is flooded with sunny equilibrium, and the reign of Saturn comes to an end (120). This withdrawal from the world, this freedom from the actual, is for Schiller the very prerequisite for the emergence of humanity from savagery. "A delight in *appearance*, a disposition towards *ornament* and *play*," "an indifference toward reality"— these are the conditions which define "man" (125). "So long as Man is still a savage he enjoys merely with the senses of feeling....As soon as he begins to enjoy with the eye,...he is already aesthetically free...and the play impulse has developed" (126).

It is, then, this emancipation from selfishness effected by the fine arts that is supposedly so useful to society. Beauty alone provides man with a social character. "It is through Beauty that we arrive at Freedom" (27). Taste alone, since "it has a horror of everything sharp, hard, and violent,"[24] can bring harmony to the individual by training the sensibility and ennobling the character (*Aesthetic Education*, 138). Of course, it will be a temptation for the artist to try to change the world by plunging into the present: "...glowing desire strives impatiently for action in vigorous souls" (53). At one point Schiller imagines the artist, appalled by the character of his age, returning, "terrible like Agamemnon's son, to cleanse it" (51). But it is precisely this Orestean temptation that for Schiller must be resisted. The artist cannot change life directly in this way. "The fabric of error and lawlessness will fall," he says (54). To assail one's contemporaries directly, to condemn their deeds, the banalities by which they live, is to waste one's breath and earn utter oblivion. They will never be able to tolerate the "gravity" of one's principles. The actual is not at all the artist's sphere. Flee the "sorry productions of time," resign the "sphere of the actual" to the wretch who is at home there (52). The artist in any case is certainly not. He breathes a different air. The only way the arts can change life is to approach appetitive mankind through its idleness (54). The coarse soul will tolerate the artist's projects only if he understands them to be unreal phantoms, if they are unsubstantial entertainments, if they are *not* to be taken seriously. Then the people will open themselves unconsciously to reform. Reform pleasure, says Schiller, surround people with idealized images, and you open the possibility of changing people in other ways as well (55). The Beautiful frees us from passion; the aesthetic thereby engenders the moral sense (106–107, 110–112). Schiller has faith that appearance will overpower actuality. Art will alter Nature.

It would be unfair to say that this aesthetic education plan for world reform is completely useless. Others, whose sensitivity to injustice and desire for reform are not in question, have continued to give Schiller's theories ever new adaptive possibilities over the years. Though art is *Schein* (illusion), it can create a "cosmos of hope," a "holiday reality" within "everyday reality"; it can keep alive a utopian, reformist element in a world almost totally colonized by false consciousness.[25] One finds these adaptations in Frankfurt School theorists like Herbert Marcuse (*The Aesthetic Dimension*), Ernst Bloch (*The Principle of Hope*), and to some extent in Fredric Jameson, who can locate utopian elements in some of the strangest corners of "postmodern" culture.[26]

One problem with these adaptations and with Schiller, surely, is that they locate hope at such a distance, or see the efficacy of the aesthetic mediated by the reflection of so many mirrors that one begins to wonder whether this distance does not suggest a kind of self-defeating compulsion—similar to a fear of germs or a horror of dirt. Albert Speer claimed that had he written fewer essays about literature and concentrated more on "problems of society," he and his generation might not have been so "without defenses when exposed to the new techniques for influencing opinion."[27] This comment suggests again that Schiller's hope for art as playfully reforming human character is delusive, at least in Speer's case and in that of his generation, if Speer is as representative as he claims to be. Art's unreal images do not in fact effect a substantial moral improvement of reality. On the contrary, actuality seems regularly to overpower appearance. Speer's essays on literary topics, which without any doubt at all included Schiller, did not help him much later when he took the plunge into time and made decisions which, in his words, led to the "crushing of justice and the elevation of every evil."[28] Schiller asserts that it is so well known that a "developed feeling for Beauty" ennobles people, refines their manners, that there is no need to prove the idea (*Aesthetic Education*, 55). Yet in the same letter he admits that, historically, when the arts are flourishing, humanity tends to be in decline, that history cannot produce "a single example where a high degree...of aesthetic culture has gone hand in hand with...civic virtue, fine manners with good morals, or refinement with truth of conduct" (58). But, Schiller says, this is hardly compelling evidence, and comes from "keep[ing] solely to what experience has taught us..." (59).

What is wrong here, aside from the repression of history by a historian of some repute? Where, come to think of it, are art's idealizing agents supposed to come from? We find the answer to this in perhaps the most feverish of

Schiller's letters, the Ninth. It comes in the passage in which Schiller is speaking of the regrettable necessity that the artist be "of" his time in any significant sense. Schiller would prefer him not to be. Nevertheless, the artist's subject matter, perhaps, *must* come from the present age. But sublimating *form* comes from a "nobler time—nay, from beyond all time, from the absolute unchangeable unity of his [the artist's] being" (51–52). There is such fury in these passages against matter in general and against subject matter in particular that later, in Letter Twenty-two, Schiller says the real artistic secret consists in…annihilating the material by means of the form" (106). He adds that "in a truly beautiful work of art the content should do nothing, the form everything.…" What does it matter that Roman religion decayed, that the gods became objects of universal ridicule (52)? What did that matter when the temples themselves stood bleaching nobly in the Mediterranean sun, monuments, like Hegel's symbolic Egyptian pyramid, to dead ideas, houses for a perfumed corpse, "immense crystals," in Hegel's words, "now built by art to conceal an interior that is to be kept forever separate from all that is purely natural."[29] In the Ninth Letter, this physical, natural, historical matter appears at its most putrefacient and fecal, while the artist appears at his purest and most Icarian: "Here, from the pure aether of his daemonic nature, flows forth the well-spring of Beauty, untainted by the corruption of the generations and ages which wallow in the dark eddies below it" (*Aesthetic Education*, 52). The Ideal is certainly elsewhere: "Those who do not venture out beyond actuality will never capture Truth" (60).

The humiliating dependency on matter here in Schiller makes him widely relevant in the context of debates to come throughout the nineteenth century. For Marx Schiller's position will be embedded in the "German Ideology," which sees products of consciousness as more important than the material conditions which in fact generate them. This is a position for Marx which causes man and his circumstances to "appear upside down, as in a camera obscura."[30] In fact the whole business of consciousness, law, literature, culture, religion, are for Marx "phantoms" which have no independence from the material life process, but are "sublimates" of that process, its "direct efflux." "Life is not determined by consciousness," says Marx, in the famous formulation, "but consciousness by life."[31] The tendency in both Darwin and Freud to see the essence of human life as a function of extremely primitive behavior which humans share with, say, communities of anthropoid apes is not by any means irrelevant here. Darwin derives incest prohibition not from any intrinsic fastidiousness, instinctive dread of inbreeding, or innate moral sense, but simply from the tyrannical possessiveness of the strongest male in a community, who drives younger males away when they become a competitive threat where the females are concerned.[32] In Freud these exiled, repressed males will return to murder and eat the patriarch, and it is the material ingestation, the food shared between them, which forges new community solidarity and brotherhood.[33] Kinship implies participation in a common material substance, just as the law of *xenia*, hospitality to an outsider, will endure as long as the food which has been eaten in common remains in the body. To last, however, the bond must be constantly renewed.

What flows forth most clearly from Schiller's text and from others, like Matthew Arnold's, which it has helped engender, and which in turn have engendered, immaculately, colleges of the liberal arts, is that this conception of art and of art's role in society is based on a massive repression of materiality. Not that Schiller is unaware of the power of the physical: "Man in his *physical* condition is subject to the power of nature alone; he shakes of this power in the *aesthetic*, and he controls it in the *moral* condition" (*Aesthetic Education*, 113). Consider also the last paragraphs of Letter Twenty-seven. Schiller is speaking of the "aesthetic State" here. It is difficult to decide whether Schiller means to remain within the metaphorical (the artwork as ideal "State") or whether the metaphor has indeed been actualized in "a few select circles" where "People's own lovely nature governs conduct" (140). In any case, the hostility to the body which has been obvious all through our account of the aesthetic taming of the senses, here reaches a kind of Puritanical apogee: "Taste spreads out its soothing veil over physical need, which in its naked shape affronts the dignity of free spirits, and conceals from us the degrading relationship with matter by a delightful illusion of freedom" (139). We are not really free of matter and physical need, says Schiller. But they affront our dignity, degrade and circumscribe our freedom. What art is unable to face, indeed, what art conceals, lies about, are its own origins in materiality, its birth from the primal slime, the admittedly appalling notion that thought is the phosphorescence, the swampy luminosity of the bowels. It is a thought certainly that would appall Lukács—and did. He wrote an essay on "Healthy or Sick Art" and identified a "decaying class society" precisely by this tendency for the viscera to seize power from the head.[34] Decadence is a *Putsch*, the noble battlements of the brow overrun by "the bellowing waves of the viscera," in Bataille's phrase:

Man willingly imagines himself to be like the god Neptune, stilling his own waves, with majesty; nevertheless, the bellowing waves of the viscera, in more or less incessant inflation and upheaval, brusquely put an end to his dignity.[35]

One might further add, continuing with the outrageous Bataille to torment the shade of Lukács, that grace and dignity are difficult to reconcile with the principle of toes. In his meditation on "The Big Toe," Bataille points out that, though this toe is the most human part of the body in the sense that it is the most unlike the corresponding body parts of the anthropoid ape, no longer arboreal in function, "applied to the ground on the same plane as the other toes,"[36] it is precisely the toe, and the foot to which it is attached, that evoke secret horror and apoplectic rage—and any number of attempts to conceal and repress it and all its fellows. Schiller and Lukács must have had toes. To think about their toes, however, is not tasteful. Taste would like to censor this thought, no doubt because of the "hilarity commonly produced by imaging the toes." Toes are derisible because they are base. Their baseness is due in turn to the mud in which they are usually found. Myths of our origin involve molding figures out of mud and breathing life into them— brown Euphrates mud, black Nile mud, red Alabama mud. Mud is dirt, moist dust, clay. We turn back into this element when we die. Is this then why the viscera bellow, bewailing in advance the transient flesh, the cadaverous, yet somehow still dignified, toe? "Since by its physical attitude the human race distances itself as much as it can from terrestrial mud…one can imagine that a toe, always more or less damaged and humiliating, is psychologically analogous to the brutal fall of man—in other words, to death."[37]

What taste censors, finally, what the monument covers and conceals, is not just the senses, history, physicality, undignified orifices and organs of the body, the principle of matter, the lower classes ("Communist workers appear to the bourgeois to be as ugly and dirty as hairy sexual organs, or lower parts"[38]), the dark races, the Third World, germs, crazy people, Arabs, writing (as opposed to speaking), the darkness of night, but that which for the mind, for the European Enlightenment, for philosophy, for theory itself has always been the very womb of all the other horrors—what taste and aesthetic education most want to censor is death. Think of the vaguely erotic recumbency of the Robert E. Lee marble in Lexington's Lee Chapel: death, not as sleep, but as a wet dream. The entirely understandable motivation behind this opus must be, as Schiller says, the restoration of the lost dignity of man; and death, not the toe, not the viscera, not the animal drives or the senses that the aesthetic leads us away from, but death is the ultimate indignity. "Humanity has lost its dignity," says Schiller, "but Art has rescued it and preserved it in significant stone" (*Aesthetic Education*, 52).

This is the role that our culture expects the arts to play, to dignify, ennoble human life: "men obstinately imagine a tide that will permanently elevate them, never to return, into pure space."[39] Such purity and elevation is what the dean expects when we ask him for money. He would be comforted to think that we would prevent all future embarrassments, prevent all future Albert Speers from designing cathedrals of ice with his klieg-lights at party rallies.[40] But we can't promise to prevent such things. In fact, we taught Speer all he knew. What, indeed, he appeared to be doing with the help of his leader, another artist, not incidentally, for a certain kind of proletarian upheaval, was ennobling, dignifying, and sanctifying the "dejected and impoverished life of the proletariat."[41] Fascism, which, as Bataille says, has close ties to the impoverished classes (closer certainly than classical royal society does or than elitist educators do, though they themselves are largely impoverished[42]), was in the process of collecting the revolutionary ferment of the furious, excluded, and undignified, and perverting it, pouring it into the sadistic geometry, the aggressive rigidity, of the military parade, in which effervescent heterogeneity becomes dominated again by a new kind of imperative sovereignty (the leader), thus necessitating the next revolution.[43]

Perhaps the dignifying, ennobling side of art is precisely the problem. When we say that this sweetness is the essence of the arts, we are usually talking to people with discretionary accounts and travel grants. Perhaps we should continue to lie to them (and delude ourselves). I don't know how they would react to the truth. On second thought, we had better tell them. The sooner they know we are a worthy substitute for military spending, the sooner we may get some respect. What is art, then? In Thomas Middleton's *The Changeling*, De Flores has just murdered Piracquo and cut off his finger onstage. Why has he done that? De Flores can't get Piracquo's engagement ring off. Art is about that. De Flores is the foulest, most repulsive, verminous, carbuncular, standing toad-pool of a murderer ever to wear the buskin. The virgin Beatrice-Joanna finds him loathsome, "as youth and beauty hates a sepulchre." Not surprisingly, then, she becomes his lover. Explains De Flores:

> Hunger and pleasure, they'll commend sometimes
> Slovenly dishes, and feed heartily on 'em,
> Nay, which is stronger, refuse daintier for 'em.
> Some women are odd feeders.
>
> (Act 2, Scene 2, lines 150–3)

Art is about that, too. Art is also about a wise, good man who murders his father, marries his mother, and begets daughters who are his sisters. This accomplished, he stabs out his own eyes with his hanged wife's hairpins. It is this work which Aristotle identifies as the greatest paradigm of its genre. Art is about fathers who sacrifice virgin daughters to retrieve whores. It is about fathers who eat their own children by accident after their uncle has killed them and cooked them up in a stew. It is about a mother who stabs her two sons to death to spite an errant husband. She also takes care of her husband's new girlfriend and the girlfriend's father, incinerating them with a trick napalm dress. It is about a man who comes home after twenty years of wandering to find his house filled with other men who want his wife. He kills all 108 of them. They fall down and bleed in the food. Then he allows his son the fun of hanging the serving women who have entertained the suitors. One could go on. I have scarcely mentioned the theme of adultery, so inspirational for the fine arts that Tony Tanner in *Adultery in the Novel* is tempted to identify the theme with the narrational urge. Consciousness itself, as Bataille says, is scandal.[44]

In these contexts, what do we mean when we say that literary art represents "the best that is known and thought in the world" and that critical activity is an effort to "learn and propagate" this best? If art consists of negative examples, which are designed to teach us how *not* to live, doesn't it go too far, finally? How will such nightmarish material "console us, sustain us"? How will it ultimately complete science and provide a substitute for religion and philosophy, as Arnold, following Schiller, says it will, after the "melancholy, long withdrawing roar" has roared its last?[45]

III.

We can understand how art can do these things largely through the work of Georges Bataille, whose reflections on entrails and toes we have had occasion to refer to earlier. Bataille is a theorist so appalling to literary history that even surrealism took pains to eliminate him.[46] He is extremely difficult to talk about, to paraphrase. Every time one tries, one runs the risk of being considered seriously morbid or mad. The people who have, though at the time untenured, brought his work into English now—Allan Stoekl, Alastair Hamilton, and others—have to be recognized not only for their meticulous research but also for their great courage.[47] Bataille's general unavailability has surely been one of the reasons why it was so difficult for Anglo-Saxons to absorb developments in literary theory during the past twenty years. The difficulty is not just the Anglo-Saxon tradition of seeing literature as the unproblematic transmission of elevated moral values, a heritage generated only in part by the likes of Matthew Arnold. Writers from other traditions, like E. M. Cioran, claim to have found the entire English example "bewildering." "Thanks to the conformism and enlightened stupidity of her citizens," he says, the country "has not produced a single anarchist."[48] The homogenizing weight, the relentless health of the Great Tradition, with its veiling of the tenebrous and marginal, with its common sense, geniality, and clarity, tends to find Continental developments tortured and perverse anyway, and so much the more so for coming in at an advanced stage in the Continental discourse; for how much less strange it would seem to hear that history is the repression of writing and the privileging of voice if one were acquainted with what Bataille had already said in his various studies of the fastidious tradition, its obsession with the prefix "sur," its efforts to repress the heterogeneous, its Icarian longing for the aether.[49] Derrida's interests in the sun in his essay "White Mythology" seem less unexpected in the contexts of "The Jesuve" or "Rotten Sun." The entire project of "deconstruction" was simply to do what Bataille was already trying to do, namely discover what had been swept under the rug, to loosen up a "hardened" tradition, to dissolve its various "concealments," to let the springs of Being flow in their purity—or putrefaction.

For Bataille, human culture and community are based on the observance of shared taboos (*Literature and Evil*, 172). There are rules, laws, a system of morality which serve to ensure the survival of society (6). To follow these rules is to be reasonable. To follow the path of reason is to be good. To be good and reasonable is to be obedient and submissive (169). Work, the production of useful goods, is supposedly our reason for being here, the fulfillment of our human destiny (*Visions of Excess*, 138). True, this reasonableness is a state of half death, but the people who dominate life in this form, politicians, fathers, tycoons, tenured faculty, scientists, university administrators, require servility and subordination; and certainly there is a kind of security in obedience, caution, in husbanding our vital substance, spending rationally, receiving a modest return on our investments, keeping our accounts balanced and in order (97). And there is in this approved world a kind of communication, a possibility of banal exchange of standard phrases and faint signs of life, which do not disturb the easy, homogenized flow of the everyday (*Literature and Evil*, 170–1). In this sense the opium of the people is "not so much religion as it is accepted boredom" (*Visions of Excess*, 167). "It is a law of present-day life that an ordinary man must be incapable of thinking about anything at all, and be tied down in every way by completely servile occupations, which drain him of reality" (211). It is of course, those who do not participate directly in the production of goods who are moved to establish a morality regularizing "for their own profit the circulation of goods" (99). If morality fails, they have the police guarding their houses, their silver, their oriental rugs, the plate glass windows of their banks.

This state of affairs will hold true until the timid and exploited wretch they depend on "abandons the world of the civilized and its light" (*Visions of Excess*, 179). Being "reasonable and educated" has led to "a life without appeal." Unless we "refuse boredom," unless we become "completely different," living only for fascination (179), seeing "all the moralistic buffoons as so many dogs" (101), we will completely cease to *be* in any but the most degraded sense. Our existence will "end up crumbling into dust" (117), a contradiction homologous with the father's "malevolent solicitude" for his son. The father willingly recognizes some of the son's needs—food, shelter, clothing, a little harmless recreation, if Junior absolutely insists. But the son has no right to speak about "what really gives him a fever." "In this respect...*conscious humanity has remained a minor*" (117). Really to speak of this fever is to approach the boundaries of horror; to act on it is to release orgiastic, destructive explosions of energy, to sweep away lethargy, inertia, and boredom. Bataille claims, finally, that this was the fundamental appeal of the Fascists. "The world is at the mercy...of those who provide at least the semblance of an escape from boredom" (167). Collective exaltation will come from "words that touch not the reason but the passions of the masses."

These words would constitute significant, "powerful" communication (*Literature and Evil*, 171), not the "feeble communication," the distant platitudes to which we are accustomed. They would necessarily draw their power from scandal (171), from the violation of taboos, "the negation of some interdict" (173), from criminality, from the overturning of idols, and butchering of sacred cows; from rents, wounds, bloody, painful losses and memorable lacerations (*Visions of Excess*, 251). There was enough in the ritual circumcision of Abraham and his entire household in *Genesis* to make the establishment of the covenant truly a memorable event for all concerned. "Privileged moments of powerful communication," "the convulsive communication of what is ordinarily stifled" (242), are "based on the emotions of sensuality, festivity, drama, love, separation, and death" (*Literature and Evil*, 171–2). Literature which deals with these things is—it must be admitted—a poor substitute for human sacrifice, self-mutilation, and lopping off the head of the king, for the potlatch destruction of whole villages, smashing of canoe flotillas, and the throwing of vast fortunes into the sea (*Visions of Excess*, 121–2). "The most rending visions" of art have never forged much more than a "fugitive link between the people they have touched," even compared for example to the primitive, primal friction, the profoundly silent, burning passion of lovers, a source of ecstasis worthy of the name (229). Generally speaking, poetry is hardly "less debased than religion," so often ending up appropriated by some "aesthetic homology" or other (97). Real poetry, though, is close to the sacred wastage and divine intoxication of "expenditure" and "sacrifice" (120). The world and class to which we belong display such a horror of "unproductive expenditure" of any sort precisely because the bourgeoisie, when it came to power, defined itself against the "prodigality of feudal society" by developing its own universally mean, secretive, small-minded, rapacious habits of accumulation (124–5). The allegory of its great enemy, Sade, is that of the imprisoned aristocrat, unable to assert his exorbitant rights of mastery through murder and therefore forced to resort to transgression in writing (*Visions of Excess*, 93; *Literature and Evil*, 10, 87, 101). Actual violence is transmuted into literary sadism, and writing becomes a radical alibi for inaction, "formally abandoned to the impotence of servile beings" (*Literature and Evil*, 65). Poetry may trample verbally on the established order but is hardly, for Bataille, a substitute for the real thing (23). Literary enterprise is defined as "useful for ambitions moderated by the impotence of present-day man" (*Visions of Excess*, 93).

But writing feeds on our most intimate dreams. Literature is the "dream of sacred violence which no settlement with organized society can attenuate" (*Literature and Evil*, 11). That is why literature is dangerous and irresponsible, and that is why it is "evil" in the sense that it is opposed to the greater evil of being respectable. Literature simply must not "assume the task of regulating collective necessity," that is, to commit us to the laws of the city, show us the path of the Good (12). We must find in art that which proper bourgeois life denies us. If human life did not contain this violent instinct, the extreme of which would be the Aztec or Hebraic hecatombs (of *Numbers* 31, for example), "we could dispense with the arts" (51). Boredom is the dream of scaffolds, says Baudelaire, and evil is the dream of the good, the expression of the "most ethical," of those in whom the ethical is "most deeply rooted" (8; 12); otherwise literature would really be dangerous. The existence of evil and the necessity for literature come into being at the same time—with the establishment of the social bond and its definitions of decency. Good is our very reason for doing evil (159). It is on the bosom of the legal, in fact, that the criminal is conceived. Marriage brings adultery into existence. But the criminal in turn reaffirms the legal, as adultery reconfirms marriage. (And this is the turn in Bataille's thought that confirms Bataille's inevitable respectability and the reappropriation of the outrageous by the normal.)[50]

The inextricable entanglement between antinomical cultural elements in Bataille seems more radical than Freud's sublimation theory which commits itself eventually to an Enlightenment view of human progress. Freud's rather blatant adaptation of Schiller's three *Triebe*, the drives of "sense," "form," and "play," into the triple partitioning of our psychic home, indicates the path that Freud's plan of sublimation will necessarily take.[51] In Freud's view it must become clear even to a testosterone-driven horde that we cannot follow every impulse that our aggression provides, that it is impossible for every male to copulate with every female for whom he has a gust of desire. The forces of competition that are unleashed by such behavior threaten the very existence of society.[52] The impulsions of desire, then, must be drained off into higher forms of cultural production than orgasmic transgression. "Instinctual satisfaction" must be sacrificed for the "benefit of the whole community."[53] Hence the paradigm of civilized man in Freud is a neurotic artist, forever discontented and forever at work, spinning his *Divine Comedy* out of his desperate longing for an unreachable Beatrice.

Matthew Arnold, too, will side with the enlightenment against those darker, thanatotic, materialist impulses of the world that fill him with such shudders of horror. He, like Schiller, is powerfully aware of the pressure of the contingent, of the bestial, of all those conditions that make of us *terrae filii*.[54] He is not without compassion for those poor souls who are hopelessly entangled in things of the earth. He traces material misery to the very material progress celebrated in the practical epoch of expansion that was his own historical context. Those who are exuberant in their complacency and self-satisfaction have become so at the expense of the girl named "Wragg," who lived at the workhouse, was illegitimately pregnant, and strangled her newly born child on Mapperly Hills at Nottingham. But it is the ugliness of the girl's name, finally, that permits Arnold to escape the material horror and get back to what Marx would consider the reassuringly ideological. And with the ideological, Arnold commits himself to a certain kind of elitism. "Such hideous names," he moans, still speaking of Wragg and of the Higgenbottoms, Stigginses, and Buggs: natural growths from the grossness in our race.[55] Then he adds an idealizingly Hellenic touch which can be only technically true. "By the Ilissus there was no Wragg, poor thing!" The grinding shock of his historical context leads Arnold to give up on "the mass of mankind."[56] Such folk will always be content with very inadequate ideas.

Unlike himself and his fellow Oxford graduates, the common folk will never have much passion for "seeing things as they are." By "things as they are," very possibly, the sensitive Arnold must mean something like "things as they are not," since surely if anyone saw things as they are, for the mercifully short interval of her appalling life, it was the seduced, traduced, and abandoned Miss Wragg. Salvation must be restricted, Arnold insists, to a "very small circle," which will not include her. It will be this elite group who must effect such change from above as will eventually trickle down, perhaps, to the benighted many. The superstructure will change the base, if ever there will be change. It is not the base, *pace* Marx, that will change the superstructure. Meanwhile the very small circle on high will "propagate the best that is known and thought in the world."[57] They will maintain the "touchstones" in good working order until such time as the promised land heaves into view again.[58] Such touchstones, isolated literary fragments of great delicacy and beauty, will sustain us in our time of dearth, console us, replacing the "false shows" of religion and philosophy which, in our day, can no longer be taken seriously.[59]

As we search for consolation, then, it is frightening to think that Emily Brontë could have produced one of our touchstones. Not sweetness and light, but only the savage turmoil of the primal horde, only the murky, antinomical nature of things could explain the existence of a book like *Wuthering Heights*. Emily Bronte, living obscurely, austerely, in a primitive Yorkshire vicarage, with apparently no personal experience of love, but living along with her sisters in a "frenzy" of literary activity, is precisely the person to produce "the most beautiful and most profoundly violent love story" (*Literature and Evil*, 3). The fiendish sadism of this book is, indeed, breathtaking. Everyone pinches, slaps, bruises, flogs, sheds blood, tears hair, hangs puppies, and dreams of "slow vivisection" to amuse themselves of an evening (8). "One of man's attributes," says Bataille, "is the derivation of pleasure from the suffering of other" (*Visions of Excess*, 101). He speaks of the "measureless hate that divides men" (127). And we remember that Aristotle erected his notion of art's pathological discharge upon the recognition of this notion. For Bataille, this discharge is "erotic," a "lubricious participation in that agony" of the other (101). Not everyone will admit this fact, but they are "cowards afraid of their own joyful excesses" (101). One reason art is the representation of mutilation and violence is that the origins of tragedy lie in the primitive convulsions of sacrifice. The original actor in tragedy seems likely to have been Dionysus, part of whose ritual involved *omophagia*, the eating of the god by his worshippers. In the absence of the god, a human or animal stand-in would do. Wine was involved, the chewing of laurel leaves (containing potassium cyanide), and the tearing apart of the living sacrifice and eating of his still-quivering flesh.[60] The scene in Euripides' *Bacchae* in which Pentheus, dressed as a woman, is torn apart by the Maenads, apparently alludes to this part of the cult. Certainly Christians mime this rite themselves every Sunday in the reenactment of their own divine Communion narrative. Art retains the kernel of this mysticism which is the "asocial aspect of religion" (Bataille, *Literature and Evil*, 12).

Matthew Arnold, then, is partially right that art is religion, though in a way that would have horrified him. And Schiller is right that art is play (*Spiel*) and pretending (*Schein*), but not epiphenomenally. De Flores amputates the Piracquian finger with its obstinately clinging engagement ring because nothing less will discharge our maniacal hostility for the institution which the ringed flesh represents, except perhaps the actual mutilation of a sexual rival. But this is an evil, a criminality of which we deeply ethical types, committed as we are to all the institutions of a well-ordered society, are permitted only to dream. Only to dream it, not to do it, permits us to live to dream again, and, as Bataille would say, in this dreaming, again to live.

Notes

1. Georges Bataille, *Visions of Excess. Selected Writings, 1927–1939*, trans. Allan Stoekl with Carl R. Lovitt and Donald M. Leslie, Jr. (Minneapolis: University of Minnesota Press, 1985), 116.
2. Friedrich Schiller, *On the Aesthetic Education of Man*, trans. with an introduction by Reginald Snell (New York: Ungar, 1983), 26. All quotations are from this particular translation unless otherwise indicated.
3. Judith Miller, "Study Links Drop in Support to Elitist Attitude in the Arts," *New York Times* (13 October 1997): A1.
4. The statistics on the military's involvement in the U. S. economy and U. S. universities come from an article by Don Graff, "If Ike Could See Us Now," *Opelika-Auburn News* (1986). A more recent account of the "militarization of the economy" and the consequent docility of the American intelligentsia would include Noam Chomsky, *World Orders Old and New* (New York: Columbia University Press, 1994), especially 108 ff and 178 ff. "With the Cold War gone, new fears have been stimulated to sustain the Pentagon funnel for the public subsidy" (101). "The terms 'defense,' 'national security,' etc., never wilt, no matter how much light pours on them" (103). See also Chomsky, *Chronicles of Dissent, Interviews with David Barsamian*, intro. by Alexander Cockburn (Monroe, ME: Common Courage, 1992), especially "State Economic Planning," 179ff, "Introduction," and "Foreign Policy and the Intelligentsia";

Chomsky, *Language and Responsibility* (New York: Pantheon, 1977), especially "Politics"; Chomsky, *Manufacturing Consent* (New York: Pantheon, 1988), 18 ff; and Albert Speer, *Inside the Third Reich*, trans. Richard and Clara Winston (New York: Macmillan, 1970). Hereafter Speer.

5. See Fredric Jameson, "Postmodernism and Consumer Society," in Hal Foster, *The Anti-Aesthetic, Essays on Postmodern Culture* (Port Townsend, Washington: The Bay Press, 1983).

6. See Allan Bloom, *The Closing of the American Mind* (New York: Simon and Schuster, 1987), 344. Also E. D. Hirsch, *Cultural Literacy: What Every American Needs to Know* (Boston: Houghton Mifflin, 1987). Also by Hirsch, *The Dictionary of Cultural Literacy* (Boston: Houghton Mifflin, 1993). William Bennett, *The De-Valuing of America: The Fight for Our Culture and Our Children* (New York: Summit Books, 1992).

7. Speer, 35, 36.

8. Speer, 102.

9. See Hans Christoph Buch, "Writers and Dictators: On the Double Bind Between Mind and Power," trans. Dan Latimer, *Southern Humanities Review* XX (Fall 1986) 317–324. Buch's main interest is the violence of the cultured toward culture, quoting Karl Radek's *bon mot*: "When I hear the word 'culture,' I reach for my Browning."

10. Nadezhda Mandelstam, *Hope Against Hope, A Memoir*, trans. Max Hayward (New York: Atheneum, 1970), 84. For the "Kremlin mountaineer" reference, see poem number 286 (November 1933) in *The Complete Poetry of Osip Mandelstam*, trans. Burton Raffel and Alla Burago (Albany: State University of New York Press, 1973), 228. Mandelstam's poem on Stalin refers not only to fingers like fat worms and to "cockroach whiskers," but also to Stalin's incredible ferocity. Stalin was a Georgian, possibly an Ossetian, reputed to honor the custom of munching a raspberry to celebrate the death of an enemy. Mandelstam's demise is also connected to an incident of 1932 involving the writer Amir Sargidzhan and his mistress, Tatyana Dubinskaya, who lived in the same building as Osip and Nadezhda. Every time the Mandelstams received visitors Sargidzhan and Dubinskaya would appear as well, though uninvited. Eventually blows were exchanged, and the subsequent trial at the Writers' Union was presided over by Aleksey Tolstoy, who did not give Mandelstam satisfaction. So Mandelstam slapped Tolstoy's face. Rumor has persistently associated Tolstoy with Mandelstam's death. See Clarence Brown, *Mandelstam* (Cambridge: Cambridge University Press, 1973) 127–9, 131. For the writer as killer, see Elias Canetti, *The Play of the Eyes*, trans. Ralph Manheim (New York: Farrar Straus & Giroux, 1986), 282–3. Authors' accounts of their fellow writers are generally dreary, mean-spirited affairs. Canetti's are no exception.

11. George Lichtheim, *George Lukács* (New York: Viking Press, 1970), 38–43.

12. Georg Lukács, *Geschichte und Klassenbewusstwein* (Darmstadt und Neuwied: Luchterhand, 1977), 52. The translation is my own, as "Tatik and Ethik" can only be found in the German, but not in the English version of *History and Class*. See also Lichtheim, 43; Rudolf Tökes, *Bela Kun and the Hungarian Soviet Republic* (New York: Praeger, 1967), 197.

13. Lichtheim, 43. The "historian" is Lajos Lassak.

14. Matthew Arnold, *Culture and Anarchy*, ed. R. H. Super (Ann Arbor: Michigan University Press, 1965), 91. The piece was originally published in 1869. Quotations are

from Chapter 1, "Sweetness and Light," 90–114.

15. Arnold, 112.
16. Schiller, *On the Aesthetic Education of Man*, 26.
17. Arnold, 91.
18. Tertullian, *Tertulliani Opera II. Corpus Christianorum, Series Latina*, ed. J. G. P. Borleffs, E. Dekkers, et al. (Turnholti: Typographi Brepols, 1953), *De Carne Christi*, Chapter V. Tertullian was speaking of the nature of Christ, "*credibile quia ineptum est.*"
19. Arnold, 112.
20. *Aesthetic Education*, 30.
21. Friedrich Schiller, *Essays Aesthetical and Philosophical* (London: George Bell, 1884), 122; *Aesthetic Education*, 117.
22. *Essays*, 122.
23. *Essays*, 122.
24. *Essays*, 122.
25. Herbert Marcuse, *The Aesthetic Dimension* (Boston: Beacon Press, 1977), 49.
26. See Fredric Jameson, "Postmodernism, Or, The Cultural Logic of Late Capitalism," *New Left Review* 146 (July-August, 1984), 53–92.
27. Speer, 35.
28. Speer, 50.
29. G. W. F. Hegel, *Hegel: On the Arts*, ed. and trans. Henry Paolucci (New York: Ungar, 1979), 14. See also Jacques Derrida's "The Pit and the Pyramid: Introduction to Hegel's Semiology," in *Margins of Philosophy*, trans. Alan Bass (Chicago: University of Chicago Press, 1982), 71–108, for an account of this passage, and related ones, in Hegel.
30. Karl Marx and Frederick Engels, *The German Ideology* (Moscow: Progress Publishers, 1964), 37.
31. Marx, 38.
32. Charles Darwin, *The Variation of Animals and Plants under Domestication*, vol. 2, ed. Paul Barrett and R. B. Freeman (London: William Pickering, 1988), 2.127.
33. Sigmund Freud, *Totem and Taboo*, trans. James Strachey (New York: Norton, 1961), 134 ff.
34. Georg Lukács, *Writer and Critic and Other Essays*, trans. Arthur Kahn (London: The Merlin Press, 1970), 105.
35. Georges Bataille, *Visions of Excess, Selected Writings, 1927–1939*, trans. Allan Stoekl, with Carl R. Lovitt and Donald M. Leslie, Jr. (Minneapolis: University of Minnesota Press, 1985), 8.
36. Ibid., 20
37. Ibid., 22.
38. Ibid., 22. See also Edward Said, *Orientalism* (New York: Random House/Vintage, 1978).
39. *Visions of Excess*, 20.
40. Speer, 97.
41. *Visions of Excess*, 154.
42. See Cary Nelson, ed., *Will Teach for Food: Academic Labor in Crisis* (Minneapolis: Univ. of Minnesota Press, 1997).

43. Bataille, 154.

44. Georges Bataille, *Literature and Evil*, trans. Alastair Hamilton (New York: Urizen Books, 1973), 171. Tony Tanner, *Adultery in the Novel* (Baltimore and London: Johns Hopkins, 1979), 14–15.

45. "It is not unintentionally that I have placed religion and taste in one and the same class; the reason is that both one and the other have the merit, similar in effect,…to take the place of virtue properly so called." See "The Moral Utility of Aesthetic Manners" in Schiller, *Essays*, 128. See also Matthew Arnold, *English Literature and Irish Politics*, ed. R. H. Super (Ann Arbor: University of Michigan Press, 1973), 162.

46. For the Surrealist attack on Bataille, see André Breton, *Manifestoes of Surrealism*, trans. Richard Seaver and Helen R. Lane (Ann Arbor: University of Michigan Press, 1969), 180 ff.

47. The pioneering books have been Bataille, *Literature and Evil*, trans. Alastair Hamilton, and Georges Bataille, *Visions of Excess*, trans. Allan Stoekl. Marguerite Duras (*Outside: Selected Writings* [Boston: Beacon Press, 1986]) wondered when the time would finally come that one could speak of Bataille. Julian Prefanis, who quotes Duras, considers the study of Bataille as a matter of risking one's reputation. See his *Heterology and the Postmodern* (Durham, NC: Duke Univ. Press, 1991).

48. E. M. Cioran, *Histoire et utopie* (Paris: Gallimard, 1960).

49. *Visions of Excess*, 32ff. See Terry Eagleton's account of F. R. Leavis and "The Great Tradition" in *Literary Theory. An Introduction* (Minneapolis: University of Minnesota Press, 1983), 37ff.

50. Michel Beaujour, "Eros and Nonsense: Georges Bataille," in *Modern French Criticism*, ed. John Simon (Chicago and London: University of Chicago Press, 1972), 154.

51. Sigmund Freud, *Introductory Lectures on Psychoanalysis*, trans. James Strachey (New York: Norton, 1966), 11, 23.

52. Sigmund Freud, *Civilizations and its Discontents*, trans. James Strachey (New York: Norton, 1961), 59.

53. Freud, *Introductory Lectures on Psychoanalysis*, 23.

54. Matthew Arnold, *Lectures and Essays in Criticism*, ed. R. H. Super (Ann Arbor: Univ. of Michigan Press, 1962), 276.

55. *Lectures and Essays*, 273.

56. Ibid., 274.

57. Ibid., 282.

58. Arnold, *English Literature and Irish Politics*, 168.

59. Ibid., 162.

60. Charles Rowan Beye, *Ancient Greek Literature and Society* (Garden City, N. Y.: Anchor/Doubleday, 1975), 166. Robert Graves, *The Greek Myths*, 2 vols. (Harmondsworth: Penguin, 1960), vol. 1: 17, 57; see also 107 ff.

The Making of the Postmodern Minimal Self: Rousseau and the Denial of Dialogical Politics
by Kent Brudney

> When roused by passion I can sometimes find the right words to say, but in ordinary conversation I can find none, none at all. I find conversation unbearable owing to the very fact that I am obliged to speak.
> Jean-Jacques Rousseau, The Confessions

Rousseau hit upon one of the major dilemmas of modernity: how does one define the self and protect the self in a world that makes the establishment of a unified self problematic and that poses any number of threats to the authentic self—to a self that is true to itself?

Rousseau saw his world dominated by the hegemonic story of the egoistic, materialistic, vainglorious individual, a story that served to legitimate repressive political, social, and religious institutions. This pervasive story about human nature Rousseau believed responsible for his and others' alienation from the authentic and unencumbered self: the Hobbesian story denied men and citizens self-esteem. Rousseau sought to create a new story about men and citizens: in the *Discourse on the Origin of Inequality*, he provided an alternative account to the Fall and to the Hobbesian story of human nature and in *The Social Contract* an alternative account to the Hobbesian and Lockean stories of secular salvation. He offered the human capacity of imagination and feeling as the means by which men and citizens could both escape and transcend the conditions imposed by the hegemonic story of his time.

Rousseau sought to expose the contingent character of the dominant story. By rejecting the constraints of tradition and the concealments and manipulation of egoistic reason, Rousseau suggested the exposure of modernity (and now postmodernity) to a heartless world without a haven. He wanted to assert an authentic self against the repression of tradition and against the impositions of political and cultural life. But this self had to be invented, and it had to be invented without recourse to the standards provided by tradition and without recourse to the standard of disinterested reason. It was, finally, a search for authenticity that turned in on itself. The search could locate the impositions and contradictions of the past and the present, but it could not chart the path to the future.

What is missing in the Rousseauvian deconstruction of the dominant story of the egoistic self is a reference point beyond the Rousseauvian ambiguous and fluid selfhood. Quite unwittingly, Rousseau suggested another dilemma of modernity: if I must to my own self be true, who am I? How do I know who I am, and how do I know what it is that must be protected against a venal and imposing world? Rousseau understood the perils to the self in the modern world, but he could not very well protect it because the self he wanted to protect was so minimal and so frail. Rousseau, by abandoning the premodern sources of the self and rejecting modernity's recourse to self-interest or to reason, was at cross purposes: his minimal self was not likely to withstand the threats to it.

Rousseau's minimal self represents the bridge between modern and postmodern notions of the self. The Rousseauvian self is more narcissistic than egoistic—less the interest-driven, inner-directed individual of liberalism than the fragile self of postmodernism.[1] Contrary to the claims of so much of postmodern literature, the outstanding characteristic of the late-modern identity is not its bourgeois egoism and self-interest, but the lack of a sense of self—a non-integrated, fragile self. Narcissus fell in love with his own reflection not because he knowingly fell in love with himself, but because he did not recognize himself.[2] The possessive individualist, the object of postmodern scorn and Rousseau's wrath, has been supplanted by a self that lives from moment to moment in the tentative politics of survival.

The main features of the so-called postmodern identity are already evident in modernity. Rousseau's rage against a remote and threatening world that imperils the authentic self, that imposes systems of power that appear to negate self-definition and self-recognition, is the opening battle in postmodernism's rage against modernity. The current preoccupation with selfhood, identity, and recognition—the politics of identity— emerges as the very possibility of a unitary self is called into question by the requirements of survival in a heartless world. Rousseau, in *The Reveries*, acknowledged the frailty of his authentic self:

Night was coming on. I saw the sky, some stars, and a few leaves. This first sensation was a moment of delight. I was conscious of nothing else. In this instant I was being born again, and it seemed as if all I perceived was filled with my frail existence. Entirely taken up by the present, I could remember nothing; I had no notion of myself as a person nor had I the least idea of what had just happened to me.[3]

The fragile self fears conflict because it threatens to obliterate whatever remains of the self. It thus seeks to blend into an undifferentiated community, one which protects the self by abolishing not only otherness, but also difference. The minimal self cannot tolerate the conflicts of ordinary politics, because conflict is perceived as threatening the self with annihilation. What Charles Taylor calls the "politics of recognition" (multicultural politics) is commonly less rooted in a commitment to the value of difference per se than in similarly situated groups seeking enclaves of survival.[4] The multicultural celebration of difference is paradoxically rooted in a fear of difference and a search for unity with others who mirror the fragile self; the group that seeks the recognition of difference is afraid—perhaps for good reason—of being obliterated by the others. It fears that its identity cannot withstand exposure to the give and take of conflictual pluralistic politics. As I will argue below, Rousseau's distrust of dialogical politics is related to his minimal self's fear of difference; that is, public discourse will only expose the latent differences among citizens.[5]

There is a paradoxical relationship between Rousseau's insistence on authenticity and the multiple selves of postmodernism. On one hand, Rousseau wanted to insist on the possibility of an integrated, unitary self—one that remains intact despite the impositions of the external world. This is why he took such precautions to protect the self against the myriad of perceived threats to it. It is also why he had to invent himself as an outsider. To be an insider was to risk capture by forces that seek to impose themselves on the self.

On the other hand, Rousseau's search for authenticity was actually a search for integration among his multiple, fluid selves, selves that he could not successfully integrate because he acknowledged no independent standard by which to determine what would constitute an integrated, unitary self:

> If this revolution had done no more than restore me to myself and had stopped there, all would have been well. But unfortunately it did go further, and carried me rapidly to the opposite extreme. From that time my soul has been in a state of disturbance, and has enjoyed only a passing moment's equilibrium. For its perpetual oscillations have prevented its ever holding a true line.[6]

This authentic self is neither Christian nor classical (because both would insist on truths which the self internalizes as it establishes itself); it is instead a bundle of feelings, intuitions, and potentialities that are inevitably subject to molding by contexts and discourses.

Rousseau, in the *Confessions*, showed himself to be chameleon-like ("On my own I was generally reckoned a complete cipher in all respects...''[7]): he absorbed his contexts, always suspecting that he was being robbed of something, but lacking a sense of self sufficient to determine what had been stolen. Rousseau's Hobson's choice was between a carefully nurtured and protected minimal self, on one side, and fragmentation and corruption, on the other. Rousseau's lifelong attempt to manufacture an authentic self ends in the *Reveries*, where the self is finally obliterated in a Narcissus-like separation from time and a delusional creation of an omnipotent existence: "What is the source of our happiness in such a state? Nothing external to us, nothing apart from ourselves and our own existence; as long as this state lasts we are self-sufficient like God."[8]

Rousseau's modernity meets postmodernity in shared positing of a self too fragile to allow for the possibility of a vibrant, pluralistic, dialogical politics: "The startling implication of Rousseau's theory therefore is that in a free republic assemblies have a purely ritual function, and real politics in the sense of public action and discussion is redundant."[9]

As much as Rousseau wanted to supplant the Hobbesian story of human nature, he could not escape the Hobbesian account of vainglory. Whereas he insisted that the natural condition of man evinced *amour de soi*, but not *amour propre*, Rousseau conceded that sociability necessarily entailed comparison, pride, and vanity.[10] For Rousseau, as for Hobbes, men, once with others, live in the eyes of others, and they can only define themselves positively by gaining the esteem of others. The Rousseauvian self is so fragile that it can only remain itself by protecting itself from others or by being protected from others. The Rousseauvian self, once thrust from the pristine state of nature, is so in risk of acquiring the vices of sociability that it must experience solitude even in the midst of legislative assemblies.

Hobbes's apparent egoism was no more rooted in an independently defined self-interest than was Rousseau's.[11] Rousseau is out to abolish Hobbesian self-interest, but in order to do it, he also has to obliterate sociability, precisely because he allows Hobbes to define man's social nature for him. Similarly, Rousseau's distrust of reason stemmed from his having tacitly conceded the Hobbesian notion that reason is the hand-maiden of the passions. This has all kinds of consequences for the possibility of dialogical politics.

Rousseau's notion of willing, as it is explicated in *The Social Contract*, was rational in a limited, reflective sense: citizens must make sense out of their own instincts and feelings, and they must intuit the relationship of their own wills to the general will. The willing, however, was not rational in a dialogical sense; it did not require, indeed it prohibited, a mutual engagement among citizens to figure out what the community's interest might be. Such engagement would subject each citizen to the manipulation of others; it would bring into play all the vices of Hobbesian sociability. In this sense, Rousseau's story and Hobbes's story merge: freedom is finally the right to be left alone. Despite the common association between Rousseau and participatory democracy, the Rousseauvian citizen is largely mute. The legislative assembly seeks a kind of feel-good consensus about the general will; it does not seek the exercise of the rhetorical art by which the eloquent manipulate and by which diverse opinions and interests are exposed.[12]

Similarly, Rousseau's notion of the persuasive skills required of the Legislator ("persuade without convincing"[13]) is neither dialogical nor deliberative. It is rooted instead in a kind of pacified Machiavellianism; that is, in the use of symbol and ritual to inspire awe and to foster the development of habits and customs that will keep citizens in the Legislator's persuasion.[14] The very act of political creation by the Legislator suggests Rousseau's distrust of ordinary dialogical politics: the great patriarch must create politics for citizens, who in turn become dependent on him and who are expected to defer their politics to him.[15] An analogous use of symbolism and ritual occurs commonly in American political rhetoric in which the cultists of the Constitution and of the "framers' intentions" have turned the truly deliberative character of the American founding into ancestral worship, seeking to preclude the ongoing conversations of republican politics by insisting that it was all settled in Philadelphia.[16]

Judith Shklar argues that Rousseau's public life lacks the true spirit of democracy; that is, it lacks genuine participation in making the laws by which one lives. Instead, it requires the vigilance necessary to prevent the usurpation of the alleged autonomy of individual citizens:

> Given the difficulties of democratic government, there is always the potential for tyranny, and only a watchful citizenry can prevent its emergence. This is why active participation is necessary. The people do not assemble to make new laws. That is to be avoided, as is all change. The popular assemblies exist to preserve

the republic, not to better it or adapt its laws. Their chief purpose is to express
their confidence in or dissatisfaction with magistrates and to confirm the original
laws.[17]

Shklar also saw that the Rousseauvian autonomous citizen suggested
"not the solitude of Prometheus, but the self-protective flight of the
incurably weak who are afraid of being bossed."[18] As they are afraid of
being bossed, they do not themselves know how to be bosses.

Rousseau wanted politics to come first from the heart and then from
the acquired habits of the heart. This politics of the heart explains both
Rousseau's emphasis on the spectacles of the *patria* over reasoned
discourse and his attraction to Sparta and Machiavelli's Roman
republicanism. But Rousseau misread Machiavelli, who, although he had
not fully explored the dialogical character of politics, frequently
acknowledged in the *Discourses* and in *The History of Florence* the
importance of public conversations, who did understand the conflictual
nature of politics, and who did find among the ancients and even among
some of his own contemporaries the fortitude to withstand the fierce
debates of the public world. Whereas Machiavelli noted multiple
identities—the difference between the life of a citizen and personal life—
he assumed selves that were sufficiently integrated to allow for the
diversity of roles that are part of the human condition—without
fragmentation and without fear of annihilation.[19]

Rousseau's suspicion of dialogical politics is rooted, in part, in his
ambivalence about language. On one hand, there is no truth deeper than
language is capable of conveying; the feelings of the heart must find
linguistic expression, or else man is forever a stupid beast. Language is
the vehicle of self-revelation. On the other hand, language is the means
of concealment and manipulation. With the passage of time (and akin to
the corruption of man), language loses its pristine utility, and it comes to
display the vices of sociability:

> Anyone who studies history and progress of the tongues will see that the more
> words become monotonous, the more the consonants multiply; that, as accents fall
> into disuse and quantities are neutralized, they are replaced by grammatical
> combinations and new articulations. But only the pressure of time brings these
> changes about. To the degree that needs multiply, that affairs become
> complicated, that light is shed, language changes its character. It becomes more
> regular and less passionate. It substitutes ideas for feelings. It no longer speaks to
> the heart, but to reason....Language becomes more exact and clearer, but more
> prolix, duller, and colder.[20]

Since the corruption of language allows some citizens to persuade (convince) others to serve their wills and their interests, Rousseau resolved that it must be kept to a minimum in politics. A simple "yes" or "no" can reveal the authenticity of the will in public votes. As the use of language in public settings expands, so does the possibility of manipulation, and mastery—the old Hobbesian vices. Rousseau himself was most successful when his written language was self-revelatory— when his writing had its source in the sentiments of the authentic self. He was less successful in (and finally came to disavow) political writing, because political communication is based on conventions of argument, evidence, and persuasion (persuasion in the rhetorical sense, not in Rousseau's sense of inspiring awe); these conventions pose continuing threats to the fragile self. By the time he wrote the *Reveries*, Rousseau recalled his earlier political self with anxiety and pain. His new self, apparently his true self, emerged in his own escape from sociability: "These hours of solitude and meditation are the only ones in the day when I am completely myself and my own master, with nothing to distract or hinder me, the only ones when I can truly say that I am what nature meant me to be."[21]

Postmodernists and some feminists attack the notion of a unified self because they associate it with traditional political, economic, and gendered forms of power, domination, and imposition.[22] The idea of the unified self is cast as a large part of Western modernity's system of control; the promulgation of the notion of the unified self supports the patriarchal, capitalistic oppressions of Western socio-economic development. The dissolution of the unified self thus permits the deconstruction of the mutually reinforcing systems of control. The much heralded coming of postmodern fluid, multiple selves conveniently posits an individual who is too playful and too slippery to be pinned down by the myriad forces of social, economic, and political control. Postmodernists, by first rejecting and then deconstructing the traditional sources of the modern self, abet the process of the self's fragmentation.[23]

There is a certain empirical acumen in postmodernism's announcement of the fluid, multiple self: casual observation tells us that something has happened, and the postmodernists seem to know what it is. Their only glaring empirical error is historical; that is, postmodernists neglect the continuity between the postmodern self and the Rousseauvian alienated, authentic self. Rousseau's minimal self is really postmodern multiple selves with one major difference: Rousseau still thought the search for authenticity crucial, whereas the postmodernists have abandoned it. Rousseau bemoaned the fragile status of the self, but many postmodernists see its passing as the harbinger of a new age of liberation from the constraints of egoism and patriarchy.

Postmodernist theorizing about the emergence of the multiple, fluid self has a perilously abstract character, one that glosses over much of the evidence we now have about multiple selves.[24] Despite the Foucault-inspired critique of institutional power (including the definition and treatment of mental illness) and of hegemonic discourses, James Glass shows that multiple personality disorder (MPD)—the real manifestation of the postmodern theory of multiple selves—is anything but liberating:

> In none of the accounts offered here did I see that the phenomenon of multiplicity of identity was a creative or playful or regenerative experience. It is not an aesthetic; it is not self-awareness without the constraints or limits of historical knowledge or conventional moralities. It is not symbolically enriching. Multiplicity of identity becomes for these women an ongoing torment, a horror that because of the incessant pain and confusion of living with this condition totally incapacitates them.[25]

Glass also shows that language, rather than being the means by which the self is imposed upon, is instead the means by which multiple selves of those inflicted with the illness announce themselves, so that diagnosis and treatment can proceed. Language is also the means by which the external power that has imposed the illness (usually a sexually abusive father of a female child) is overcome, the means by which the multiple selves are integrated. Language here is not imposition (the imposition is an act of physical aggression, an act that has no respect for an independent, unitary self); it is, instead, the means of diagnosis and cure.

Finally, Glass shows that the origins of MPD are in fact prepolitical and prelinguistic; its origin is in the pure terror and power of the father's conquest, in the Hobbesian state of nature. The postmodernists, on Glass's view, have mistakenly construed language not as the vehicle for understanding and agency, but as their opposite: "What distinguishes the citizen and the political dissident from the madman is the command of the agency of language....In its disorganization it leads to self-destruction. Language becomes an end not to political transformation or self-transformation but to an even greater confusion as to the boundaries between inside and outside [the self]."[26]

However much postmodernism wants to sever our ties with the

traditions of premodernity and modernity that precede it, its own abandonment of dialogical politics can be traced to Rousseauvian suspicions of public discourse.[27] If everything external to the self (or selves) is imposition, then why try to persuade? Why not dismiss the politics of dialogical civility by insisting that the other side "just doesn't get it," and that the issue will be decided by the politics of power, the politics of play (extravagance), or by disengagement and retreat? James Glass suggests that there is a connection between delusion and the suspicion of traditions and language: "Delusion, then, may be seen as a denial of history, the language of history, and the archives of a historical culture."[28]

Rousseau's language of the heart, the language of authenticity, is highly symbolic and highly idiosyncratic. It expresses a self that has no public context and no reference point beyond the self. This self-referential language not only denies the possibility of consensual, conventional discourse, but also denies the possibility of a self that is capable of knowing itself. The language of the heart can only reflect the confusion of the self; it can comment on the wounds suffered by the self in some apolitical state, but by denying common, consensual meanings, it abandons the shared narratives by which the self organizes itself.[29]

It is delusional to think that the human action in the present and into the future can be maintained in the face of fragmenting, multiple, minimal selves that have no past. It is, however, also delusional to think that the unified self is a given in human nature. The self, as Rousseau and postmodernists understand it, is constructed: the self is a product of our own narrative traditions.[30] But these stories that construct the self are deconstructed at our own risk; we risk the loss of the recognizably human subject and the prospect of agency and substitute narcissistic rage and what symptomatically appears to be mental illness. The constructed self—what C. Fred Alford calls "the virtuous noble lie"—cannot be abandoned:

> What I am recommending with the virtuous noble lie is that the social theorist take over this artistic task. The virtuous noble lie is this artistic championing of the self, one with will and consciousness. To the social scientist, who sees in this program only the confusion of myth and reality, I have but two responses. First, in abandoning such virtuous noble lies, be careful that you are not abandoning more of the Western tradition than you recognize....[A] concern with the self as a center of value in its own right may be the last thread holding this tradition together. Second, be sure to tell only the truth: that the regimes you recommend

generally serve the interests of social order against the subject. Hobbes came closest to this truth, and it is not pretty.[31]

The final irony of the postmodern critique of the authentic self is that it provides late modernity with the philosophical justification for the obsessive and delusional absorption in the self. Charles Taylor identifies this surprising affinity between the alienated self of Rousseauvian modernity and the multiple selves of postmodernity:

> The impact of [Derrida and Foucault] is paradoxical. They carry their Nietzchean challenge to our ordinary categories to the point of even 'deconstructing' the ideal of authenticity and the very notion of the self. But in fact, the Nietzchean critique of all 'values' as created cannot but exalt and entrench anthropocentrism. In the end, it leaves the agent, even with all of his or her doubts about the category of the 'self', with a sense of untrammeled power and freedom before a world that imposes no standards, ready to engage in free play or to indulge in the aesthetics of the self....[I]t further strengthens the self-centered modes, giving them a certain patina of deeper philosophical justification.[32]

The postmodern hostility to dialogical politics implies its continuing ties to the Rousseauvian notion of authenticity. Without the tacit recognition of the authentic self, we have no way of determining what is being imposed upon or what is being oppressed. More important, we have no basis for caring about how the linguistic and institutional structures that postmodernists urge us to deconstruct affect us. Rousseau believed that there was something, however frail, worth preserving in the face of modernity's onslaught. Postmodernity insists that there is no there there, and still somehow expects us to struggle and to care.

In postmodernity's abandonment of the unified self, yet again "Minerva's owl is beginning to falter," and again its "screech is a noise both of warning and of pain."[33]

Notes

1. See my review essay, "Christopher Lasch and the Withering of the American Adam," *Political Theory* 15 (February 1987): 127–137.
2. I owe this insight to Christopher Lasch, in *The Minimal Self, Psychic Survival in Troubled Times* (New York: Norton, 1983).
3. *Reveries of the Solitary Walker*, trans. Peter France (London: Penguin, 1979), 39.
4. *Multiculturalism and 'the Politics of Recognition'* (Princeton: Princeton Univ. Press, 1992).

5. See C. Fred Alford, *The Self in Social Theory* (New Haven: Yale Univ. Press, 1991), 156–270.

6. *Confessions*, trans. J. M. Cohen (London: Penguin, 1953), 389.

7. *Confessions*, 383.

8. *Reveries*, 89.

9. Margaret Canovan, "Arendt, Rousseau, and Human Plurality in Politics," *Journal of Politics* 45 (May 1983): 286–302.

10. *Amour de soi* is equivalent to self-esteem; that is, a healthy respect for the self, not dependent on the evaluation of others. *Amour propre* is equivalent to vanity, the socialized translation of self-esteem in which respect for the self becomes dependent on the opinion of others.

11. See James M. Glass, "Hobbes and Narcissism: Pathology in the State of Nature," *Political Theory* 8 (August 1980): 335–363.

12. James David Barber, in *Strong Democracy: Participatory Politics for a New Age* (Berkeley: Univ. of California Press, 1984), is one of those who has popularized the participatory interpretation of Rousseau's thought.

13. *The Social Contract*, 45, in *The Social Contract and the Discourse on the Origin of Inequality* (New York: Washington Square Press, 1967).

14. See Christopher Kelly, "'To Persuade without Convincing': The Language of Rousseau's Legislator," *American Journal of Political Science* 31 (May 1987): 321–334.

15. Hannah Pitkin, in *Fortune Is a Woman: Gender Politics in the Thought of Niccolo Machiavelli* (Berkeley: Univ. of California Press, 1984), makes a similar argument about the patriarchal character of Machiavelli's notion of founding.

16. I make an argument for the deliberative republican character of the American Founding in "Machiavellian Lessons in America: Republican Foundings, Original Principles, and Political Empowerment," in Wilson Carey McWilliams and Michael Gibbons, eds., *Federalists, Antifederalists, and the American Political Tradition* (New York: Greenwood Press, 1992): 13–26.

17. Judith N. Shklar, "J. J. Rousseau and Equality," 269, in Alan Ritter and Julia Conway Bondanella, eds., *Rousseau's Political Writings* (New York: Norton, 1988): 260–274.

18. Shklar, 271.

19. James Glass, *Shattered Selves: Multiple Personality in a Postmodern World* (Ithaca: Cornell Univ. Press, 1993), shows that postmodernism blurs the important distinction between self and identity: postmodernists want to pluralize the former, when it is the latter that is (and must be) plural, and which can only remain functionally plural to the extent that the former is singular.

20. Jean-Jacques Rousseau, "Essay on the Origin of Languages," 5:16, in John H. Moran and Alexander Goode, trans. *On the Origin of Language* (Chicago: Univ. of Chicago Press, 1966).

21. *Reveries*, 35.

22. See, for example, William Corlett, *Community without Unity: A Politics of Derridian Extravagance* (Durham: Duke Univ. Press, 1989); and Gilles Deleuze and Felix Guattari, *Anti-Oedipus, Capitalism, and Schizophrenia* (Minneapolis: Univ. of Minnesota Press, 1990).

23. See Charles Taylor, *Sources of the Self The Making of the Modern Identity* (Cambridge: Harvard University Press, 1989).

24. For a discussion of the problems of the postmodern theorizing about the self, see Carole Lambert's essay in this volume.

25. Glass, *Shattered Selves: Multiple Personality in a Postmodern World*, xvi. Charles Taylor cogently responds to Foucault on the impositional character of discourse: first, if all previous discourse has been an imposition, now that we recognize its impositional character (thanks to Foucault), can't we do better?; second, can't we make significant distinctions among degrees of imposition and can't we see that the impositional character of discourse has changed historically (and often for the better); for example, the erasure of women at the American founding versus the vibrant, pervasive public disclosure about women today? See "Connolly, Foucault, and Truth," *Political Theory* 13 (August 1983): 377–385.

26. Glass, *Shattered Selves*, 142.

27. For a recent discussion of the possibility of dialogical politics in a postmodern world, see Dana R. Villa, "Postmodernism and the Public Sphere," *American Political Science Review* 86 (September 1992): 712–724; see also the subsequent exchange between Villa and James Johnson, in *American Political Science Review* 88 (June 1994): 427–433.

28. James M. Glass, *Delusion: Internal Dimensions of Political Life* (Chicago: University of Chicago Press, 1985), 14.

29. Ibid., 108.

30. The idea of the self constructed from narrative traditions is from Alasdair MacIntyre, *After Virtue* (Notre Dame: Univ. of Notre Dame Press, 1981).

31. Alford, 191.

32. *The Ethics of Authenticity* (Cambridge: Harvard Univ. Press, 1991), 60–61.

33. Sheldon Wolin, "Political Theory as a Vocation," *American Political Science Review* 63 (December 1969), 1082. I am indebted to the National Endowment for the Humanities for a grant to attend a summer seminar, led by Leo Damrosch of Harvard University, during which the research for this essay was completed.

Rousseau and Communitarian Individualism in "Late Modern" America: The Interpretation of Benjamin Barber
by W. Jay Reedy[1]

One of the most discussed trends in American political thought and policy-making recently is "Communitarianism." Reflected in the campaign rhetoric of Bill Clinton in 1992, the Communitarian outlook has attracted interest in various quarters. One can count among those who consistently or occasionally take Communitarian positions such philosophers, social scientists, and commentators as Benjamin Barber, Charles Taylor, William Galston, Amitai Etzioni, Sheldon Wolin, Amy Gutmann, Alan Wolfe, John Keane, Michael Sandel, Hans Jonas, and Robert Bellah and associates.[2] Numerous others might be nominated to fit within this porous ambit, too.

Supporters of this "movement" affiliate it with neither what passes for the "Right" nor the "Left" in mainstream American politics. Purportedly, it represents a "third way." A "Communitarian Platform" has been endorsed by a variety of public and academic figures.[3] Communitarian "teach-ins" have been held—one included Vice President Al Gore while also appealing to Jack Kemp and Henry Cisneros—and a Communitarian quarterly, *The Responsive Community*, is published. Those attracted to this camp disagree on important topics, especially where civil liberties and "free-enterprise" economics are at issue. However, Communitarians do hold certain views in common. In particular, they share a concern about the vacuous "moral" condition of what they see as the atomized individualism and "interest-group" politics of the contemporary United States.

Sensitive to anti-communal tendencies in the American past and present—and broadly agreeing with the "civic republicanism" which scholars claim guided Anglo-American politics before the mid-nineteenth century[4]—Communitarians question what they see as the "anarchic" bases of liberalism and criticize the disintegrative policies those bases warrant. From the Communitarian standpoint, "classical" liberalism—implanted in the "rights language" described by Louis

Hartz[5]—is a distortive sociopolitical ethos which the "deregulatory," even Social Darwinistic, proclivities of the Reagan administration found easy to magnify. For practical as much as theoretical reasons, aver Communitarians, some of liberalism's laissez-fairist influence must be curbed. Self-centered "privatism" threatens national cohesion, economic planning, and individuals' success in finding meaningful lives. They contend that the "unencumbered self" of the "original position" in the welfarist liberalism of John Rawls's *A Theory of Justice* is an unconvincing image of humanity, one that neglects the social preconditions of selfhood. Liberalism's perspective on human nature, say Communitarians, is artificial inasmuch as it depreciates mankind's social interdependence, and this perspective, in turn, produces a liberal conception of society that is riven with antinomies.[6]

The consequences of liberalism's "atomistic" theory of individualism, declare Communitarian analysts, is apparent on personal no less than on institutional levels of American life where participation in government and a sense of community, cooperativeness, and public responsibility are withering. This enervation, goes their argument, accelerates several of the dire problems (e.g., declining educational achievement, mounting crime rates, the breakdown of the family, etc.) facing Americans. Unchecked, hollow individualism is not just philosophically or sociologically untenable, insist Communitarians. It makes our society, our polity, and our "selves" unsatisfying. Despite differences among their diagnoses, Communitarians conclude—shades of Emile Durkheim here!—that egocentrism and anomie are flaws inherent to liberal doctrines that have been worsened by a consumers' enchantment by "symbolic" material goods and the demographical trend of withdrawal to the suburbs. Communitarians believe that widely accepted elements of Americans' individualism and definition of freedom must be reconsidered if they wish to have a society that is ethically and politically renewed.

Communitarianism constructs its case against the present-day sociopolitical situation by relying almost exclusively on America's own heritage of ideas and predispositions. It is scarcely surprising, of course, that Communitarians concentrate on the intellectual history of their own country. Tocqueville, turn-of-the-century Populists, the democratic socialist Eugene V. Debs, the Protestant moralist and historian Reinhold Niebuhr, and, most importantly, the early-twentieth century philosophers William James, John Dewey and Josiah Royce are among those whose ideas are invoked. Communitarian tracts echo with Dewey's condemnation of "lonely individualism" and promotion of "anchored liberalism."[7] Unfortunately, this American bias neglects other sources for "communitarian individualism" within the history of political thought. One European thinker who has insights to offer any "recentering" of individualism but who is intentionally or unintentionally overlooked by most Communitarians is Jean-Jacques Rousseau. Benjamin R. Barber is one of the few Communitarians to appreciate his salutary relevance. But whether even Barber fathoms the depth of Rousseau's criticisms and maintains the height of his ideals is another matter. This question occupies the essay at hand.

It is tempting to explain the Communitarians' disregard of Rousseau as due to the interpretive problems posed by that thinker's writings. The obscurities within Rousseau's works as well as the troubles of his personal life are, indeed, obstacles to easy access.[8] Rousseau has been glorified as the inspirer of Jacobin radicalism during the French Revolution, on the one hand, and condemned as a distant architect of totalitarian Leninism and Fascism, on the other.[9] The fact that Rousseau's targets included facets of Enlightenment "modernity" as well as the "tradition" of Europe's pre-Revolutionary societies and states compounds readers' frustration. Yet, these obstacles can be overblown. Large portions of Rousseau's *oeuvre* conduct a quest for a democratic political society that is profound and lucid. They do so, moreover, based upon a "moral" understanding of democracy which, because it is neither apparently majoritarian nor interest-based, transcends the patrician or bourgeois definitions of representative oligarchy broached by Locke, Montesquieu, and the American Founding Fathers.

Rousseau's books and essays attribute "natural goodness" to early, unantagonistic humanity and defame *amour-propre* and its sophisticated reifications, intertwined themes which should appeal to Communitarians disaffected with American society today. The occasional vagueness of Rousseau's words cannot justify a Communitarian's reluctance to learn from his socializing *cum* liberating ideas. Like them, Rousseau was conscious of the liabilities of extreme egalitarianism and was attracted by the moral ambience of community-based government. But by no means did he turn against all manifestations of individualism. So why have not Communitarians regularly drawn upon Rousseau's politics of socially sensitive autonomy? A possible answer is conveyed by Michael Walzer's verdict on Communitarian thought: its motif of anti-atomization, rather than being a subversion of the liberal *status quo*, is "a consistently intermittent feature of liberal politics and social organization."[10] On the other hand, if the Communitarian agenda aims at more than a subtle rebalancing of Anglo-American liberalism, then Rousseau and the genealogy of European radical and social democratic thought should be among their objects of study.

Benjamin R. Barber's version of Communitarianism combines an inspection of classical liberalism's postulates with suggestions on how to modify its individualism to lessen its deleterious "real world" consequences. Justice cannot be done to every feature of his thought here, though it should be remarked that his views are less freighted with reactionary urges than those of some Communitarians. Generally, Barber's analyses are representative of the Communitarian orientation. They also reveal, however, how even a philosophically and historically adept Communitarian has borrowed from Rousseau's formulations but has then dulled their thrust. My focus on Barber's views is thus no accident. Rousseau is mentioned on many pages of his works, almost always with approval. One could argue, in fact, that Barber uses Rousseau—albeit *his* Rousseau—as the guiding template for his vision of "strong democracy."

All this does not simplify the job of comparing these two writers, however. The notions of individual, society, and government in Rousseau can prove elusive even while they are provocative. Jean-Jacques the "sentimental" reasoner seldom worried about his points being pellucid or conjunctive. Sometimes he concentrated on praising the "virtue" of the warrior-citizens of ancient Sparta or bucolic Switzerland; sometimes on the solitariness of pre-civilized mankind (his parodied "noble savage" theme); sometimes on the careful tutoring of the unspoiled child; and sometimes, toward the end of his life, on the outcast entranced by nature's wonders.[11] Thus, it is undoubtedly true that the categories of "citizen" and "man" form a knotty complementarity throughout Rousseau's *oeuvre*.[12]

Barber's Communitarian desiderata are summarized in his "Strong Democracy Program."[13] Its presuppositions, however, are more germane to our purpose than its particular dicta, especially Barber's contention that Americans' hostility or apathy towards government, their "programmed" opinions, and their decreasing sense of intergenerational responsibility, are at the same time causes and results of a non-participatory political life, of today's "thin" representative democracy.

These characteristics, he asserts, permit the "free" market and the bureaucracy of the state to fill the void. Our representative system now presides over a nation not of committed citizens but of indifferent voters (and non-voters) who see government, at worst, as the source of heavy taxation and "red tape" and, at best, as the ineffectual provider of "entitled" services legitimately pursued by aggregates of individuals with hypertrophic desires and atrophic responsibilities.[14] Modern Americans resist politics—no longer just certain politicians and policies—presumes Barber. Not many are actively involved in governing themselves; most have even forgotten that they ought to want to be. It is as part of this inquiry into American democracy's "corruption" that Barber adapts, dilutes, or refocuses Rousseau's critique of modernity. Fearing to stray far beyond the bounds of our political culture and vocabulary, Barber, we shall find, closes his eyes to the full scope of Rousseau's discontents and correctives.

Barber's first major book, *The Death of Communal Liberty* (1974), grew out of his Harvard dissertation. Rousseau and his misgivings about Enlightenment-style liberalism hover in the background of this analysis of democracy in eastern Switzerland, as Barber himself stresses.[15] Jean-Jacques' Protestant Swiss background is common knowledge. More important, Swiss village government in the eighteenth century (that of Neuchatel more than that of the larger Geneva) served him to highlight democracy's promise. Barber's book on local democracy in the eastern Swiss (formerly Raetian) canton of Graubunden is not an example of disinterested historiography. In fact, he begins it by underscoring the relevance for modern societies of the Swiss experience; it ends with a discussion of the threats to Graubunden's communal democracies from the central government and the socioeconomic changes of the late 19th and 20th centuries. Clearly, he admires the participatory aspects of the immemorial unit of governance known as a "neighborhood" (*Nachbarschaft*), 227 of which existed in the autonomous area of Raetia prior to federation with Switzerland in the 1850s.[16]

In the traditional Raetian village, Barber approvingly observes, politics was not just voting, regular assemblies of the electorate, or even the choice of local officers by lot. Rather, civic life there and elsewhere in Switzerland—albeit an exclusively male affair until the 1970s when women won the ballot!—included universal military service and "common work." He stresses, too, that the referendum remains a device through which Alpine neighbors/citizens frame and refine their own policies rather than, as in modern America, merely register "yehs" or "nays" to proposals from a distant capital, politician, or administrative bureau.[17] In short, Barber touts Swiss practices as exemplars, which, if tailored to the United States, could enliven and popularize our governmental practices.[18] Referring to Hannah Arendt along with Rousseau, he notes that in the premodern era "the individual Raetian's involvement in neighborhood self-government was his obligation to participate in the concrete implementation of the policies he...ratified. Citizenship brought with it the obligation to *do* and to *act* as well as to *will* and to *vote*....It was as if the neighborhood citizen had taken Rousseau's injunction that the will, being inalienable, cannot be represented, and adjusted it to the peculiar forms of his own political life." Barber concludes from this that before the mid-twentieth century the Swiss "appeared to experience none of that atomization that attends freedom in representative systems, none of the alienation which so often emerges as the obverse side of individuality in liberal regimes. The sense of self given by his citizenship defined him as an autonomous man *within* the structure of his polity....How far is this formula from Rousseau's construction of freedom as obedience to 'a law which we prescribe to ourselves?'"[19]

Unfortunately, his history of Swiss democracy does not have a happy ending. Barber has a hard time resisting nostalgia for medieval Graubunden. The mountain citizenry, overtaken by modern concentrations of power and wealth, left their slopes and valleys in burgeoning numbers for city jobs and attractions in recent decades,[20] an internal emigration that he paints as a fall from the grace of *Gemeinschaft*: "Thus, from traditional communal man comes modern economic man....ready for solitary life of affluence in the jungle of cities. Materialism in [today's] Switzerland seems at least in part to act as consolation to men who have lost their citizenship....It is the ghost of Peter Laslett's *World We Have Lost*, haunting the world that has replaced it."[21] In the end, Barber's paean to direct democracy in the Alps becomes a wistful eulogy.

Communitarian treatments of premodern political community are prone to irrelevance due to such anachronistic ruminating. Whether the Swiss experience of the past can be anything more than an embarrassment to our complacency, whether, that is, it pertains to the situation of a huge and heterogeneous society like the United States, remains an open question. Favoring an increase in common bonds in the late twentieth century can tempt Communitarians into seeming like yearners after some vanished (whether Athenian, medieval or Hegelian) society, but selective approval of features of traditional community need not turn into quixotic or reactionary revery. There is no *a priori* reason that elements of traditionalism cannot contribute to a society's "subversion" and revision.[22] Rousseau's many references to ancient polities as touchstone rather than blueprint show how well he understood this.

Barber's most sustained exegesis of Rousseau's world-view is to be found in his 1978 essay on the Genevan's notion of the "dramatic imagination." Rousseau's assessment of this subject provides Barber with a basis for his own diagnoses of today's America. Barber realizes that the French thinker's judgment on the human imaginative faculty is Janus-faced. The Genevan was "equally inspired by and directed against the imagination."[23] The first "fall," in Rousseau's story, occurred when independent mankind misused its creativity by polarizing *amour-propre* and compassionate conscience (*"pitié"*).[24] This polarization, in turn, stimulated the establishment of private property and the laws and institutions protecting it, unfortunate developments that made happy and sociable selfhood and any non-oppressive order of society impossible to achieve.[25] That Rousseau disapproved of the insouciant "cultivation" of the ego endorsed by the *philosophes* (e.g., Voltaire, Diderot) is plain. Barber knows about Rousseau's disapproval of the Enlightenment's sophisticatedly secular and utilitarian worldview.[26] The abstract and amoral rationality of the "century of light" was false for Rousseau because it encouraged abstract and amoral individualism.[27] The selfhood encouraged in the Parisian *salons* condescended to *le peuple*; it could not rescue mankind from its historically shaped psychological and sociopolitical defects.

For Rousseau, according to Barber, imagination in history had frequently operated as a malign force. In a famous published letter of 1757, Rousseau, disagreeing with d'Alembert, supported the Genevan magistrates' ban on theatrical productions. Yet, this condemnation of artistic mimesis resists Plato's elitist sweep. Rousseau admitted that the theater could benefit a corrupt society (i.e., Old Regime Paris) by playing with alternatives.[28] His objection to performances in less degenerate societies, notes Barber, was that in the "theater…with the insidious help of the imagination, passion overwhelmed reason, and stimulation and pretence…expelled authenticity and action." A playwright's success flows more from entertaining audiences than from strengthening their mores. Drama dissimulates. What ails the dramatic arts is the same thing that mars the imaginary of "civilized" mankind in general: a proclivity for self-gratifying illusions and masks.[29] The solipsistic imagination Rousseau finds behind all simulations—including forms of representation (either linguistic or political), the practice of wet-nursing, masturbation, etc.—spurs "inauthenticity." Falsified experiences encourage narcissistic passivity. Despite evidence from *The Confessions* and *Rousseau juge de Jean-Jacques* that he was a "chameleon" (his own description[30]) plagued by neurotic turmoil, as a theorist he favored an uplifting imbrication—not a smothering identification—of personality and humane community. Only thus would the twin corruptions of emotional solipsism and sociopolitical privatism in modern life be defeated.

The founders of admirable polities of the past whom Rousseau venerates strove for something different from what the concoctions of melodrama proffer. Lawgivers like Moses, Lycurgus, Numa, or Calvin provided guidelines for less "denaturalized," more moral communities. With assistance, they believed individuals could divest themselves of inherited, erroneous conventions. Barber seems on the mark in stating that Rousseau was unable to ally with Platonism because of its authoritarian propensities. Rousseau's ideals castigate not freedom but the amorality that contaminated twisted forms of it, and, though Rousseau's autobiographical works register the anguish of maladjusted genius, his theoretical texts struggle against the "fragmentation of the modern self, alienated from the world and from its own nature."[31] Rousseau's labyrinthine, sincerity seeking subjectivity is impelled by a false civilization as much as by particular neuroses. His ego—uniquely attractive and unattractive in its literary self-exposure—vets rather than acclaims the "sickness" of its soul.

Barber's interpretation of Rousseau's critique of the malign imagination of the "civilized" is a prelude to *Strong Democracy*, especially its "argument against liberalism." There, Barber looks at the conceptual deficiencies of the Cartesian, Hobbesian, and Newtonian paradigms that have anchored liberal thinking since the late seventeenth century.[32] He locates one fountainhead of America's "thin" democracy in Hobbes's pseudo-scientific assumption that "natural" (or naturalistic) individuals are aggressive "atoms" chasing pleasure and power.[33] John Locke merely modified this approach in insisting that "the great and chief end...of men...putting themselves under government...is the mutual preservation of their lives, liberties and estates, which I call by the general name property."[34] Given this instrumentalist viewpoint, comments Barber, it is predictable that either unrestricted capitalism or statist coercion will shadow the classical liberal's philosophy. Only solitude or contacts for advantage result from devaluing the empathetic relationships essential to the completely human condition—that lost condition mourned by Rousseau. For Barber, liberalism's ancestry explains why Americans guard their private liberties so obsessively even as they marginalize that "public space" where self-governance itself must transpire.[35]

Barber sees an escape from this morass in the "recreative" role which Rousseau believed a beneficial form of imagination could fill. Rousseau posited a moral, rational, and voluntarist version of imagination, one capable of healing crippled, asocial authenticity. This reading of Rousseau accords with that of Robert Wokler. Wokler holds that Rousseau was skeptical about Enlightenment "progress"—a "progress" that produced "moral corpses," according to Rousseau.[36] But he points out that this stance was accompanied by Rousseau's novel conception of "perfectibility" which "joined together a highly optimistic idea of human potentialities with a deeply pessimistic vision of man's worldly accomplishments [thus far]."[37]

The archetypal example of such a recreative use of imagination in Rousseau, emphasizes Barber, is his description of how humans' innate capacity for "pity"[38] connects every observer with observed victims of villainy or misfortune.[39] Both the *Second Discourse* and *Emile* hypothesize that amid civilized corruption it may seem that "a really happy man is a hermit." And yet, it is "only God [who] enjoys happiness" of that kind.[40] As ungodlike humans, our worries, inadequacies, and setbacks "draw our hearts to our fellow-creatures," provided that our natural feelings are undeformed by customs permeated by hypocrisy. This compassionate imagination succors those afflicted by calamity or injustice and also enables individuals together to craft autonomy within community.

To Rousseau's mind, the techno-rational "progress" favored by the *philosophes* frequently enlarges modernity's "spiritual" vacuum, but he resisted blaming "modernization" for our tribulations. People themselves have forged and passed along their lonely "prison." Ontology and polity are not unrelated. Despite the fact that existing civilization appears to be the leading culprit in the two *Discourses*, "the paradox of the imagination suggests that nature itself—the natural faculty of imagination—is at fault." However, our species' previous choice of a falsely "enlightened" civilization never leads Rousseau to think that mankind would be better off without intelligence or freedom. Creative choice, from which error and misery can always spring, is also the place from which liberation can begin. The teacher-priest of *Emile* rejects the opinion that humanity would benefit from having instincts alone. Rousseau maintains that humanity, now trapped by what it invented, can remake itself once its faculties are self-purified. All is not lost even for societies pervaded by "advanced" unnaturalness. Their reformation, although difficult, is attainable via imaginatively-improved goals and actions that can restructure political society, "[s]ince we are developmental animals by nature."[41]

In its commiserating, mutualized form, imagination is praiseworthy for Rousseau. With it, Barber notes, he expected people to overcome the *amour-propre* which condemned human abilities to the role of tools of competition and lacerating alienation. No longer the servant of self-love turned sour, imagination as creativity can produce a "general will" and expand our fraternity. Potentially, such imagination is the cognitive/affective starting-point for compassion among freely social individuals—the goal espoused by the *Social Contract*. Rejecting the opinion that self-centeredness is congenital, Rousseau promoted the "moral promise" of people's simultaneous rethinking of themselves and their sociopolitical environment. Rousseau was, indeed, an unprecedented "dreamer of democracy."[42]

Paradoxically, Barber travels further with Rousseau the "dreamer" than with Rousseau the critic of the *status quo*. What Barber has distilled from Rousseau is a watered down formulation of his tonic for democratizing modernity. While even this buoys his Commmunitarianism, it deprives the original of its boldness. Barber's assimilation of Rousseau turns timid. This is evident in Barber's reluctance to confront America's reigning values and institutions head on, something he justifies on the grounds that theorizing is anathema to politicking.[43]

Properly suspicious of the "scientistic" veneer of classical liberalism, Barber overreacts. He prohibits philosophizing about political life: "[P]olitics is the search for reasonable choices....Abstract rationality is not at stake, for that concept suggests some prepolitical standard of truth....Yet in reality it is precisely the absence of such norms that gives rise to politics....A reasonable choice or a reasonable settlement is not necessarily rational at all, but it will be seen as deliberate, nonrandom, uncoercive, and in a practical sense fair."[44] Stated succinctly, "[p]olitics is what men do when metaphysics fails."[45] This dialogic aspect of Barber's thought indicts the deontological approaches of Hobbes and Habermas, Nozick and the "mature" Marx, in the same breath. Of course, this ban testifies to a commendable mistrust of government directed by a Leninist or any other oligarchy of the "wise" or "scientific." The price for this anti-theoretical standpoint, however, is high, namely, the concession of all normative and objective judgments in the sociopolitical realm. This price Rousseau was unprepared to pay, and with good reason. He realized that eschewing critical theorizing redounds to the benefit of established "facts" and persons in power. For Rousseau, intelligent civic living requires not a contentless pragmatism but (to borrow from Aristotle as well as Kant) "practical reason," a quasi-transcendental yet wholly human responsibility that is antiauthoritarian because it consists of the self-imposed commitments of individuals affected by community.

Barber's deflation of theorizing sounds temperate and beneficial. Nonetheless, it is oblivious to the problem of habituated ideology which Marx calls "false consciousness," Gramsci describes as "hegemony," and Marcuse implies by "one-dimensional man." Barber's lack of critical thrust, his abandonment of Rousseauist "practical reason," is a characteristic found as well in the neo-pragmatic philosopher Richard Rorty. Rorty's writings show that pragmatism is liberalism's latest "fellow-traveller," one so indeterminate that it undercuts concerns with the epistemologically "true" and ethically "good."[46] The cultural "conversation" it cherishes is interior monolgue, the (Henry) Jamesian ruminations of refined and well-off individuals detached from a grimmer social cosmos that seldom vexes their broadminded aesthetic sensibilities.[47] The pitfall of a position like Rorty's and at times Barber's is that, lacking even a "weak" deontology, its reformist sentiments end up looking like arbitrary preferences. The vacuous formalism of this pragmatism collapses into prudent non-interference with the "givens" of modern institutions and the attitudes and behaviors under their tutelage.

The triumph of a democratic community, realized Rousseau, depends upon arguments and actions that expose the present's shortcomings while assisting to make the ideal "real." A noncommittal stance, on the other hand, is the likely result of Barber's disinclination to probe what needs to be done to correct both those perceptions and the sociopolitical actualities which are their *raison d'etre*. Vaunting democracy's procedural openness blurs substantive ideas of the "good life"—not the "goods" of a manic, middle-class "lifestyle"—while forgetting those vestiges of community which, one might think, should occupy any "Communitarianism." Hopes of transcending liberalism that refuses first to dissect liberalism's failings attenuates even mild misgivings about America's sociopolitical situation. There may seem little to dissent from in Barber's pronouncement that politics "should be something done by, not to, citizens."[48] However, the threat of anti-intellectual populism lurking in that statement is uncommendable. Pragmatic relativism is irreconcilable with the intentions behind Rousseau's "general will."[49] It also reinforces the "playfulness" of those postmodernists whom Barber himself condemns as purveyors of "hyperskepticism." The desirability of dialogue—which Barber equates with an absence of independent grounds for judgment in democracy—need not connote a flight from examining what advances and what obstructs democratic government, society and economy. Because he ignores this, the core of Barber's Communitarianism is strangely barren. His single-minded concentration on the process of democracy omits the prior values without which such a process is either nugatory or a scramble for control among vested interests. It is almost as unlikely that democracy will arise from an insubstantial pragmatism as that it will descend from inflexible dogmatism. Banishing pointed criticisms is a recipe for democracy's perpetual postponement. Although a number of its caveats about our predicament ring true, Communitarianism tends to remain unwilling to specify the structural causes of the problems it treats. It could gain a keener critical edge by acquiring a Rousseauist insistence stronger than the one tendered by Barber.

Barber looks for credentials for his pragmatism by tying Rousseau to the customary approach to government advocated by Edmund Burke. He portrays them as like-minded opponents of "foundationalist" thinking. There may, indeed, be scant reason to think Rousseau would have concurred with the format of Kant's "categorical imperative."[50] Nonetheless, Rousseau and Kant stand together—contra Burke and Barber—as partisans of non-relativistic ethics and rational politics, the first even claiming that "universal justice...springs from reason alone."[51] This point is confirmed by the fact that Rousseau concentrates on the preconditions for democratic community rather than inscribing what policies citizens imbued with a "general will" might take. He claims that his dicta concerning democracy "take men as they are, and laws as they ought to be." Rousseau's idea of what corrupted humanity is nowhere as vacuously "situationalist" as Barber implies. In the end, Barber's "Jean-Jacques as pragmatist" tells us about his own tactics but much less about the principles motivating Rousseau as critic.

Notwithstanding his penchant for pragmatism, Barber is attracted to the transformative possibilities depicted by Rousseau: "Economic man as a calculator of self-interest imperils democracy....The danger is...that the self-interested competitor...will be deprived of the only faculties that make possible common willing and the creation of political communities....Liberal democracy makes of this limitation a virtue by treating politics as an arena of market competition that is indistinguishable from economics—'interest-group politics,' as it is known."[52] But because he refuses to take a philosophical stand, Barber can reprimand Milton Friedman's academic variation on the theme "greed is good" only hypothetically. His pragmatic Communitarianism is, therefore, ripe for cooptation.

How to abet communal democracy under modern conditions is the issue tackled in the final sections of the *Social Contract*. There, Rousseau counts on learning to unmask those amoral/irrational social/personal forces that mold behavior and which democracy's vilifiers from Plato to William Riker present as irremediable shortcomings of the "masses." Not just a few paternalistic philosophers but *all* citizens can become intelligent and active custodians of public well-being. Barber observes that one of Rousseau's main achievements was setting forth "conditions under which self-interested beings can act disinterestedly and thus virtuously in a fashion that curbs their private interests without compromising their natural self-love (*amour de soi*). In this light, the General Will may be understood as advice which...rediscovers and gives social force to the natural powers of compassion (right instinct)."[53]

Barber's faith in dialogue *tout court* discards Rousseau's larger intentions. More important it is untenable as the sole prerequisite to democratic society. When history is looked at, we notice that the *pro forma* opportunity for discussion among citizens—whether in fifth-century Athens or 1950s America—has not consistently produced humane policies. The tenacity of militarism, racist legislation, or fascist-like regimes that "deliver the goods" demonstrates this even for presumably democratic nations. The conundrum that Barber wrestles with is analogous to the one that tested Rousseau. Either norms of "practical reason" must be discovered and upheld or those with the greatest clout and wealth or the sharpest skills of flattery or deception will dominate.[54] The Communitarianism of Barber frustrates the pursuit of truth and ethical values with a pragmatic pliability that invites inaction. Therefore, it is not surprising that his works prefer to skirt issues of class, race, and gender. They evade consideration of that "repressive tolerance" of sham and impotent individuality which inures Americans to the painful sociopolitical absurdities around them.

Given the fact that the Old Regime's "corporatist" structure protected privilege more than pluralism, Rousseau's disapproval of interest groups—a similar distaste for political parties prevailed in the nascent United States—should not be misunderstood.[55] Rousseau's refusal to believe that participatory politics is achievable simply through the unfettered expression of existing prejudgments and anti-egalitarian arrangements makes Barber, like numerous readers of Rousseau, uneasy.[56] Certainly if "interest-group" democracy is the measuring-rod, then "forced to be free" smacks of tyranny. But the textual context of that phrase in the *Social Contract* indicates Rousseau never defines democracy as a contest or "con game" for offices or economic perquisites. Such a definition—close to our present politics though it seems—in his view nullifies democratic community.

For Rousseau, arriving at the meaning of freedom connotes educative means for diminishing parochial perspectives based on unequal authority and property relations, relations that affect even representative governments and which are attended by *amour-propre* among rich and poor alike. Releasing modern people from the "repressed memory" of their civilization's founding trauma of suspicion and inequality is what is sought. His infamous phrase thus implies not bullying or manipulation but the sensitizing of individuals, preferably while they are still growing up, to a reciprocity which nourishes accord and liberty.[57] Rousseau may not have been a pillar of personal rectitude or adjustment—"I am made unlike any one I have ever met"[58]—but he was committed to a democratic society. Only communal democracy can return contentment along with moral freedom to a nation's individuals.

The oxymoronic aura clinging to "forced to be free" throws into relief the dilemma of merging communal needs and personal desires for most people. It is this dilemma that moves Rousseau to propose a lawgiving "shaman"—his "Legislator"—as a guide for escaping from undemocratic, atomistic civilization. In the thought-experiment that is the *Social Contract*, a non-dictatorial "therapist" contributes to the coming of democracy by exorcising modern individuals' "internal" and modern society's "external" constraints.[59] Unflinching social *cum* self-examination could nurture "an ego without any of the 'pain' associated with the frenzy of a decadent historical process."[60] Thus, Rousseau's "Legislator" is not a would-be authoritarian but "the engineer who invents the machine; [whereas] the prince is merely the mechanic who sets it up and operates it.…[J]ust as he who has command over men must not have command over laws, neither must he who has command over laws have command over men."[61] If Barber were to pay due attention to Rousseau's "Legislator," perhaps he would grasp why developing democracy implies cultivating critics.

Like Rousseau, Barber recognizes a concomitant to participatory democracy in education. Both writers concentrate not on technical skills or bookish knowledge but on tutoring "applied," humanistic citizenship. Barber, in particular, follows Rousseau in asserting that educators should focus on an autonomy-enhancing formation of the student's character. He dismisses the neo-conservative diatribes of Allan Bloom[62] and walks a thin line between those bent on preserving the "canon" and "politically correct" educators who carry a commendable multiculturalism to faddish excess. Barber compliments the educational program of *Emile* for its view of learning as "a lifetime task of which schooling represented only a phase."[63] Yet, though one section of his *Superman and Common Men* opens with a quote from *Emile* on why the good teacher must build a wall around his charge's soul.[64] he does not really elaborate on Rousseau's assertion that future citizens should be taught how to discover for themselves what authentic freedom feels like. Barber's is not a "pedagogy of the oppressed" in the vein of what Paulo Freire or Henry Giroux outline. Still, he takes with seriousness Rousseau's notion that freeing consciousness requires sublimation through mentoring. A quest for "emancipatory authority" may strike moderns as menacing, but only if "negative liberty"—i.e., lack of compulsion, including compelling knowledge—is the shallow and sole dimension of freedom venerated.[65]

Barber, then, is aware of the reason the *Social Contract* and *Emile* recommend fostering solidarity through "civil religion," rites, and symbols.[66] Some "deprogramming" through which we unlearn the antisocial messages of marketers and libertarians as preparation for social existence of a less guarded, less instrumental sort might be necessary in our age. Acquaintance with community is not procured through disingenuous techniques for "making friends and influencing people;" it stems rather from myriad, sentiment laden interactions that teach the mutuality of autonomy.[67] Barber anticipates that raising Americans' desire for democratic involvement will require "mandatory citizen education and community service."[68] Through cooperative "service" projects directed at community improvement and undertaken by citizens of all strata, the dominant "language of consent" in our politics ("*me* language") might be reforged into a "language of participation" ("*we* language"). Once it becomes a complete "form of life," this kind of parlance leads not to "[monistic] unity, no[r] voices disciplined into unison, but musical harmony in its technical sense."[69] Here, Barber grasps at least one of Rousseau's deep doubts about liberal modernity.

Advocating the "unlearning" of prejudices and anti-communal definitions of liberty, Barber knows, pits his position against "the shibboleths that have comprised traditional liberal ideas of education" in America. Liberalism fetishes tolerance, according to Barber, as a means of bolstering a laissez-fairist indifference toward society. The apolitical and ethically neutral "marketplace" liberalism of this century—more perhaps than the early modern versions of Locke and Smith— "demoralizes" the social setting to which individuals owe their maturity and emotional well-being.[70]

The exact extent of Barber's dissatisfaction with "late" capitalist society and culture is hard to ascertain. In places, he reviews, without heartily embracing, radical charges against modern political economy. Contrary to these flirtations with the Left, however, is his expressed belief that "economic individualism" is so ingrained in the American "soul" that it is impervious to attack. The critic who stages such an attack, he implies, will encounter deaf ears or be labelled "un-American." In the introduction to the fourth printing (1990) of *Strong Democracy*, Barber even reassures "middle-of-the-road" readers that his is not "a call for major economic change....[M]arkets have proven to be immensely productive, while systems that subordinate economic choice to planning and control...have often wound up serving neither choice nor justice, as the extraordinary rebellion against command economies and one-party rule in the formerly communist world attests."[71] For Barber, prudence entails that democratic reformers speak softly about the tragic injustices that litter the social landscape under capitalism.

Barber does not everywhere give in to his own counsel of prudence, however. Despite the plaudits he pays economic individualism—as a liberation from premodern authorities—he is aware that capitalism persistently generates many baleful effects for individuals and societies alike. Barber charts the decline of citizenship and its language of "virtue" after the Renaissance thus:

> [T]he privileging of economic activity as the basis for social growth, and the concomitant stress on individual activity and private choice, both shaped and placed limits on the [civic] republican revival....Democracy was...reborn in the modern world with capitalism as its midwife....This capitalism...transformed the classical values that constituted its own core. More and more people shared in a [state] power that meant less and less....[T]he rights of citizens...were reactive and cautionary rather than empowering and anticipatory—giving them protection...but little control.[72]

Nonetheless, these reservations are in the margins of Barber's thought, especially in his works of the Reagan-Bush years. Often his critical comments are amorphously or tepidly expressed. His best-known writings acquiese to the claim that the capitalist economy is a precinct of liberty and equality unconnected to the governmental situation Americans revile. It is significant that Barber's misgivings about the socioeconomic underpinnings of America are clearest in one of his earliest books, *Liberating Feminism*.[73] Tellingly, the pragmatic meekness of his Communitarian thinking began as the 1970s ended.

One looks in vain for any sustained critique of America's institutional panoply in Barber. Too frequently, his works simply chide but then quite thoroughly accommodate the "logic" of a capitalism whose premise is that we are creatures molded not by a changeable culture but by a congenital nature indentured to injurious strife or conformist strivings. Barber's idea for encouraging voting parades its cautiousness by urging that Americans be paid to go to the polls. As an afterthought, he admits that "the outlook and realities of modern monopoly capitalism...interfere with and finally jeopardize strong democracy." But this is followed by a clubbing of Marxist socialism and corporate/consumerist capitalism with the same blunt hammer. Both are alleged to deny the "autonomy of politics" in an identical manner. Both, declares Barber, instill an anti-political "economic determinism."[74]

In the face of this statement, one feels bound to reiterate that Marx believed in democracy, opposed the extent to which the modern mode of production warps modern society, and was a staunch proponent of community. That aside, why does Barber expect his own idealization of "face-to-face" politics, detached as it is from a thorough analysis of capitalism and its consequences, to show the way toward less interest-based democracy? The hegemony exercised by today's global economy, its maldistribution of wealth among and within nations, and its clichés about "equal opportunity" and "freedom" through insularity need reanalysis. Are not the types of communities exemplified in twentieth-century Scandinavia or in the conceptions of socialists—foreign and domestic—more in line with Barber's complaints against liberalism than the fine-tuning of America's institutions and assumptions which his writings have come to settle for? Since Barber and most of his persuasion avoid seriously investigating "un-American" options in economic, social, and political organization, the tacit Communitarian answer is "no."

Rousseau was never as epistemologically or ethically elastic a thinker as Barber has become. Though he lived before the expansion of industrial, let alone multinational, capitalism, his arresting caricature of possessing/governing elites—"[t]he rich...being so to speak sensitive in every part of their Goods"[75]—expresses an indictment which Barber mutes. That the "open" communicativeness prized by Barber can develop in a citizenry conditioned by a milieu that often turns a blind eye to individual success through deception and divisiveness seems unlikely. Rousseau went beyond anything in Barber by deriding the specific ways in which "possessive individualism" (C. B. Macpherson) feeds the drive for prestige and negates sociability: "I would prove that if one sees a handful of powerful and rich men at the pinnacle of greatness and fortune while the mass crawls in obscurity and misery, it is because the former value the things they enjoy only to the extent that the others are deprived of them, and they would cease to be happy if, without any change in their own state, the People ceased to be miserable."[76]

Rousseau insisted that imaginative social recreation is thwarted by the oppression of the "have-nots" and by the endless pursuit of satisfaction through "luxury" on the part of the "haves."[77] One can agree with Barber that the power of the few over the many will only be defeated when democratic process is manifested through the wills and deeds of individuals who have become habituated to isolation. But what if individuals' freedom to imagine this remains blocked by the weight of monolithic institutions and by the "programming" of electronic marketers whose fare of privatized fantasies are the enemy of democratic sociability? Breaking out of that kind of a vicious circle remains a formidable undertaking. This predicament must be faced *before* communication and participation by citizens can produce an actual politics of "free" community.

In the end, Barber's "strong democracy" is less a replacement for the pseudo-democracy Rousseau found unacceptable[78] than a mid-course correction of our trajectory.[79] Its ken remains shortsighted because Barber avoids interrogating American history and culture and the established boundaries of the acceptable. Even a tame Communitarianism, of course, may disturb those for whom "America as we know it began with the death of community."[80] However, what must trouble anyone looking for significant change is that Communitarian thinkers seldom investigate the structural underpinnings of the liberal credo, especially the social and economic system whose imprimatur it is. Communitarians, Barber included, never thoroughly appraise liberalism as an entrenched matrix of institutionalized practices. In short, they pull their punches regarding the liberal ideology's partnership with a socioeconomic dominion which, as much as non-responsive government, presides over America and much of the world.

Barber has learned a lot from Rousseau's works. Perhaps Rousseau could have benefitted from the former's brief for syncretic politics as dialogical parleying. In any case, the Rousseauist *aperçu* that "society must be studied in the individual and the individual in society" has been absorbed by Barber. He perceives that politics, ethics, and economic equity treated separately will all be miscomprehended. However, in marrying Rousseau's democratic imagination to a circumspect pragmatism, Barber's Communitarianism mollifies Rousseau's abrasive reflections on modern society. Lauding the democratic pragmatics of dialogue without interrogating the "systematically distorted communication" (Habermas) that permeates the present is insufficient. Rousseau's writings, by contrast, dug into that underside of modernity's institutions and values below the formally political. Seldom did Rousseau deal with politics—as Barber's all too American Communitarianism is wont to do—apart from incisive analyses of the inequalites that precondition the workings of government.

For better or worse, Rousseau was no pragmatist.[81] A singular regulative ideal motivates Rousseau's theorizing: how to achieve a diverse but just community of autonomous and different yet responsible and caring individuals. One of his insights that even Marx could have learned more from is that capitalism is an all-encompassing "form of life," one that obstructs authenticity within as well as outside the ego.[82] Concentrating on political procedures—even announcing sound principles without showing what prevents their realization—will not lead to the removal of that obstruction. This is a point Barber seems aware of but which he fails to press home; too often he merely alludes to the underlying impediments to democratic society in today's America. As opposed to Barber—let alone most Communitarians—Rousseau did not temporize when he assailed the factors that keep modern people from achieving full democracy.[83]

Rousseau's troubled life, it is true, foreshadows the evanescent "postmodern" individualism of our incredibly commodified late twentieth century. But the prototypical individual in community of his philosophical social criticism rebukes this fashionably postulated condition. The communal democracy of Rousseau's vision is anything but contentless. It sharply judges the ignobility of bourgeois civilization and frames this denunciation as a necessary prelude to the emergence of a free, socialized humanity. To make discussion of liberation through communally conscious self-legislation possible, Rousseau, unlike Barber's Communitarianism, excoriated an economy that spurned equality, a social order that militated against cooperativeness, and a spurious individuality that was (and is) the cohort of both. In moods pessimistic and optimistic, Rousseau prodded himself and others toward the realization that *we* construct and can reconstruct not only politics but also its socioeconomic correlates and ourselves as well. Genuine Communitarians at the end of the twentieth century would do well to keep this in mind.

Notes

1. This essay benefits from the advice of Prof. Michael E. Hobart as well as Prof. Leo Damrosch and the participants in his NEH Summer Seminar on Blake and Rousseau held at Harvard University in 1993. The views expressed, of course, are the author's responsibility.

2. Cf. Shlomo Avineri and Avner De-Shalit, eds., *Communitarianism and Individualism* (Oxford: Oxford Univ. Press, 1992).

3. Appended to Etzioni's *The Spirit of Community: Rights, Responsibilities, and the*

Communitarian Agenda (New York: Crown Publishers, 1993).

4. Cf. J. G. A. Pocock, *The Machiavellian Moment* (Princeton: Princeton Univ. Press, 1975).
5. Cf. Hartz, *The Liberal Tradition in America* (New York: Harcourt, Brace, 1955).
6. Cf. Michael Sandel, "The Procedural Republic and the Unencumbered Self," *Political Theory* 12 (1984): 81–96.
7. See Dewey, *Individualism, Old and New* (New York: Minton, Balch, 1930), 90.
8. Cf. Jean Starobinski, *Jean-Jacques Rousseau: Transparency and Obstruction*, trans. A. Goldhammer (Chicago: Univ. of Chicago Press, 1988).
9. See Roger Barny, "Rousseau dans la Revolution," *Dix-Huitième Siecle* 6 (1974): 59–98; and Jacob Talmon, *The Rise of Totalitarian Democracy* (New York: Praeger, 1954).
10. Walzer "The Communitarian Critique of Liberalism," *Political Theory* 18 (1990): 6.
11. These are the dominating ideals of, respectively, *The Social Contract*, *Emile*, and *The Reveries of the Solitary Walker*.
12. Cf. Judith N. Shklar, *Man and Citizen: A Study of Rousseau's Thought* (Cambridge: Cambridge Univ. Press, 1969).
13. Barber's agenda is appended to *Strong Democracy: Participatory Politics for A New Age* (Berkeley: Univ. of California Press, 1984), 307.
14. See Barber, "Political Participation and the Creation of Res Publica," in A. Ritter and Julia C. Bondanella, eds., *Rousseau's Political Writings* (New York: W. W. Norton, 1988), 293, 302.
15. *The Death of Communal Liberty* (Princeton: Princeton Univ. Press, 1974), 8.
16. Ibid., 7–8, 173.
17. Ibid., 170–203 *passim*.
18. Cf. "Political Participation and the Creation of Res Publica," 296.
19. *The Death of Communal Liberty*, 176–177.
20. Rousseau (in his *Projet de constitution pour la Corse*) says the Swiss forfeited happiness when they began cultivating finance and a taste for luxuries.
21. *The Death of Communal Liberty*, 272.
22. Cf. David Gross, *The Past in Ruins: Tradition and the Critique of Modernity* (Amherst, MA: Univ. of Massachusetts Press, 1992).
23. Barber, "Rousseau and the Paradoxes of the Dramatic Imagination" *Daedalus* 107 (1978): 79.
24. *Emile*, trans. B. Foxley (London: J.M. Dent, 1974), 252.
25. Rousseau, *Second Discourse*, 184 in *The First and Second Discourses and Essay on the Origin of Languages*, ed. and trans. V. Gourevitch (New York: Harper and Row, 1986). He was not opposed to a modicum of private property fairly distributed.
26. Cf. Victor Gourevitch, "Rousseau on the Arts and Sciences," *Journal of Philosophy* 69 (1972): 737–754; and Julia Simon-Ingram, "Alienation, Individuation, and Enlightenment in Rousseau's Social Theory," *Eighteenth-Century Studies* 24 (1991): 315–335.
27. *Emile*, 230–237.
28. See Benjamin Barber and Janis Forman, eds. and trans., "A Preface to Narcisse; or the Lover of Himself, "*Political Theory* 6 (1978): 543–554.
29. "Rousseau and the Paradoxes," 84; *Emile*, 191.

30. Rousseau, "Second Dialogue," in *Rousseau, Judge of Jean-Jacques*, eds. R. Masters and C. Kelly (Hanover, NH: Univ. of New England Press, 1990), 143.

31. Barber, "Rousseau and the Paradoxes," 79. Cf. Charles Taylor, *Sources of the Self: The Making of the Modern Identity* (Cambridge, MA: Harvard Univ. Press, 1989), especially 356–365.

32. See, generally, Barber, *Strong Democracy*, 3–116; and Barber, *Superman and Common Men: Freedom, Anarchy and Revolution* (New York: F. Praeger, 1971), 40–51.

33. Rousseau contradicts Hobbes's view of mankind; cf. Rousseau, *Second Discourse*, 159–160.

34. Locke, *The Second Treatise of Civil Government*; quoted in Barber, *Strong Democracy*, 7.

35. Barber, *Strong Democracy*, 113 and *passim*.

36. Rousseau, *Second Discourse*, 149.

37. Wokler, "A Reply to Charvet: Rousseau and the Perfectibility of Man," *History of Political Thought* 1 (1980): 90.

38. Rousseau, *Second Discourse*, 161.

39. "Human association depends on imagination: the capacity to see in others beings like ourselves....subjects of tolerance and respect" (Barber, *An Aristocracy of Everyone: The Politics of Education and the Future of America* [New York: Ballatine Books, 1992], 5).

40. *Emile*; quoted in Barber, "Rousseau and the Paradoxes...," 92.

41. Ibid.," 90; cf. *Emile*, 244.

42. Cf. James Miller, *Rousseau, Dreamer of Democracy* (New Haven: Yale Univ. Press, 1984).

43. Cf. Barber, *The Conquest of Politics: Liberal Philosophy in Democratic Times* (Princeton: Princeton Univ. Press, 1988), 3–22, 193–212.

44. *Strong Democracy*, 127.

45. Ibid., 209. Cf. *The Conquest of Politics*, 205.

46. Cf. Ian Shapiro, *Political Criticism* (Berkeley: Univ. of California Press, 1990), 36–54.

47. Cf. Rorty, *Contingency, Irony, and Solidarity* (Cambridge: Cambridge Univ. Press, 1989).

48. *Strong Democracy*, 24.

49. Rousseau insists that "[i]ndividuals must be obliged to subordinate their will to their reason" (*The Social Contract*, trans. M. Cranston [Harmondsworth: Penguin, 1968], 83). The resulting "general will" is no recipe for tyranny, however: "[F]or the body of government to have an existence, a real life *apart from* the body of the state..., it must have a particular ego, a consciousness common to its members, a force, a will of it own tending to its preservation" (Ibid., 106).

50. *The Conquest of Politics*, 6, 12–13, 204.

51. *Social Contract*, 80.

52. *Strong Democracy*, 254–255. For Rousseau's view of "self-interest" as an "acquired idea," see *Emile*, 252–253.

53. "Rousseau and the Paradoxes...," 90.

54. See Allan Gilbert's attack on the pragmatic position in the name of "radical

democracy" (*Democratic Individuality* [Cambridge: Cambridge Univ. Press, 1990], 78).

55. It should be noted that Rousseau was *not* opposed to close-knit associations that cultivate camaraderie or affection, but only to those that oppressed or protected privilege; cf. *Social Contract*, 73.
56. *The Conquest of Politics*, 208.
57. Cf. *Emile*, 182–185.
58. Rousseau, *The Confessions*, tr. J. M. Cohen (Harmondsworth: Penguin, 1953), 17.
59. Cf. Rick Matthews and David Ingersoll, "The Therapist and the Lawgiver: Rousseau's Political Vision," *Canadian Journal of Political and Social Theory* 4 (1980), 94, 96.
60. James M. Glass, "Political Philosophy as Therapy: Rousseau and the Pre-Social Origins of Consciousness," *Political Theory* 4 (1976), 180.
61. *Social Contract*, 84–85.
62. Barber, *An Aristocracy of Everyone*, 151–191 *passim*.
63. Ibid., 133–151 *passim*.
64. Rousseau adds that Emile's tutor teaches how to resist seeking "his pleasure in domination and in the sufferings of others" (*Emile*, 213).
65. *Superman and Common Men*, 73.
66. *Social Contract*, 185–186.
67. *An Aristocracy of Everyone*, 7.
68. Ibid., 246, 251. Cf. *Social Contract*, 140.
69. Barber, "Liberal Democracy and the Costs of Consent," in N. Rosenblum (ed.), *Liberalism and the Moral Life* (Cambridge, MA: Cambridge Univ. Press, 1989), 65.
70. *Superman and Common Men*, 75, 95–97.
71. *Strong Democracy*, xv.
72. *An Aristocracy of Everyone*, 241–242.
73. *Liberating Feminism* (New York: Seabury Press, 1975), 146.
74. "Political Participation and the Creation of Res Publica," 299; *Strong Democracy* 253.
75. *Second Discourse*, 185. Cf. *Government of Poland*, trans. W. Kendall (Indianapolis: Hackett, 1972), 68–70.
76. *Second Discourse*, 195. Cf. "Political Economy," in *The Social Contract plus the Dedication from the "Second Discourse" and "On Political Economy"*, trans. and ed. C. Sherover (New York: New American Books, 1974), 271.
77. *Social Contract*, 96.
78. *Social Contract*, 141.
79. Communitarianism as pernicious anti-liberal nostalgia is the theme of Derek Phillips, *Looking Backward: A Critical Appraisal of Communitarian Thought* (Princeton: Princeton Univ. Press, 1993).
80. H. N. Hirsch, "The Threnody of Liberalism," *Political Theory* 14 (1986), 440.
81. "Propose nothing but what is feasible, people are constantly telling me. It is as if they were saying, propose only what we are already doing" (Quoted in Bernard Manin, "Rousseau," in F. Furet and M. Ozouf, eds., *A Critical Dictionary of the French Revolution* [Cambridge, MA: Harvard Univ. Press, 1989], 838).
82. Wokler, "Rousseau and Marx," in D. Miller and L. Seidentop, eds., *The Nature of*

Political Theory (Oxford: Blackwell, 1983), 233.

83. Cf. Barber, "A New Language for the Left," *Harper's* (Nov., 1986): 47–52.

Studies on Themes and Motifs in Literature

The series is designed to advance the publication of research pertaining to themes and motifs in literature. The studies cover cross-cultural patterns as well as the entire range of national literatures. They trace the development and use of themes and motifs over extended periods, elucidate the significance of specific themes or motifs for the formation of period styles, and analyze the unique structural function of themes and motifs. By examining themes or motifs in the work of an author or period, the studies point to the impulses authors received from literary tradition, the choices made, and the creative transformation of the cultural heritage. The series will include publications of colloquia and theoretical studies that contribute to a greater understanding of literature.

For additional information about this series or for the submission of manuscripts, please contact:

Peter Lang Publishing
Acquisitions Dept.
516 N. Charles St., 2nd Floor
Baltimore, MD 21201

To order other books in this series, please contact our Customer Service Department:

800-770-LANG (within the U.S.)
212-647-7706 (outside the U.S.)
212-647-7707 FAX

Or browse online by series at:

www.peterlang.com